Explore the world

NELLES GUIDE

TUSCANY

Authors:
Ulrike Bleek, Christiane Büld Campetti,
Stephan Bleek

An Up-to-date travel guide
with 162 color photos
and 19 maps

W9-AMU-940

Dear Reader: Being up-to-date is the main goal of the Nelles series. Our correspondents help keep us abreast of the latest developments in the travel scene, while our cartographers see to it that the maps are kept completely current. However, as the travel world is constantly changing, we cannot guarantee that all of the information contained in our books is always valid. Should you come across a discrepancy, please contact us at: Nelles Verlag, Schleißheimer Str. 371B, D-80935 Munich, Germany, tel: +(49) 89 35 71 940, fax: +(49) 89 35 71 94 30, e-mail: Nelles.Verlag@t-online.de.

Note: Distances and measurements, including temperatures, used in this guide are metric. For conversion information, please see the *Guidelines* section of this book.

LEGEND

★★	Main Attraction *(on map)*	**Volterra** *(Town)*	Places Highlighted in Yellow Appear in Text	National Border
★★	*(in text)*	S. Galgano *(Sight)*		Tollway
★	Worth Seeing *(on map)*	◄ ◄	Int'l, Nat'l Airport	Expressway
★	*(in text)*			Principal Highway
❽	Orientation Number in Text and on Map	**Mte. Amiata** · 1738	Mountain (altitude in meters)	Main Road
▦	Public or Significant Building	\ 13 /	Distance in Kilometers	Secondary Road
▦	Hotel	☀	Beach	Ferry
▦	Market	♠	National Park	Parking
✝ ♦	Church	🛈	Tourist Information	ⓈⓈⓈ Luxury Hotel Category
⬛	Castle	∴	Ancient site	ⓈⓈ Moderate Hotel Category
		†	Cemetery	Ⓢ Budget Hotel Category

(for price information see "Accomodation" in Guidelines section)

TUSCANY
© Nelles Verlag GmbH, 80935 München
All rights reserved

Second Revised Edition 2000
ISBN 3-88618-209-6
Printed in Slovenia

Publisher:	Günter Nelles	**Translations**:	Angelika Funkhauser
Managing Editor:	Berthold Schwarz		Ross Greville, Kent Lyon, Janet Mayer
Project Editor:	Ulrike Bleek	**Cartography**:	Nelles Verlag GmbH,
English Edition			Munich
Editor:	Rebekah Rollo	**Lithos**:	Priegnitz, Munich
Photo Editor:	K. Bärmann-Thümmel	**Printed by**:	Gorenjski Tisk

TABLE OF CONTENTS

TABLE OF CONTENTS

GUIDELINES

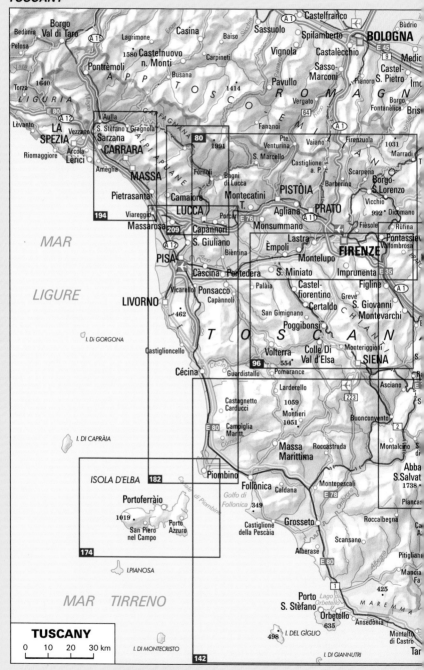

MAP LIST

HISTORY
AND CULTURE

THE LAND OF DREAMS

Tuscany – just the sound of this magical word is enough to make eyes sparkle and awaken a profound sense of yearning. It is synonymous with culture, beauty and enjoyment. Its cities are themselves enormous works of art and its landscapes seem to imitate paintings. In short, it is a Mecca for lovers of art, the destination *par excellence* for romantic dreamers.

The countryside, seductive and full of promise, attracts not only artists hoping to draw inspiration from this culture-soaked land, but also those seeking refuge from civilization, who yearn for the simple life in a still-innocent world.

Three thousand years ago, the Etruscans created the first civilization on the Apennine Peninsula. Six hundred years ago, the Renaissance and its ideals of humanism ushered in the modern age. Dante, Boccaccio and Petrarch, Brunelleschi, Arnolfo di Cambio, Nicola and Giovanni Pisano, Ghiberti, Donatello, Giotto, Piero della Francesca, Michelangelo and Leonardo da Vinci – their names are forever linked with cities such as Florence, Pisa, Lucca, Siena, Arezzo. Tuscany has a veritable surplus of art and culture.

And yet there is more. The landscape, shaped by men who intuitively knew where to build their simple stone houses and how to most effectively group their cypresses and pines, is as much a feast for the eyes as any sculpture by Donatello or fresco by Piero della Francesca. And nature, in Tuscany, has many countenances. There are inaccessible mountain areas,

Previous Pages: For many a landscape of dreams. An Annunciation fresco by Fra Angelico in the monastery of San Marco. Left: A street scene in Florence; detail of a painting by Masolino.

thick forests where rare species of animals can still be found, lonely river valleys dotted with ancient monasteries and forgotten villages and hamlets, gently rolling hills, sandy beaches fringed with pine woods, and islands large and small. Anyone seeking untouched nature will find it here, and hikers or cyclists will be in seventh heaven.

If beach life is more to your taste, there is always the coast, where luxurious thermal springs offer a place for the weary body to rest, and bon vivants can recover from the effects of extravagant living – only to succumb anew to the temptations of the Tuscan cuisine and cellar.

If it is your intention really to get to know Tuscany, a single trip will be woefully inadequate. The visitor who has only seen the main tourist attractions and checked off the best-known works of art in his guidebook will have missed a lot of what Tuscany has to offer. If you are interested in the land and the people, you will have to seek out the small towns with no spectacular monuments to boast of. You will have to get off the beaten track.

Chianti, the Maremma, the Crete – every traveler to Tuscany is smitten with these dream landscapes. And many travelers simply decide to stay. A large number of houses here, occasionally entire villages, are owned by foreigners, mostly Germans, Swiss or British. In the 1950s, the rural population began to migrate to the cities, leaving many idyllically located farmsteads to slowly decay. Wealthy foreigners were quick to act. They snapped up these houses, restored them – usually very tastefully, in a traditional style – and proceeded to live there, some for a few weeks each year, others year round.

Every lover of Italy has probably harbored, at some time or another, the dream of owning a house in Tuscany; a dream that has come true for a variety of people. Many of those who have taken up permanent residence here try their hands at be-

13

What do the Tuscans think about all of this? People born in Tuscany tend to consider themselves singularly blessed by fate. And one cannot disagree entirely. After all, the Tuscans not only look back on a glorious past, they are also spoiled by the fact that they happen to live in one of the most beautiful places on earth.

And even if, just as in the old days, the Pisans can't stand the Sienese, and the San Gimignans can't abide the Lucchese, and in fact everyone hates everyone else, and the Florentines worst of all, there is one point on which everyone agrees: their homeland is one vast work of art that their forebears created in the truest sense of the word. Accordingly, they all have a deep awareness of their own traditions and are prepared actively to defend their valuable heritage, while being ready, at the same time, to welcome progress.

Fortunately, some recognized the downside of progress early on. People are again giving priority to quality of life, rethinking, and sometimes abandoning, projects that were based purely on profit motives. Happily, even if an industrial project does besmirch the landscape in a certain area, Tuscany is too large and too multifaceted for it to seriously damage the region's natural beauty.

Because of this, Tuscany, with its art, landscapes, mild climate, excellent cuisine and delightful wines, will continue to be a favorite destination for the tourist hordes. You shouldn't, however, let the crowds prevent you from exploring Tuscany. To avoid them, simply schedule your trip for the late autumn or winter, when the focus of the tourist industry shifts to the southern hemisphere. In the off-season, Tuscany is virtually deserted. You don't have to stand in line in the museums, hotel staff are friendlier and more obliging, more care goes into the preparation of your meals, and everything is warmer, more human, more Italian. The only thing you can't enjoy in the off-season is a swim in the ocean.

ing vintners, or press their own olives, or keep a few sheep. Most have a hard time if they have to make a living this way.

Often enough, there follows a rude awakening: disputes with Italian authorities, integration problems and communication difficulties. Even Italian neighbors sometimes have trouble getting along with these foreign settlers who strive to be more Tuscan than the Tuscans themselves. Still, these foreigners are a sight better than the tourists.

The tourist industry is an important sector of the Tuscan economy, and the main source of income for countless local residents. At the same time, the visiting hordes have helped to inflict almost irreparable damage on the works of art that drew them here in the first place. Tuscany is sick, and drastic measures and a lot of money are needed to save what can still be salvaged, before it is too late.

Above: Stone Age art. Right: A pitcher with an equestrian figure – an example of the bucchero ceramics of the Etruscans.

THE TURBULENT COURSE OF TUSCAN HISTORY

Early Traces

Traces of the first human settlement in Tuscany date back to the Paleolithic era. Ancient stone tools that are 30,000 years old have been found in the foothills of the Apennines near Prato, while near Arezzo, excavators have even found the remains of a Paleolithic man. The Arno valley and the island of Elba, on the other hand, have yielded numerous items from the transitional time between the Paleolithic and Mesolithic eras; such finds have, in fact, been made all along the Tyrrhenian coast from Liguria to Sicily.

Permanent settlements with farming and cattle breeding did not, however, develop until the Bronze Age (ca. 1500 to 1000 B.C.) on the slopes of the Apennines. Finds from this period have included attractive pots with geometrical patterns and countless tools made of stone, metal and bone.

This historical period commences during the transition from the Bronze to the Iron Age. It was the time of the so-called Villanova culture (named after a small village near Bologna), a society that practiced cremation rather than tomb interment as in the Bronze Age.

The Villanova culture has also furnished the first examples of artistically decorated tools and weapons of bronze, as well as small, stylized figures representing human beings or animals. This culture extended across northern Italy and the region that would later to become Tuscany, and flourished between ca. 950 and 450 B.C. Around 700 B.C. it was superseded in this area by Etruscan culture, which would to develop into central Italy's first advanced civilization.

The Etruscans

"Once upon a time, a farmer from Tarquinia was plowing his field not far from town. Thrusting his plowshare deeper into the earth than usual, and turn-

15

ing over the clump of sod, he found a boy with feet like serpents, the countenance of a mature man, and a head of white hair. He was Tages, son of a local deity and the grandson of Jupiter. The farmer shouted until people ran to see what the matter was. His shouts even drew the *lucomos*, the chiefs of the twelve cities of the Etruscan League. In the midst of this assembly, the wondrous earth-child began to sing his wisdom; and the lucomos wrote down every word as he sang it. These became the Etruscans' *Tagetic Books*, a body of learning that is passed from generation to generation as a priceless treasure. When Tages finished singing, he fell back into the earth and died."

This, then, is the Etruscan myth of their creation. And although more than three thousand years have passed since this wonderful event, much remains obscure about their origins and the development of their nation and their culture.

Above: An Etruscan grave from the 7th-5th centuries B.C., near Populonia.

They emerged from the mists of antiquity during the first millennium B.C., and had returned to obscurity before written history begins. Even their language, which most authorities do not consider to be part of the Indo-European linguistic family, still has not been deciphered, despite the many attempts to do so.

The ancient realm of the Etruscans was bounded by the Arno and Tiber Rivers, and the Tyrrhenian Sea, a body of water named for the Tyrrhenians, as the Greeks referred to the Etruscans. Tyrrhenus was a prince of Lydia who led part of his people to Italy to escape a famine that was ravaging their homeland. The Romans, on the other hand, called them Etrusci or Tusci, and these words gave rise to the later terms Etruria and eventually Tuscany.

The first physical signs of their presence in what is now the region of Tuscany go back to the 8th century B.C. As to their ultimate origin, there are various theories, and even the scholars of antiquity were not able to agree with one another. In all probability they did come from Lydia, crossing the sea and settling Etruria from the coast, working inland and mixing with the indigenous peoples of the Villanova culture. This was the hypothesis of the Greek historian Herodotus, and there are many indications, both in art and religion, to support his theory.

In his *Antiquites Romanae* Dionysius of Halicarnassus, another Greek, postulated that the Etruscans were an autochthonous people who developed out of the Villanova culture's Proto-Italians.

A third theory, supported by a number of scholars in the 19th century, holds that the Etruscans, who themselves used the name Rasenna (from *Raeti*, the inhabitants of the Rhaetic Alps), are to be counted amongst the groups of Indo-Germanic peoples who migrated across the Alps and onto the Italian peninsula from ca. 2000 B.C. onwards. This theory is supposedly supported by inscriptions found in Trentino that bear a certain resemblance to examples of Etruscan epigraphy. Unfortunately, these inscriptions date from as late as the 4th century B.C., and thus only serve to demonstrate that the Etruscans were also present in this area.

Whatever the truth of the matter is, the riddle of their origins cannot, at present, be solved. Happily, it is possible and interesting to examine how the Etruscan people, with their advanced culture, developed.

There is no disputing the fact that the Etruscans, starting from the cities of Vetulonia and Populonia on the coast, and their early inland settlements of Volterra and Chiusi, spread into Umbria and Latium. They founded cities and settlements, ploughed the land, drained the swamplands of the Maremma with their ingenious drainage systems, and mined the ores and minerals of the wooded Colline Metallifere.

Etruria was organized into city-states on the Greek model, and ruled on the basis of an aristocratic constitution, with a priest-king, the *lucomo*, at the top. The cities themselves were autonomous. In the 6th century B.C., the twelve most important cities, including Arezzo, Cortona, Volterra, Chiusi, Roselle and Vetulonia, joined to form a loosely-knit defensive federation. At the same time, the Etruscans extended their dominion northwards beyond the Apennines, as far as the Po River plain, and founded the cities of Adria and Spina on the Adriatic coast.

The Etruscans were also a seafaring people. As pirates they were feared, as trading partners they were valued. Allied with Carthage, the fleet of the League of the Twelve Cities defeated the Greeks off Corsica in 540 B.C. After this, the Etruscans effectively held sway over the entire northwestern Mediterranean, and their maritime trading activities were secured.

Between the 7th and 5th centuries B.C., Etruscan art and culture blossomed as never before. Strong Greek influence can be detected in their script, their religious pantheon and in their coins. The Etruscans also looked to Greek models in their art, something that can be seen, for example, in their vase painting. Yet, despite outside influence, their works had a unique, distinctive flavor. In their small-scale sculptures, they simplified and stylized shapes, giving their works a lifelike vividness of expression quite removed from the distant, enlightened serenity seen in Greek sculptures.

Another feature of Etruscan art, seen almost exclusively in cult objects, is the excellent technical quality of their workmanship. Their goldsmiths were masters of highly developed granulation and filigree techniques, and others developed a high degree of mastery in such artisan skills as working metals into basins, mirrors and candelabras, carving ivory, or in the production of *bucchero* ceramics (bucchero is a brilliant black substance similar to clay).

Ironically, one characteristic of this people who had such a love of life was a

preoccupation with the next world, the afterlife, and a very distinctive cult of the dead. The Etruscans furnished their necropolises, which lay outside the city walls, with everything that had made life and living pleasant. The tombs were built like dwellings or homes amidst a network of roads and lanes modeled on the city of the living. The tomb's inner walls were decorated with gaily-colored frescoes depicting scenes of life and death. Copious trinkets were left so the deceased need lack for nothing in the hereafter. Vaulted cottage tombs consisted of multiple levels and rooms, with space enough for a family's successive generations. In the north these necropolises were built of stone, while in the south they were hewn out of the volcanic tuff. Tombs were designed to last an eternity, unlike homes and temples of wood and terra-cotta tiles, which didn't survived the millennia.

Above: An alabaster figure of a dead man (Etruscan Museum, Chiusi). Right: An Etruscan doorway arch in Volterra.

The Etruscans' contemporaries found their rituals strange, especially since their religion was otherwise basically Hellenistic; it was particularly marked by a strong dependence on the involvement of the gods in their fate. In accordance with the procedures laid down in the *Etrusca disciplina*, the Etruscans observed natural phenomena, the flight of birds and the innards of animals, and their priests interpreted what they saw. Essentially, if the gods were to be pleased, their will had to be clearly understood. These methods of soothsaying were later adopted by the Romans, as were the Etruscans' music, theater and gladiatorial games.

A thorn in the side of patriarchal societies such as Ancient Greece and Rome must have been the fact that Etruscan women clearly enjoyed a position of equality with the men, and a broad spectrum of matriarchal rights. As priestesses, women had an important role to play in the spiritual leadership of the people, and could even participate in banquets, contests and competitions.

The Etruscans were thus, "a people who don't resemble any other, either in their language or in their customs," as Dionysius of Halicarnassus summarized in his findings.

Then began the decline of Etruscan culture. They lost a naval battle to the Syracusan fleet in 474 B.C., and this ushered in a gradual loss of their power over the seas. Also, Rome, which was initially very much under the influence of the Etruscan aristocracy and had become rich and powerful in just a short time under the rule of the seven legendary Etruscan kings (Romulus, Numa Pompilius, Tullus Hostilius, Ancus Marcus Tarquinius Priscus, and Tarquinius Superbus), was increasingly acting as a rival. The conquest of Etruria can be said to have started with the fall of Veii in 396 B.C., after a siege that had lasted ten years. One by one the city-states fell under the rule of Rome until the last of them, Volsinii (Bolsena on the Lago di Bolsena) was destroyed in 265 B.C. By 100 B.C., the Romans had completely absorbed the Etruscan world

and their religious and cultural identities were all the Etruscans were able to maintain in the coming years.

The fact that the Etruscans play such a subordinate role in Roman historiography seems to indicate that there must have been a certain degree of Roman jealousy of this highly-civilized people. This may also be the reason so few written testimonies of the Etruscans have survived the centuries. Accordingly, scholars attempting to decipher their language have only the relatively short grave inscriptions and a small number of manuscript fragments to go on. At the same time, numerous examples of their architecture still survive, among them, remnants of city walls in Roselle, Vetulonia, Populonia, Cortone, Fiesole and Volterra (where the Porta dell'Arco, the famous gate with the Etruscan heads, still stands), and also the necropolises with their precious grave trinkets, which can be seen in many museum collections, such as those of the Museo Archeologico in Florence and the Museo Etrusco Guarnacci in Volterra.

Roman Etruria

The Romans were skilled at handling the peoples they conquered. Cities were permitted to retain a certain degree of formal autonomy while the entire corresponding region was incorporated into a system of federation. This is why a number of Etruscan cities in the north – Arezzo, Cortona and Perugia – accorded the Romans a friendly reception. During the Punic Wars and in the battles with the Celts, Romans and Etruscans fought together as allies, and in 91 B.C., the Etruscans were granted Roman citizenship.

During the first century of Roman rule the region initially continued to flourish. Roman colonies were founded and wide roads were built to connect Rome and Etruria. The first of these roads, the *Via Aurelia*, built along the coastline, was begun in 241 B.C. After 225 B.C., *Via Clodia* led from Veii to the Aurelian Way.

Above: Roman amphitheater in Fiesole. Right: A bronze statue of Charlemagne, ca. A.D. 870.

From ca. 220 B.C., the *Via Cassia* connected Rome and Fiesole. The year 187 B.C. saw completion of the *Via Flaminia*, which passed through Arezzo and over the Apennines into Emilia.

Not very many buildings or works of art from the Roman era have survived in Tuscany; most traces were destroyed in the Middle Ages and Renaissance. Occasionally, however, remnants of the typical Roman civil works can still be seen: amphitheaters (Luni, Volterra and Fiesole), temples (Fiesole) and thermal baths (Pisa and Fiesole). To this we may add the remains of Roman patrician villas on Monte Argentario near Porto Santo Stefano, and on the island of Giannutri.

The last century of the Roman Republic also ushered in the final downfall for Etruria. Parts of the region were used as battlefields in the Civil Wars, resulting in the destruction and devastation of wide tracts of land.

As malaria increasingly spread along the coastline, settlements there had to be abandoned and the people fled inland.

It no longer paid to grow corn locally, since cheaper grain was being imported from Asia, Egypt and Sicily. The same applied to the mining of ore.

Emperor Augustus tried to improve the dismal economic situation in the country and in the course of an administrative reorganization of Italy, Etruria was declared the VIIth Region, the borders of which were the Magra River and the Apennines in the north and northeast respectively, the Tiber River in the southeast and the coast as far as the mouth of the Tiber in the west.

During the 3rd century A.D., under Emperor Diocletian, Etruria – now called Tuscia – went to Umbria and a *corrector* took over the office of chief administrator. His residence was in Florentia, a Roman veterans' colony on the Arno, which had been founded in the days of Caesar.

The Period of the Barbarian Migrations

The insurgence of the barbarians resulted in Tuscia's political and economic downfall. The country was destroyed and some cities, particularly those located on the major highways leading to Rome, never recovered. After the Alemanni and the Ostrogoths, there was a brief upswing under the Byzantines (A.D. 553-569), but the Lombards, who settled principally on the Po River plain, had only a military interest in Tuscia, which had been virtually destroyed and thus had little to offer. Fortified settlements were erected along the Apennines and from the Garfagnana, via the Mugello River, into the Chiusi region as a defense against the Byzantines.

The Lombards made Tuscia an archduchy, subdividing it into smaller duchies. The most important city at the time was Lucca, which was probably the first city to be conquered by the Lombards when they invaded the country via the Cisa Pass in the north. The next city to be taken was Pisa, which to a certain extent

was still involved in maritime trade. From here the Lombards sailed to conquer Sardinia and Corsica. The other cities, such as Pistoia, Fiesole, Florence and Arezzo, were in a state of utter decay at this time. Siena was involved in a century-long dispute with Arezzo involving the ownership of certain parishes, and Chiusi was threatened by the Chiana valley's spreading marshlands.

In the year A.D. 774, with the conquest of Pavia, Charlemagne brought the kingdom of the Lombards into the kingdom of the Franks. Under Charlemagne, who no longer regarded Tuscia as an enemy territory to be exploited, there began a new era of recovery. Commerce flourished once more, prosperity increased, and cities gained in importance. Lucca, Siena, San Gimignano and Colle di Val d'Elsa profited from the newly built *Via Francigena* (the Frankish road), which extended though the interior of the country, connecting Pavia and Rome. Pilgrim hostels were built, as well as trade centers and monasteries, including the Abbazia di

San Salvatore on Monte Amiata. Other cities, however, which had once benefited from their location on the Roman consular roads, such as Florence, Arezzo and Chiusi, were now too far removed from the new trading and pilgrimage routes to participate in this economic recovery. At this time, the population living near the coast was being forced to flee into the mountains to take refuge from the raids of both Normans and Saracens.

During the 9th century, Tuscia became a margravate, and in A.D. 934 the name *Tuscana* first appeared in a document. At this time, a feudal system recognizing both ecclesiastical and secular lords had already been established. The landed aristocracy had built numerous castles, and the monasteries were becoming richer and more powerful. However, in the cities the middle classes were gaining self-con-

Above: Emperor Henry IV with the Margravine Matilda before his Journey to Canossa (pre-1114 book illumination). Right: Dynastic towers in Lucca (14th-century illumination).

fidence because of their commercial successes and were exerting increased political influence. As early as the 9th century, popular assemblies were held to decide on administrative and building measures, and by the 11th century the first consuls were ruling in Pisa and Lucca.

The Gregorian church reforms had a strong following in many of the Episcopal cities, particularly in Pisa, Lucca and Florence; this movement later developed into the strife between the Papacy and the Empire. This new burst of religious zeal demanded stricter morals and more discipline within the church, and led to the founding of new orders everywhere. In Tuscany the orders of the Vallombrosans and the Camaldolensans dominated.

The Era of the Communes

The Margravine Matilda, on whose family estate in Canossa Henry IV had knelt before Pope Gregory VII, died in 1115. She bequeathed all her worldly possessions to the Church, which intensified the conflict between the Pope and the Emperor. The cities exploited the dispute to undermine the power of both the bishopric and the margravate, thereby winning more independence for themselves. In the 12th century, the larger cities were to all intents and purposes autonomous and were developing into independent communes, although they continued to be governed by the aristocracy.

As a result of the crusades and the trade in the eastern Mediterranean, Pisa had in the meantime experienced a rapid ascent. It was in Pisa that the crusaders were provided with transportation, military escorts and provisions. Thus, Pisa remained Tuscany's most important city throughout the 12th century. Sudden economic upswings were also felt in the other cities. Siena's banks and money-lenders had connections that extended as far as Rome, northern Italy and France; Lucca and Florence made a modest start to their tex-

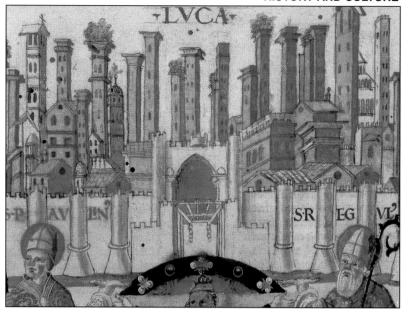

tile industry, which soon brought flourishing bank activities to Florence.

The demand for unrestricted commerce without road tolls gradually led to the dissolution of the feudal system. Minor landed aristocrats were encouraged or forced to take up residence in the cities. Only larger families such as the Guidi, the Aldobrandeschi and the Malaspina were able to maintain the traditional system for a longer period. This struggle against feudal lords continued throughout the 12th century. At the same time, Pisa, Lucca and Florence started to fight for supremacy over their neighboring, and rival, cities. The first victim was Fiesole, which was razed to the ground by Florence in 1125.

Soon everyone was fighting everyone else in alliances that were as quickly dissolved as made. Florence and Pisa were especially bitter rivals because Florence required unimpeded access to the sea for its booming wool trade. However, for years Florence had also been in conflict with Siena because it was wealthy and was thought to be an especially dangerous competitor in this particular line of trade.

Guelphs and Ghibellines

The incessant disputes between the Pope and the Emperor served as a pretext for these battles, the real purpose of which clearly was the struggle for supreme power.

The Emperor's supporters called themselves the Ghibellines, after the Swabian city of Waiblingen, home of the Hohenstaufen dynasty, and were primarily members of the aristocracy who expected the old order to be upheld and maintained by the power of the Emperor. The new upper strata of the middle class, which included wealthy merchants and bankers who were not very interested in a return to the old order, were adherents of the Guelph party, named after the Guelph king crowned as Emperor Otto IV by Pope Innocence III. The Guelphs expected greater trading possibilities as a

result of the Church's extensive connections.

Social tension grew within the cities and feuds developed between the different parties, finding visible expression in the fortress-like towers that the various noble families were erecting everywhere.

The cities' wealth manifested itself at this time in the construction of many great monuments. In Florence, the church of San Minato al Monte was built and the Baptistry took on its present form; Pisa developed a style of its own, which blended northern architecture with oriental elements. Florence's Duomo and Baptistry are outstanding examples of this type of architecture, but it is also reflected in cathedrals in Prato, Pistoia and along the coast up to Carrara. In Lucca, the Pisan style found an additional, typically Lucchese variant, and a mixture of the two

Above: A Romanesque capital in San Antimo, Maître de Chambestany. Right: First flowering of Tuscan painting – Cimabue's Madonna and Child Enthroned (1272-74).

was realized in the cathedrals of Volterra and Massa Marittima.

Siena and Arezzo, on the other hand, continued to maintain a style of their own. In Siena, in particular, there are few relics of Romanesque architecture. However, the abbey of Sant'Antimo, in the south of the region, is one of the most exquisite Romanesque churches in all of Tuscany.

Also in the cities, alongside the great ecclesiastical buildings, the palaces of the temporal governing powers were built, including the Palazzi del Popolo and the Palazzi del Podestà, which resembles a fortress. One very fine example of this is the Bargello in Florence. Also from this era, Prato can still boast a special type of edifice that is otherwise only found in Apulia and Sicily: the Castello Imperiale, Emperor Frederick II's imperial castle.

During the 12th century, Pisa became the center for Tuscan sculpture, the city where the great sculptor Nicola Pisano made his first mark. The field of painting saw the development of marvelously

24

painted wooden crucifixes, which demonstrate a strong Byzantine influence. A masterwork of this art, a cross painted in 1138 by Guglielmo, who was probably from Lucca, is in Sarzana's cathedral.

At the end of the 13th century, Cimabue, considered to be one of the most important painters in the development of Tuscan art, and a forerunner of Giotto, was working in Rome, Assisi and Pisa. In Siena, Duccio di Buoninsegna was at work. He was the first outstanding master of the Sienese School in whose art one can already detect Gothic elements.

At the beginning of the 13th century, the outcome of the struggle for regional supremacy was gradually becoming clear. Pisa had dissipated its energy in its endeavor to obtain supremacy in the Mediterranean and did not have the strength to secure its hinterland. Siena was repeatedly defeated by Florence and was forced to concentrate its interests on the south of the country, which was nowhere near as economically lucrative as the area between Siena and Florence.

At this time, Florence was the center of Guelph resistance to Emperor Frederick II. However, he had the Guelphs expelled from the city. In the constitution of what came to be known as the *primo popolo* (1250), the people organized themselves against the Ghibelline aristocracy and summoned the Guelphs to return. The region's first popular regime lasted some ten years. At its head was the *capitano del popolo* (captain of the people) who was supported by a council of twelve elders. Under the parallel authorities of the commune (headed by the *podestà*) and the people, the city experienced a decade of strong economic and political growth. In 1252, the first gold florin was minted, a visible sign Florence's power and a coin that was soon highly regarded across Europe.

In the Battle of Montaperti (1260), Guelph Florence and its *primo popolo* was crushingly defeated by its great rival

Siena, which had entered an alliance with the banished Ghibellines. This, however, meant only a temporary postponement of Florence's supremacy in Tuscany.

The Guilds

In order to counterbalance the all-powerful nobility, who continued to keep a firm grip on the reins of political power, the merchants, bankers and craftsmen started to join together in *arti* (guilds). Membership in these associations was on a voluntary basis, but anyone who did not join had to make do without a whole series of benefits, since the guilds not only defended professional interests at the commune level, but also protected their members from the demands of their employees. Wages and salaries were specified in a special ordinance, and the guilds can thus be seen as an early form of the trade union.

Each guild had its own coat of arms, which was depicted on banners and seals, and usually illustrated a specific feature

of the profession. The guild of the cloth merchants, for example, had a golden eagle, holding a bale of cloth in its claws, on a red background. The guild of the blacksmiths had a pair of tongs on a white background. The locksmiths and kettle makers had silver keys on a red background. And the guild of the stonemasons and carpenters had an axe on a red background. In addition to a coat of arms, every guild also had its own patron saint and was thus obliged to celebrate certain holidays.

The regulations of the guilds closely followed the constitution of the commune. Every year consuls were elected to lead each guild. They mediated disputes between guild members and punished those who did not abide by the rules. A treasurer and a notary ensured that each guild's statutes were observed.

Above: A relief representation of the architects' guild on the Orsanmichele in Florence.
Right: Dante Alighieri, painted by Michelino.
Far Right: Giotto's Campanile in Florence.

The guild members were industrious and clever and often controlled the markets of entire areas. Over the years they gradually gained influence until they finally pushed the nobility out of city governments. After the late-13th century, the guilds essentially controlled the political arena. They made all of the appointments to political and military offices and, by keeping a close watch on and frequently changing who held various government positions, made sure that no one could obtain absolute power.

In addition to their political activities, the guilds played an important role in the artistic and cultural development of the region's cities. They were constantly competing with each other, and one way in which they demonstrated their power and greatness was by commissioning magnificent works of art.

At this time, Florence had consolidated its predominance over the other Tuscan cities, and Prato, Pistoia, Arezzo, Colle di Val d'Elsa, San Gimignano, Volterra and Cortona already came under its sphere of

influence. The expansion of this sphere was not always accomplished by military force; in many cases, it was accompanied by the jingle of coins.

Florence was also the center of a flourishing cultural life. It is no coincidence that Italy's greatest poet, Dante Alighieri, who was the first to write in the Italian vernacular, was a Florentine; after 1340, the celebrated poet Boccaccio also lived in the city. The painter Giotto, whose style influenced art all over Italy, and many of whose students and followers were also to attain renown, was also from Florence. It was here that the monumental Duomo, the city's cathedral, was built according to the design of Arnolfo di Cambio, who was also responsible for the Franciscan church of Santa Croce. Next to the Duomo, the Campanile is visible proof of Giotto's architectural genius. This period also saw the building of Santa Maria Novella.

But such development wasn't unique to Florence; there are outstanding cultural monuments dating from the 14th century in other parts of Tuscany, as well. Siena's Palazzo Pubblico epitomizes Sienese pride, as do the great families' palazzi in typical Gothic-Sienese style. Exceptional monuments were erected elsewhere in Tuscany, such as the Camposanto and the church of Santa Maria della Spina in Pisa. Pisa and Siena were the leading cities for sculpture (Giovanni and Andrea Pisano), and in painting the Sienese school matched the Florentine (in particular, Simone Martini and Pietro and Ambrogio Lorenzetti).

It is astonishing that such a vast amount of excellent art could be produced at a time that was so marked by internal and external calamities. In Florence, in 1378, there was an uprising of the *ciompi* (wool-combers), and a similar rebellion broke out in Siena. There were also grave bank crises, and in 1348 a severe outbreak of the plague devastated Europe, killing two-thirds of the country's population.

But none of these blows meted out by fate could block the rise of Florence. By the mid-1300s, the only cities that had not

yet capitulated to her dominance were Pisa, Lucca and Siena. And by 1406, even the Republic of Pisa succumbed and entered the official Florentine domain.

The Medici

The Florentine conquest of Pisa meant that the city had finally gained free access to the sea. It also meant that Lucca was now the only city in northern Tuscany that was still independent. Siena, Florence's strongest rival in the south, was able to maintain its independence until 1555, when it was forced to surrender after a ten-year siege in which troops of Charles V took part. Four years later Siena and all of its possessions fell under Florentine rule.

In the meantime, a wealthy merchant family had worked its way up to hold the

Above: The guild emblem of the wool weavers. Right: Cosimo de' Medici (il Vecchio) receives the model of the church of San Lorenzo from Brunelleschi and Ghiberti.

highest positions in Florence's government. As far back as the Ciompi Uprising, a member of the then-obscure family, one Silvestro de' Medici, attained public office. The poor had rebelled when the Guelph party did not accept the election of this democratic Medici as the *gonfaloniere* (or "standard-bearer," a kind of tribune or supervisor of the judicial authority) of the city. The people stormed the Palazzo Vecchio and actually managed to remain in power for several weeks. Then the "people's government" was forced to surrender, as the upper middle class reacted with an immediate lock-out, which would have meant starvation for the workers who depended on them.

After the rebellion had been suppressed, the aristocracy once more assumed their position at the top. This upper class was actually a mixture of the nobility and upper middle-class families who had gradually made their way into the upper echelons of society because of their wealth. The facade of democracy obscured the fact that power actually rested with just a few families. Administration of the expanded territory necessitated a vast body of civil servants, and of course the positions were only filled by people approved of by these families. This inequitable system of patronage and favoritism led to social tensions that ultimately resulted in overt crisis.

The hour of the Medici had come. Cosimo de' Medici (1389-1464), later known as *il Vecchio* or "the Elder," managed, as the leader of the popular party that formed the opposition, to come out on top against the Albizzi family. Following quarrels over the conduct of a campaign against Milan, Rignaldo degli Albizzi had sent Cosimo into exile for ten years in 1433, but the pro-Medici signory called him back in 1434 and he was enthusiastically welcomed home by the crowds. Even though the Medici family technically shared the reins of government with several other families, it was

Cosimo who was most conspicuous and made his power felt. Cosimo's mantle was later passed on to his son Piero with the approval of the city's most influential citizens. Thus began the reign of a dynasty that would last for three centuries.

The Medici were from the Mugello and belonged to the guild of Florence's cloth merchants and money-lenders, called the Calimala, the city's oldest and most respected guild, which had branches across Italy and throughout Europe. It was as bankers that the Medici family had amassed their immense wealth, which in turn brought them to such a position of power that even foreign ruling houses depended on them.

Ultimately, it was Cosimo's goal to further consolidate the power of the aristocracy. Occasionally he even implemented his own private political strategies, such as cultivating a friendship with Francesco Sforza, whom he helped become Duke of Milan after Filippo Maria Visconti died. This led to a long war against the Viscontis, which ended with the Florentines'

victory at the Battle of Angihiari (1440) and subsequently led to the alliance between Milan and Florence in 1450.

Cosimo was a skilled and clever ruler. He exerted unrestricted control over the city government and at the same time was careful not to openly violate the republican-democratic way of accomplishing things. Churches and monasteries received his generous financial support, and it was because of his close affiliations with powerful contemporaries that Pope Eugene IV resided in Florence for extended periods of time and that the 17th General Council convened there in 1439.

Florence as Europe's Cultural Center

Cosimo's rule initiated a new era for the arts and sciences as well. He provided patronage to the artists and had palaces built, the first one for himself on the Via Larga (today's Via Cavour). Designed by Michelozzo, Cosimo's favorite architect, who worked on many other palaces and churches with Leon Battista Alberti, the

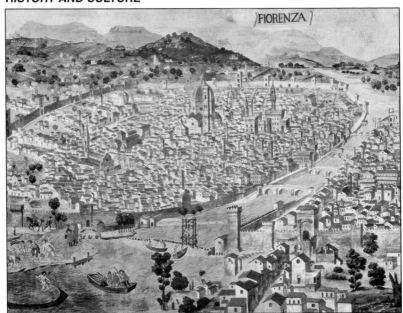

FIORENZA

wise way he eschewed making the building simply an ostentatious display of power was typical of Cosimo's reserved style. As a result, a new style that transcended Gothic and incorporated architectural elements of antiquity gradually evolved.

This new era of the Renaissance was a true Golden Age for Florence, and saw the city reach a cultural zenith. Brunelleschi, who had studied the monuments of antiquity in Rome, completed the Duomo's cupola, which at that time was considered a wonder of the art of building, and which formed an unmistakable part of the city skyline. The churches of San Lorenzo and Santo Spirito were also built, as were the Capella Pazzi and the portico of the Ospedale degli Innocenti, the Palazzo di Parte Guelfa, the Badia Fiesolana and the Palazzo Pitti in its original form.

Above: A view of Florence, ca. 1490. Right: Lorenzo il Magnifico, with Florence in the background (16th-century painting).

Meanwhile, such talented local painters as Fra Angelico, Masaccio, Andrea del Castagno and Filippo Lippi were breaking new ground with their painting techniques and their realistic representations of people and landscapes in exact, measured perspectives.

Famous local sculptors included Donatello, who was the most outstanding artist of his time, Lorenzo Ghiberti, who created the doors of the Baptistry, and terra-cotta artists Andrea and Luca della Robbia. It was also at this time that Leon Battista Alberti penned his *Ten Books of Architecture*.

Many of these Florentine artists were of humble origin. It was only through commissions from wealthy guilds at the beginning of the century, and later through the generous patronage of Cosimo and his grandson Lorenzo the Magnificent, that they were able to develop and unfold freely as artists. The results of their growth can be seen not only in Florence, but also in other cities throughout Tuscany.

Lorenzo the Magnificent

The grandson of Cosimo, Lorenzo il Magnifico (Lorenzo the Magnificent), was born in 1449 and ruled from 1469 to 1492. He was preceded by his father, Piero the Gouty, who died just five years after succeeding his father. Lorenzo, even more than his predecessors, was obsessed with absolute power, the consequence of which was mounting tensions within the ruling class that resulted, in 1478, in the conspiracy of the opposition family, the Pazzi. Lorenzo managed to escape assassination, but his brother Giuliano was not so lucky.

Pope Sixtus IV, who knew of the assassination plan in advance, was interested in the downfall of Lorenzo. With every means at his disposal he tried to break the unwholesome power of the Medici. But Lorenzo resisted his attacks, and in 1480, he set up the Council of Seventy, which consisted of the most influential families in Florence. The Council gave them a certain amount of authority, including im-portant administrative positions, and even the signory (the priories and the gonfaloniere) fell under its authority, although in reality its function would remain largely symbolic.

Lorenzo put his diplomatic skills to work outside of Tuscany, too. He established close relations with the Duke of Milan and the Kingdom of Naples. Ultimately he managed to secure an advisory position with Pope Innocence VIII. This new accord between the Church and the House of Medici was reinforced by the marriage of one of Lorenzo's daughters to the son of the Pope. The new alliance with southern Italy and the Church was naturally entirely in the economic interests of the city.

The growing power of the aristocracy was the reason so many palaces were built and decorated by famous architects and artists. The scholars and scientists, poets and artists of the time met in the Medici villas around Florence. Pico della Mirandola and Marsilio Ficino, Angelo Poliziano, Verocchio, Sandro Botticelli,

Benozzo Gozzoli, Ghirlandaio and the architect Giuliano da Sangallo were among Lorenzo's illustrious guests. But he was not only interested in intellectual discourse and the arts, but was also actively involved in the promotion of general education. Accordingly, he had the public school system expanded and in 1472 the Florentine university was founded in Pisa, although its doors were only open to the social elite.

At this point, too, Florence reached the zenith of its power in Italy. Yet patriotism in today's sense of the word did not as yet exist. The great politician and writer Niccolò Machiavelli (1469-1527) was one of the few people at this time who was capable of looking beyond his own horizons.

After Lorenzo's death, Florence was forced to relinquish pride of place to Rome in terms of the magnificence of its

Above: Niccolò Macchiavelli (painting by S. di Tito). Right: Girolamo Savonarola's execution in the Piazza della Signoria in Florence.

arts and culture. Soon after, in 1494, the Church expelled Lorenzo's son Piero from the city because in the conflict between the Church and the Milanese ruler Ludovico il Moro, Piero had sided with the French King Charles VIII who was supporting the Milanese ruler.

One other important figure of this period was the Dominican monk Girolamo Savonarola, prior of the monastery in San Marco, who gave inflammatory sermons calling for the Florentines to return to a more ascetic form of Christianity. He was responsible for drawing up a new constitution that was founded on the old republican principles. However, because of his attacks on the increasing secularization of the Church, on church corruption and often on the Pope himself, Savonarola fell into disgrace with Pope Alexander VI. He was excommunicated, and, in 1498 was hanged in the Piazza della Signoria, then burned at the stake. His republic survived him until 1512.

The Grand Duchy of Tuscany

In the course of changes in the European political power structure, Italy became a target for both French and Spanish attempts at conquest, which ultimately led to all of Italy falling under Spanish control. In addition, discovery of the New World by the Spanish and Portuguese meant that the sea trade routes had shifted to the west. These changes ushered in a period of decline for Italy, and Tuscany, too, felt the effects.

In 1512 the Medici returned to Florence. In the conflicts between France and Spain the city had sided with the French, against Pope Julius II and the Spanish. After the French were defeated, Florence was unable to defend itself, and the republic was overthrown.

But the far-sighted Lorenzo de' Medici had already entered into an alliance with the Church (in 1489 his 13-year-old son Giovanni was appointed Cardinal), and

his forethought now paid off: the Pope returned Tuscany to the Medici. In 1513, at the age of 37, Giovanni was elected to the papal throne and became Leo X. His brother Giulio succeeded him as Pope Clemens VII (1523-1534). Both popes distinguished themselves through their nepotism, distributing all manner of ecclesiastical offices, and therewith political power, to large numbers of their friends and relatives.

In Florence, Cardinal Giulio had the Medici's favorite church, San Lorenzo, extended by Michelangelo, who added the New Sacristy. Construction began in 1520. Another Medici commission was the Biblioteca Laurentiana, which Michelangelo designed a few years later.

Because of Clemens VII's pro-French politics, and his dispute with Emperor Charles V, Rome was finally conquered by the Emperor's mercenaries in 1527 in the infamous *Sacco di Roma.*

Florence's citizens seized on the weaknesses in Papal and Medici power to once again drive the Medici from the city and to proclaim a new republic. In 1528, however, it was toppled when the Pope used armed force to effect a Medici return. In 1531 Alessandro was proclaimed Duke of Florence. He abolished the democratic procedures that his predecessors had at least gone through the motions of observing for appearances' sake, and introduced a monarchical system of government. In 1537 Alessandro was murdered by his nephew Lorenzino, and succeeded by Cosimo the Great, who came from a cadet branch of the family.

Cosimo I, as he was also known, was an autocrat. He transferred the seat of his government to the Palazzo della Signoria and renamed it the *Palazzo Ducale* (Ducal Palace). The city of Florence was no longer his prime concern; he was principally interested in bringing about the political unification of Tuscany. Thus, in 1555, Cosimo I conquered Siena at the Battle of Marciano, and four years later he annexed it and its surrounding territories into his duchy. In 1569 Pope Pius V anointed him Grand Duke of Tuscany.

Now almost all of Tuscany was unified within the Grand Duchy. The only exceptions were Lucca, some parts of the Garfagnana, a portion of the Lunigiana, the *Stato dei Presidi* (along the Argentario and on the island of Elba), Piombino and the Principality of Santa Fiora, which was later sold to the Medici by the counts of Sforza-Cesarini in 1633.

But the political unification did not entail an administrative unification. Cosimo I and his successors made sure that customs barriers economically divided the old state from the new state for two hundred years. Siena, whose economy was based on arable and pastoral agriculture, suffered the most under this division: the Grand Duchy would only grant it a limited concession for one of its most important sources of income, the cultivation of cereals. Florence was still a city of craftsmanship, if not to the extent that it had

once been, and continued to be superior to other cities.

Cosimo I had public buildings erected in Florence with a view to demonstrating his power. The Uffizi were built to house the administrative offices of the Grand Duchy and the interior of the Palazzo Ducale was completely refurbished. Cosimo's favorite architect, Giorgio Vasari, built the corridor that connected the Uffizi to the Palazzo Pitti. Cosimo's wife, Eleanor of Toledo, had acquired the palace in 1549 and had it redesigned and extended as well. When the Grand Duke subsequently chose the Palazzo Pitti as his residence, the Palazzo Ducale was rechristened the Palazzo Vecchio (or Old Palace).

During the reign of the Medici, not only civil architecture, but also military works gained greatly in importance. Accordingly, it was during Alessandro's rule that the vast complex of the Fortezza da Basso was constructed, its real purpose being to intimidate the cities the Medici had conquered.

Above: Pope Leo X (by Raphael). Above Right: Duke Cosimo I Medici (by J. Carrucci). Right: Michelangelo Buonarotti.

Italy's greatest artists, such as Michelangelo, Ammanati, Benvenuto Cellini, Sansovino, Giambologna, and many others, were active in Florence at this time. The Santa Trinita Bridge, which had been destroyed by a flood, was rebuilt by Ammanati. It was a masterwork created with the help of Michelangelo, who had a consulting role. At the beginning of the 16th century Michelangelo's David, placed in front of the Palazzo Vecchio, had already set new standards for the art of sculpture. Later Michelangelo surpassed even these high standards with his monuments for the Medici tombs.

On the cultural side, Cosimo's rule was a glorious period for the academies that were being inaugurated in almost every city. One of the most important ones, which still exists today, was the *Accademia della Crusca*, which concerned itself with the care of the Italian language. In 1612 it published the first Italian dictionary, based on the dialects that were used by Dante, Boccaccio and Petrarch, thus elevating Florence's Tuscan to Italy's standard language.

In Siena, the *Collegio Tolomei* was founded as a place for scientists and students from all over Italy to come to work together. Cosimo was also the first ruler to recognize the important role the printing press could play in political power. He had a ducal printing works established that was only allowed to print works for which he had given his imprimatur.

Independent Lucca was the only city that had so far been able to assert itself against Florence; it was also the only city where the seeds of Luther's reformation fell on fertile soil and took root. In the rest of the Grand Duchy, the Church and the secular powers were able to nip in the bud any movements in this direction. But soon it was feared that the Grand Duke would use Lucca's tolerant attitude as a pretext for annexing the Luccan state. Fearing this, and the repression that would ensue, many families began to emigrate and settle abroad, mainly to the north, in Geneva.

After Cosimo's death in 1574, his son Francesco succeeded him on the throne. However, he left the government in the care of his civil servants, preferring to devote his own time and energy to scientific studies.

The next Medici, Ferdinando I (1587-1609), Francesco's brother, had a greater impact on Tuscany. All of the subsequent successors to the throne, including the last surviving male member of the family, Gian Gastone, who died in 1737 without leaving an heir, were distinguished by their obedience to Spain and the Church.

Anna Maria Ludovica, Gian Gastone's sister, died in 1743. She bequeathed the entire Medici estate to Florence, thus ensuring that the family's treasures would not be scattered to the four winds.

The Medici Grand Dukes – apart from the two outstanding personalities of Cosimo I and Ferdinando I – were on the whole unexceptional. The one project to which they all devoted themselves, with

varying degrees of enthusiasm and attention, was one of great importance to the city of Livorno: the improvement and expansion of its harbor. Under Ferdinando in particular, the city, which was also being renovated in accordance with a single unified plan, enjoyed a new period of prosperity. And as the region's major port for international trade, Livorno also became a gateway for foreign settlers of every nationality and religion. Before long it became Tuscany's second-largest city, a distinction it holds to this day.

The Reign of the Hapsburg-Lorraines

At the beginning of the 18th century, the question of succession in the Grand Duchy of Tuscany was a matter of major concern for all of Europe. Finally, in 1735 it was decided, during the preparations for the Treaty of Vienna, that Francis of Lorraine, the consort of Empress Maria

Above: Leopold I, the Grand Duke of Tuscany. Right: Napoleon Bonaparte on Elba Island.

Theresa and later Emperor of Austria, should succeed to Tuscany, provided he gave up Lorraine in return, which he did. However, Francis was too busy with other affairs to be bothered with his newly acquired Grand Duchy. He visited once in 1739, but otherwise he was satisfied to pass the administration of the state on to his regents.

His son and successor, Pietro Leopoldo, actually lived in Tuscany, residing in the Palazzo Pitti from 1765. Twenty-five years later he left Florence in order to return to Vienna as emperor. During his capable rule he implemented major reform policies, mainly in the area of agriculture, impelling Tuscany to emerge from the dull lethargic state into which it had settled under the last of the Medici grand dukes.

One example of these new policies was the establishment of the *Accademia dei Georgofili* (1753), the first European academy of agriculture, whose members included well-known names from the Tuscan patrician classes and the bourgeois intelligentsia. The Academy tried to develop scientific methods of farming and cattle breeding. For the first time, agriculture became a major focus of attention in Tuscany. Historically, crafts and commerce had been the center of regional interest.

The rule of the Hapsburg-Lorraines began under Pietro Leopoldo, who was in power until 1790, and gave Tuscany its first real autonomy. Tuscany became a model state in which peace, order and progress prevailed. The reform policies of the Grand Duke included innovations in the fields of the economy, administration, jurisdiction and the school system, which was founded on the principles that were propagated by the European Enlightenment. A new constitution was even considered. The entire country profited from these reforms and, along with Lombardy, was one of the most progressive regions in Italy.

36

The Napoleonic Interlude

Napoleon's troops brought revolutionary ideas into Tuscany in 1799, but they didn't seem to have much effect. Only in Livorno, Pisa and Florence were there a few Jacobites who greeted the French revolutionaries with open arms. The majority of the people, especially the rural population, were content with the *status quo*. Around Arezzo and Siena, in fact, the peasants were so infuriated by the intruders, particularly their atheistic attitudes, that bloody skirmishes ensued.

Fifteen years of Napoleonic rule followed the 1799 French occupation of Florence. Pietro Leopoldo's son and successor, the Grand Duke Ferdinando III, was forced to leave, and Tuscany once again fell into foreign hands. First, the so-called King of Etruria, Lodovico I, prince of the house of Bourbon-Parma, took control. He was succeeded by his son, Carlo-Lodovico (or Charles Louis), under the regency of his mother, Maria-Luisa of the Spanish house of Bourbon.

In 1808, Napoleon took over Tuscany anew, annexing it in the form of the Departements of the Arno (with Florence as its capital city), the Mediterranean, and Umbria into his empire. A year later, however, the Grand Duchy was brought back into existence for the benefit of Napoleon's sister, Elisa Bonaparte Baciocchi. During her rule, Tuscany acquired an ostensible autonomy, but in reality it was entirely dependent on Paris.

Elisa Bonaparte Baciocchi, like her predecessors, resided in the Palazzo Pitti, which she ornately refurnished in the Empire style. The French furniture she brought from Paris influenced the local style. As a result of this influence, neo-classicism, which found its true expression in Canova's paintings of Napoleon and his family, became the trend of the next few decades.

After the defeat of Napoleon and his banishment to the island of Elba in 1814, the Congress of Vienna (1814-1815) restored the Grand Duchy to Ferdinando III who returned to an enthusiastic reception.

37

The Risorgimento in Tuscany

At the time of Ferdinando III's return to Tuscany, it also included the former *Stato dei Presidi*, the principality of Piombino and the island of Elba. The only territories that had not integrated into Tuscany were the duchy of Lucca, under Maria Luisa of Bourbon, and the duchy of Massa Carrara, which was unified with Modena after the marriage of Maria Beatrice Cybo and Francesco IV from the house of Hapsburg-Este.

Ferdinando III and his successor Leopoldo II (1824-1859) resumed the reform politics of Pietro Leopoldo that had been interrupted by the French occupation. Interestingly, while he reinstated the old legislation, Ferdinando did not abolish any of the reforms that had been introduced during his exile. And it was in the prevailing liberal climate of this period

Above: A referendum in Tuscany concerning the unification of Italy, March 1860. Painting by E. Gamba (1861).

that Florence became a meeting-place for the leading figures of the Italian intelligentsia. The center of these meetings was the *Gabinetto Vieusseu*, which had been established by Jean Pierre Vieusseux as a forum for lectures, discussions and spirited exchanges. The main organ of this liberal spirit was *L'Antologia*, the most progressive newspaper in Italy at the time. *Archivo storico italiano*, which was first published in 1841, was another of the period's important scientific and cultural journals.

Because of the climate of tolerance that characterized Ferdinando's reign, the country soon became a haven for political refugees, mainly from Southern Italy. Many other foreigners, particularly the English, who were drawn by the pleasant atmosphere and warm climate, came to stay, sometimes for the rest of their lives. In Florence, along the coast of Versilia and in Livorno, a fledgling tourist industry got underway.

Under Leopoldo II, however, the government's anti-liberal tendencies and in-

creasing dependence on Vienna became more and more apparent. In 1833 the *Antologia* was shut down. When, during the critical year of 1848, democratic liberalism moved into the foreground with revolutionary agitation, the Grand Duke left Florence. Even after he returned, he continued to pursue his reactionary politics, and the chasm between him and his subjects grew wider and wider. When the Second War of Italian Independence broke out in 1859, the Grand Duke yielded to the pressure of a peaceful demonstration in Florence and once again left the country, hoping that he would be able to return when order had once again been restored.

He never did return. A referendum was held in March of 1860, and the majority of Tuscans voted in favor of a unified Italy. Despite the separatist efforts of a minority wishing to maintain the state of Tuscany's regional independence, the unification movement was pushed forward, mainly by the energetic efforts of Baron Bettino Ricasoli. From this point

on, Tuscany was no longer a grand duchy, but shared its history with the newly unified Italian state.

Tuscany in a Unified Italy

Florence was the capital of unified Italy for six years (1865-1871) and Victor Emmanuel II resided in the Palazzo Pitti. Florence's function as the country's capital meant that housing was required for the multitudes of civil servants and state officials. Old palaces, which were now used to accommodate the ministries, underwent restorations and additions. When the Papal State was captured in 1871 and Rome was declared the capital, Florence became nothing more than a major drain on the state's finances.

Following its final years as a grand duchy, the appearance of Tuscany and its cities gradually started to change. New roads were built and train tracks were laid. A train station was built in Florence. Guiseppe Poggi, a Florentine, had the old city walls torn down and replaced by

the Gothic Santa Croce was given a Neo-Gothic campanile and a marble facade.

In the countryside agriculture was still based on the traditional sharecropping or *mezzadria* system (the landlord provides capital and equipment, the tenant labor, and they divide the harvest between them), but industry was also beginning to develop. Shipbuilding, for example, got its start in Livorno, the wool industry took hold in Prato, and the mining of minerals on Elba. The working class, especially in smaller towns such as Colle di Val d'Elsa, Sesto Fiorentino, Empoli and Piombino, and also in the upper Arno valley, formed socialist organizations.

The intellectual life of the cities remained, as ever, the preserve of the upper middle class. After the expulsion of the Hapsburg-Lorraines from Florence in 1859, *La Nazione* was established. Initially moderate, over time this newspaper became increasingly conservative. *Nuova Antologia* first appeared in 1866. It was a journal that concerned itself with current affairs and was soon highly respected throughout Italy. At around this time the *Istituto degli Studi Superiori* was founded. It became a university in 1924.

Towards the end of the 19th century Tuscany fell behind Rome, Milan and Naples in intellectual importance. The only literary event of international significance was publication of Carlo Lorenzini's *Pinocchio*, the tale of a wooden puppet with the long nose that is an enchanting story children and adults alike. The Sicilian artist Emilio Grecco created a monument in Collodi (the town whose name Lorenzini used as his pen name) to commemorate the author and his puppet.

At the beginning of the 20th century intellectual life in Tuscany experienced a revival. A number of new newspapers, including *La Voce*, *Il Regno* and *L'Unità*, appeared and the great Italian publishing houses Le Monnier, Barbera, Sansoni, Salani, Olschki and Nerbini were founded in Florence.

wide avenues. He built the Viale dei Colli on the south bank of the Arno and designed the Piazzale Michelangelo as a terrace offering a panoramic view over the city. The downtown area gradually filled with sidewalk cafés, shops and arcades, and at night gas lanterns lit the streets. The first public transportation – a horse-drawn omnibus – entered service in Florence in 1865, and soon after, towards the turn of the century, the first streetcars appeared.

Of course, all this progress also had negative ramifications. In the course of the redevelopment of the town center, one of the liveliest and most beautiful sections in Florence, the Old Market and its immediate vicinity, was leveled to make space for the Piazza della Repubblica and its unattractive and bombastic buildings. The Duomo's new facade with overly ornate statues was finally completed, and

Above: Victor Emmanuel II. Right: Pinocchio, brainchild of the Florentine Carlo (Lorenzini) Collodi, has been around for over a century.

World War I took place at a time when Tuscany was experiencing an industrial boom, which initially was stimulated even more by the war. But after the war came a crisis with workers' and peasants' uprisings and strikes in protest of the high cost of living and rampant unemployment. This helped prepare the ground for fascism in Tuscany as well. Between 1920 and 1922, the new fascist movement launched attacks not only against the socialist-communist movement, but also the Popular Party, which had a large Tuscan following. After 1929 the international economic crisis hit Tuscany with full force, especially in the areas of industry and mining. The government tried to combat unemployment by means of public works projects, such as the construction of the *autostrada* between Florence and the coast and the Florence-Bologna train link.

Between the two world wars, Florence was one of Italy's cultural powerhouses. Additional publishing houses and magazines were founded and launched, the music festival *Maggio Musicale Fiorentino* was initiated, and the painters Ottone Rosai and Ardengo Soffici created new styles.

Outside Florence, other Tuscan artists making their mark include Marino Marini, a gifted sculptor from Pistoia, as well as Amedeo Modigliani from Livorno, and Lorenzo Viani from Viareggio, who are among the most important painters of the first half of the 20th century.

Works of architectural importance dating from the 1930s include the stadium in Florence and the new train station Santa Maria Novella.

During the Second World War, Tuscan cities also suffered grievously from the bombing. Particularly hard-hit were Livorno, Pisa and especially Florence, which was partially destroyed by the retreating Germans at the end of the war. All of the bridges leading across the Arno were blown up, except for the Ponte Vecchio, which was only saved because a German officer had the courage to ignore his orders. Instead, in an act that was al-

trialization, especially in the Arno valley and to the west of Florence, in Val d'Elsa and along the Tyrrhenian coast. But gradually, even in Italy, people are becoming aware of the dangers of pollution and the destruction of the environment. Tuscany has become a trendsetter for a more environmentally-conscious type of tourism. Since the 1980s the tourist and gastronomic industries have participated in demonstrations with the Green Party and environmental protection associations. Their motto: A clean sea, clean coasts and a ban on the use of pesticides in farming.

Tuscany is also ahead of other regions when it comes to urban renewal projects. Since 1987 Florence's town center – not just its historical core – has been closed to automobiles because it has been recognized that this is the only way that unique and irreplaceable works of art can be protected from being destroyed forever. Siena made this decision even earlier than Florence. Cars have been banned from its Old Town since 1956.

Not only the old town centers have been damaged in Tuscany. Since the 1950s, when the great emigration from the countryside started and more and more farmers quit their hard life as leaseholders to move to the cities, drab and ugly suburbs have been springing up on the outskirts of the region's historical centers and old cities.

But ambitious large-scale plans such as Firenze 2000, a project for a state-of-the-art city of apartments and offices north of Florence, has met with fierce resistance. Some fear that the projected area will become a ghetto for the 35,000 people who are to live and work there. Others are upset that an area of almost two square kilometers, which could otherwise be used for outdoor recreational facilities, would be covered over with pavement. Failure to reach a compromise has resulted in the whole project being put on ice. Whether the project will ever be realized remains uncertain.

most as equally reprehensible, many of the old houses at the approaches to the bridge were demolished, in order to make it more difficult for the allied troops to cross the river.

The resistance movement had many members in Tuscany, and the reprisals they had to suffer were frequent and severe.

Tuscany Today

In 1946 a referendum was held by which Italy abolished the monarchy and became a republic. In Tuscany the majority also voted for the republic, and since then the region has been ruled for the most part by the parties of the left. The only exception is Lucca. This city, which has always played a special part in Tuscan history, votes Christian Democrat.

Increasingly, the landscape of Tuscany is undergoing change as a result of indus-

Above and Right: Tourists – marveling at the sights, or worn out from shopping?

AROUND FLORENCE

FLORENCE
FIESOLE / MEDICI VILLAS
MUGELLO / SIEVE VALLEY
PRATO / PISTOIA
ARNO VALLEY / MONTALBANO

★★FLORENCE
The Blossoming City

When the French writer Stendhal visited Florence on his journey to Italy over two hundred years ago, he was so overwhelmed by the beauty of this city that he actually fell ill. To this day there are repeated instances of tourists having to be hospitalized because they are suffering from "Stendhal Syndrome." The abundance of cultural monuments that people think they absolutely must see before they leave has been known to drive some visitors into a state of hysteria bordering on nervous breakdown. According to one scientific study, only Italians appear to be immune to this phenomenon.

It's simply impossible to "see," or truly to get to know, ★★**Florence ❶** in a matter of a few days – indeed, weeks and months are hardly adequate to the task. The city is so inexhaustibly rich in sights – and not just cultural ones – that it is definitely a better idea to take your time and limit yourself to those works of art that come closest to your own personal tastes and interests. In addition, you should allow

Preceding Pages: The view of Florence from the Piazzale Michelangelo. Lungarno degli Acciaioli. Left: Graceful, open-minded and stylish – truly Florentine.

the flavor of the city itself work its magic on you. And, last but not least, you must remember to schedule some time for shopping because this is just one more area in which Florence is tempting in the extreme.

In the restricted space at our disposal here, it will, of course, be impossible to provide exhaustive information about Florence. There are plenty of detailed studies available for those who want to immerse themselves in the history, art and culture of the city, and some of these titles are listed at the back of the book. We will therefore limit ourselves to an overview of the city's most important works of art and buildings.

The City's Early History

During the time of the Etruscans there was already a settlement on the banks of the Arno and it was here that the Romans established a veterans' colony for former legionnaires in 59 B.C., at the time of Caesar. The colony was called *Colonia Florentia*, the blossoming colony, possibly because the fertile Arno valley has such an abundance of flowers. Theories abound as to the true origins of the name, but none of them are really convincing.

Because of its exposed location on the river, in the midst of Tuscany's hilly land-

ported southwards to the Mediterranean. Traders from the East who began to settle here brought with them Christianity, which began to make steady progress after A.D. 300. The 4th century saw the construction of the first two Christian churches: San Lorenzo, which at that time was located outside the city walls, and Santa Felicità, on the opposite bank of the Arno. As early as the year A.D. 313, the first bishop was appointed under the Emperor Constantine.

Under the Romans, marble palaces and temples dominated the cityscape, while an aqueduct brought water down from Monte Morelli to supply the city's residents with drinking water and fill the public baths. And a huge amphitheater was built during the 2nd century A.D. You can still detect its outlines in the curving facades of the houses on Via de' Bentaccordi and Via Torta.

scape, the settlement was hardly suitable as a military base, so we can assume that right from the start it had a primarily agricultural function. Its defense was secured by the hilltop town of Fiesole, an old Etruscan stronghold just a few kilometers away. When compared to Fiesole, *Colonia Florentia* had a fairly insignificant existence for quite some time.

The earliest plan of the city on the right bank of the Arno formed an almost perfect rectangle, the outlines of which still largely correspond to the heart of the Old Town today. Because of its favorable location on the Via Cassia, which ran from Rome through Florence and on to Lucca, and because of the connecting roads to the other most important cities in what was then the province of Etruria, Florence rapidly developed into an important trade center in the first two hundred years after its foundation. A harbor on the Arno River meant that goods could be trans-

Above: The Duomo, Campanile, and Baptistry in Florence. Right: San Miniato al Monte.

Florence in the Middle Ages

This first flowering, which may have seen the city's population swell to almost 10,000, came to an end in the confusion that was the great barbarian migrations. Florence was attacked and devastated by the Ostrogoths, the Byzantines and the Lombards in turn. After the fall of the Roman Empire traders and merchants stayed away because the new power constellation meant that trade routes had shifted west and east of the Arno valley. By the time the Western Roman Empire fell in the 5th century, the inhabited part of Florence had shrunk to a small area around the old Roman forum, which lives on today, in shape and size, in the form of the current Piazza della Repubblica.

During this period the only event of importance to the art historian was the first phase of construction of the Santa Reparata, the church that preceded the Duomo, the city's cathedral. Work may well also have started on a forerunner of the present-day Baptistry.

Not until the Franks, under Charlemagne, conquered large parts of Italy and proclaimed Tuscany a margravate did the region's economy begin to take off again. In 854 Lothar I combined the two duchies of Florence and Fiesole and established Florence as the seat of his government, which brought with it numerous privileges. Prosperity increased, Florence's population rose to 20,000, and soon the city had spread to take over the left bank of the Arno, as well. The churches of San Lorenzo and Santa Reparata were expanded, and with the construction of the monastery and the basilica of San Miniato, as well as the Baptistry, we have the first manifestations of the Florentine Romanesque style. In A.D. 978, Willa, the widow of Margrave Umberto, founded the *Badia fiorenta* and thereby the first monastery within the city itself.

The clergy, already endowed with large estates, now began to strive for more and more political power, and ecclesiastical offices were sold off to the highest bidder. The monk Giovanni Gualberto protested against the increasing immorality of the Church, but found little response from the Florentines. He left the city to live as a hermit in the Vallombrosa forest, where he founded the order of the Vallombrosans.

The 11th century was a period marked by the increasing self-confidence of the middle classes. Craftsmen, artisans and merchants were gaining in influence and their struggle for autonomy had the support of Margravine Matilda of Canossa. Matilda, in an attempt to help protect the Church from secular intervention, also sided with the Pope in his struggle against the emperor. After her death in 1115, Florence proclaimed a government of its own, which was officially recognized by the emperor in 1183.

The Period of Communal Constitution

When the empire temporarily lost its grip on Italy after the death of Henry V (1125), nothing more stood in the way of

FLORENCE

★Sant'Apollonia ⑬   ⑫ ★San Marco

Via Jacopo da Diacceto
Via L. Alamanni

Università

Pza. S. Marco

S.S.
Annunzia

Via Guelfa

Via Battisti

★San Onofrio
⑱

★Galleria
dell'Accademia ⑪

Stazione Centrale
di S. Maria Novella

ℹ

Via Nazionale

Mercato Centrale
di San Lorenzo

P ⑰

Via Faenza

Via Cavour

Via di Ginori

ℹ Via Cavour

⑭ Pza. della
Santissima
Annunziata

Ospe
d'Inf

P Pza. della
Stazione

Via Ricasoli

Via degli A

Via della Scala

Pza.
dell'Unità
Italiana

Palazzo
Medici-
Riccardi ⑮

Rotonda di
Brunelleschi

Via de Panzani

Pza. S.
Lorenzo ⑯

Via dei Pucci

Via dei Servi

★Sta. Maria
Novella ⑲

SANTA MARIA

Via Palazzuolo

Pza. S. Maria
Novella

★★San Lorenzo

Via de Martelli

SAN GIOVANNI

Ospedale
S. Maria Nuova

Borgo Ognissanti

NOVELLA

P

Via de Cerretani Pza.

★Sta. Maria del Fiore
(Duomo) ②

Via S. Egidio

⑯ Ognissanti

Pza.
D'Ognissanti

Ospedale
San Giovanni
di Dio

★★Battistero ③

S. Giovanni

Museo dell'Opera
del Duomo

Lungarno Amerigo Vespucci

Via della Spada

Via d. Agli

Campanile

Museo di
Antropologia

Via Campidoglio

Loggia del
Bigallo

Via dell'Oriuolo

Arno

Via de' Fossi

Via
degli Strozzi

Pza.
della
Repubblica

Via del Corso

Borgo degli Albizi

Via di Vigna Nuova

Via
degli Strozzi

Palazzo
Strozzi ㉓

Casa di Dante

Lungarno Soderini

Pza. di
Cestello

Pza.
Goldini

Via d. Parione

Palazzo
Corsini ㉕

Orsanmichele ④

Via del Corso

Via Dante Alighieri

Badia ⑧

Via Ghibellina

Pza.
San
Firenze ⑤

Teatro
Verdi

Pza. S. C

Lungarno Corsini

★Pza. S. Trinità

Via

Porta
Rossa

㉒ Santa
Trinità

㉑ Palazzo
Davanzati

⑳ Loggia del
Mercato
Nuovo

Pza. della
Signoria

Via d.
Gondi

Pza.
San
Bargello ⑦

Via dell'Anguillara

Via Torta

Palazzo
Vecchio

Via de' Greci

SANTA CROCE

ℹ
Cr

Ponte
Alla Carraia

Ponte
S. Trinità

Lungarno Acciaiuoli

Loggia dei
Lanzi

★★Galleria
degli
Uffizi ⑥

Via dei Neri

Via de Benci

Borgo S. Croce

Pza. del
Carmine

Lungarno Guicciardini

Via S. Spirito

Borgo S. Jacopo

★Ponte
Vecchio ㉗

Lung. Archibusieri

P

Lungarno Gen. Diaz

Biblioteca
Nazionale

Via S. Monaca

⑳ Santa Maria
del Carmine

Via de Serragli

Santo
Spirito

SANTO SPIRITO

Pza.
S. Maria Sopr.

P

Lungarno Torrigiani

Arno

Via S. Agostino

Pza.
㉘ S. Spirito

Via Maggio

Via Guicciardini

Via de Bardi

Ponte Alle Grazie

Via della Chiesa

Pza. dei Pitti

Lungarno Serristori

Giardano Torrigiani,
Porta Romana

Pza.
S. Felice

㉚ ★Palazzo Pitti

Costa di S. Giorgio

Via di S. Nicco

Via Romana

Forte di
Belvedere
㉜

㉛ ★Giardino di Boboli

FLORENCE

0   250 m   Bobolino

Around Florence

Florence's rise to independence. The conquest and destruction of Fiesole marked the start of Florentine domination of the surrounding territories, a domination that continued to expand. Commerce and trade were growing inexorably, and the city was spreading rapidly. Contacts with Pisa facilitated sea trade with countries in the eastern Mediterranean.

During the 12th century Florence proclaimed a communal constitution that gave the power of government to the aristocracy and leading members of the merchant classes. The social pre-eminence of the nobility was visibly and unmistakably expressed by the dynastic residential towers that dominated the city's skyline during these years. As a result of the savage feuds that raged between these same aristocratic families during the following decades, their towers were gradually turned into regular fortresses.

Outside the city, too, there were bloody confrontations with the feudal lords, who were gradually subjugated and stripped of their autonomy.

Eventually the disputes between noble families led to a change in the communal constitution. The business of governing was taken over by a *podestà*, a professional politician who regulated public affairs on the basis of a newly developed system of legal standards.

One typical feature of public life in Florence at that time was the formation of various associations, which then proceeded to develop active, and often bitter, rivalries between one another. This resulted in a state of political instability that, amazingly, proved to be greatly beneficial to the city's cultural development. Since each association was constantly attempting to outdo the others, they commissioned works of art and new buildings that were intended to demonstrate the status and greatness of the guild in question. This resulted in the heyday of the Romanesque style in Florence, a style that is characterized by clear lines, balanced

proportions, a restrained use of color and materials (mainly white and green marble), and geometric patterns.

At the beginning of the 13th century, various monastic orders were another major influence on the city's art and culture. The Franciscans built a small church on the site of what was later to be the basilica of Santa Croce. The Dominicans established themselves on the city's western outskirts, where Santa Maria Novella was built around the end of the century. Both churches also functioned as schools that soon enjoyed international reputations. Dante, in fact, studied here. The squares in front of the churches were arenas for festive celebrations and the competitions that were so popular with the Florentines.

In addition to these two mendicant orders, numerous other religious communities settled in Florence and built their monasteries there. One rather unusual order was the Humiliates who had emigrated from Northern Italy and were later to prove of great economic importance for Florence, turning their hands to the cloth-weaving and dyeing trades and maintaining their own workshops.

The Guilds

By far the most important of all of the associations and organizations that were formed during the 13th century were the *arti* (guilds), professional associations of merchants and craftsmen. Not only did these guilds control trade and commerce, but they also wielded considerable political power and, by constantly seeking to outdo each other, provided invaluable funding for major cultural projects.

The oldest and most influential guild was the Guild of the Calimala, whose trade connections extended from northern Europe to the Middle East. Its members were cloth traders, but they were also active as money-changers right from the

Above: A representation of the blacksmiths' guild on Orsanmichele, Florence. Right: Ponte Santa Trinità over the Arno.

start, and were soon handling not only the banking business of their trading partners, but also that of entire aristocratic families. This close affiliation between manufacturing, trade and financial matters became a trademark of Florence's economy and the secret to its tremendous success. The concrete symbol of this ascent to financial power was the florin, a gold coin that was first minted in 1252.

The power struggle between the Guelphs, the followers of the Pope, and the Ghibellines, who were loyal to the Emperor, continued to divide the city until the Guelphs finally got the upper hand after the death of Emperor Frederick II in 1250. One of the best-known victims of this feud was Italy's greatest poet, Dante Alighieri, a Ghibelline who was banished from his hometown in 1302. Nineteen years later he died in exile in Ravenna, a bitter and lonely man.

The prosperity and growing self-confidence of Florence's middle class during the 13th century was expressed in a new need to beautify the city. Numerous plazas were enlarged and new streets, which, according to the government's plan, were to be attractive, wide and straight, were built. The Ponte Santa Trinità was built across the Arno. And in 1296 work began on the magnificent Duomo, or cathedral. Work on the Palazzo Vecchio began just three years later.

By contrast the 14th century was characterized by internal and external conflicts, natural catastrophes and economic collapse. In 1333 a huge flood devastated the city. In 1348 an outbreak of the plague killed over one-third of the population. And in 1378 the city's poor rebelled in the "uprising of the *ciompi*" (wool-carders), during which they stormed the Palazzo Vecchio and forced the election of Salvestro de' Medici as the *gonfaloniere*.

After this "proletarian revolution" the city was briefly governed by the lower classes, but they soon relinquished their power to the city's great families who were quickly becoming more influential. This eventually resulted in the Medici family taking over the reigns of power.

The Medici

Despite the external difficulties and political instability, the middle classes in Florence still managed, even in this turbulent period, to maintain and indeed improve their standard of living. They were also able to continue with their numerous projects to beautify the city.

The Medici, a successful family of bankers and merchants, came to power in the city in 1434, headed by Cosimo the Elder. This marked the beginning of a period of cultural flowering that reached its zenith under Cosimo's grandson Lorenzo the Magnificent, an era that is known as the Florentine Renaissance. Names such as Botticelli, Ghirlandaio, Leonardo da Vinci and Michelangelo Buonarroti come to mind when one thinks of this epoch, which also marked the peak of Florence's political power in Italy.

What would the puritanical monk Savonarola (above) have said about the graffiti art of the 20th century (right)?

Rivalry among other patrician families climaxed with the Pazzi conspiracy in the Duomo on April 26, 1475, in the course of which Giuliano, Lorenzo's brother, was killed. Even though this attempt to overthrow Medici rule failed, Florence ultimately relinquished its leading position in the arts to Rome after Lorenzo's death in 1492.

The inflammatory machinations of the puritanical monk Girolamo Savonarola, who condemned the immoral ways of the Renaissance aristocrats, ultimately led to the Medici's expulsion from Florence and Savonarola prepared a new republican constitution that remained in effect until 1512. However, his sermons against the increasing secularization of the Church attracted the wrath of Pope Alexander VI, and he was burned at the stake in 1498, in the Piazza della Signoria.

The Medici returned to power in 1512, and several of them became popes during the course of the century. During this time wealth, power and education were in the hands of the aristocracy, who built majestic palaces for themselves and commissioned great works of art. The guilds also commissioned many Renaissance masterpieces, including Brunelleschi's dome atop the Duomo.

In 1530 Alessandro de' Medici was appointed the Grand Duke of Tuscany by Emperor Charles V, and Florence and Tuscany remained under the absolutist control of the Medici until 1743. When Gian Gastone, the last male member of the dynasty, died, the duchy was transferred to Francis of Lorraine, the consort of Empress Maria Theresa of Austria. Tuscany was governed by the Hapsburg-Lorraines until 1859 – except for a fifteen-year period between 1799 and 1814 when the French, Napoleon's sister Elisa among them, ruled Florence and held court in the city.

In 1859, Grand Duke Leopoldo II was expelled from Florence, and in 1860 Tuscany relinquished its centuries-old in-

dependence in favor of joining a unified Italy. Florence was the capital of the Kingdom of Italy from 1865-1870, until Victor Emmanuel II moved to Rome.

Florence Today

During the World War II, Florence was devastated by Allied bombing raids and later by the German troops who destroyed all of the bridges across the Arno when they retreated in 1944 – Ponte Vecchio being the sole exception.

During the catastrophic floods of November 4, 1966, when, with alarming rapidity, the Arno River rose to 5.20 meters above its normal level, many precious works of art were damaged or destroyed. The people of Florence pitched in selflessly, aided by countless helpers from all over the country, to save whatever could be saved.

The last major calamity to be suffered by the city was the car bomb that exploded in front of the Uffizi Gallery on May 27, 1993, killing five people and injuring 50 others, and seriously damaging a number of works of art.

Today Florence numbers almost half a million inhabitants, and continues to expand upriver along the Arno. In order to protect the old center of the city from the corrosive effects of exhaust fumes, private car traffic was banned there in 1988. There are attended parking lots around the edge of the downtown area and on the other side of the Arno. Since most of the city's important sights are relatively close together, Florence can be comfortably explored on foot.

A tip to aid in orientation: Florence's house-numbering system can be, to say the least, confusing. Stores and restaurants have red house numbers (the address includes a red R). Private residences and hotels, on the other hand, have black. The numbers run consecutively within their group, but the two groups are independent of each other.

And another tip: Watch out for pickpockets! Don't carry your purse or handbag on the street side. Be alert when you

are in large groups, especially when groups of gypsy women or children come begging and you are jolted or pushed. This chaos distracts you for a minute, and when you look down again you may well find that your wallet has disappeared.

The City

For an initial and breathtaking view of the city of Florence, drive up the beautiful winding road to the **Piazzale Michelangelo** ❶. Guiseppe Poggi built it for this very purpose between 1867 and 1875.

Fifty meters above the city on the south side of the Arno, this square offers a spectacular panoramic view that includes the palaces, the towers, Brunelleschi's dominating dome, the hills that enclose everything on three sides, the Arno flowing to the plain in the west, and the bridges. The view is particularly stunning at dusk,

Above: World-famous designs from very different centuries. Right: A juggler on the Piazza del Duomo.

when the sky gradually turns a soft bluish green and the first lights start to come on in the city below.

If you want to avoid the inevitable crowds of tourists that usually throng this observation terrace, drive to the Forte di Belvedere at a slightly higher elevation, where the view is just as beautiful, if not more so, and the crowds are generally smaller. As a bonus, from here you can even see the hilly landscape of Chianti to the south.

When you have drunk your fill of this picturesque view of the Duomo, the Campanile, the towers of the Palazzo Vecchio and Badia, Orsanmichele, Santa Maria Novella and Santa Croce – to name just a few of the most impressive sights – wrap yourself in equanimity and patience and plunge into the crowds of tourists that choke the streets of Florence from March to October. Florence, after all, has an enormous number of works of art – only Rome has more – all neatly packed into a very small area. And yet, despite being surrounded by exhausted tour groups and lost tourists, if you keep you eyes open and dare to venture onto the little side streets away from the main attractions, you can still experience a taste of real Italian ambience.

The *Duomo, Campanile and **Baptistry

These three monuments form the spiritual center of the city. They are located on a narrow space that had to be cleared by hand before they could be built. Perhaps the best place to get a full view of them is the **Loggia del Bigallo**, located between Via dei Calzaiuoli and Via Roma, which was built in the 14th century as the seat of the *Misericordia*, a charitable institution that is still in operation today.

The **Duomo**, or ***Santa Maria del Fiore** ❷, was begun in 1296. Arnolfo di Cambio, the architect, placed it where the Santa Reparata church once stood (the remains of which can be seen in the cathedral's crypt). After di Cambio's death work was continued by the period's best architects, including Giotto, Andrea Pisano, Francesco Talenti and Giovanni Ghini, and was finally completed with the construction of the dome in 1436. Building the dome was perhaps the greatest challenge ever faced by the architect Brunelleschi. He built it without using scaffolding, tile by tile, working from the outside in. An almost impossible technical undertaking, it was completed in the face of every conceivable obstacle. After Brunelleschi's death, Michelozzo made the lantern according to Brunelleschi's design, and Verrocchio topped it with the golden ball you see today. Cracks were recently discovered in the dome's roof, but they have probably always been there.

The cathedral's exterior is encased in marble; green from Prato, white from Carrara and red from the Maremma. The intricate and over-elaborate facade, decorated with figures, was not created until the 19th century.

The gloomy, stark interior of the cathedral covers an area of 8300 square meters and can accommodate up to 25,000 people. Interesting features include the clock above the main door: its hands run counter-clockwise; the canonical sacristy with a terra-cotta *Ascension* by Luca della Robbia above the door; the New Sacristy with its bronze door by Michelozzo and Maso di Bartolomeo, through which Lorenzo the Magnificent fled from the assassins of the Pazzi conspiracy in 1478; the restored dome painting; and in the left transept, the metal plate in the floor that has been used for astronomical measurements since the 15th century.

Another notable work of art is an equestrian painting by Paolo Uccello (1436) of Sir John Hawkwood – Giovanni Acuto to the Italians – who was the leader of the English mercenaries that fought alongside the Florentine army at the end of the 14th century. Its complicated perspectives make it an important example of Renaissance painting. A painting of Dante (on the same wall) standing in

front of a mediaeval Florence is a Florentine tribute to Italy's greatest poet, as well as a gesture of atonement for the fact that he was banished from his hometown.

Next to the Duomo is one of the most magnificent towers in the world, Giotto's **Campanile**. Construction of this Gothic masterpiece, which stands almost 85 meters high, began in 1334. After Giotto's death it was completed by Andrea Pisano and Francesco Talenti between 1336 and 1359.

The base of this fine and seemingly weightless tower is decorated with two rows of bas-reliefs by Pisano and Luca della Robbia (the originals are in the Cathedral Museum). Its ogival windows get larger the higher up you go, and convey an almost filigree lightness to the tower. From its top, reached after climbing 414 steps, there is an impressive view of the dome of the Duomo and its surroundings.

Above: The Baptistry's "Gate of Paradise." Right: Luc Della Robbia's chior loft in the Cathedral Museum (detail).

The ****Baptistry** ❸, like the Duomo and the Campanile, is clad with polychrome marble and is one of the oldest buildings in Florence. There is still some dispute as to exactly when *Il bel San Giovanni* – as Dante referred to the church where he was baptized – was built. It is assumed that its structure dates from the 11th or 12th century and that it was erected on the site of an older building from the 4th to the 6th century. The octagonal church, which is reminiscent of ancient Roman buildings, is crowned by an eight-sided white pyramidal roof, which conceals the cupola beneath it. The interior of the cupola is lined with magnificent 13th-century mosaics representing the medieval concept of Heaven, Hell and Purgatory. Also noteworthy is the tomb of the antipope John XXIII, which was designed jointly by Donatello (actually Donato di Niccolò di Betto Bardi) and Michelozzo around 1425.

The most beautiful aspect of the Baptistry is, however, the three famous bronze doors that are a highlight of Western sculpture. The **South Door**, oldest of the three, was created by Andrea Pisano and represents the sunset of Gothic sculpture in Florence. The **North Door** was started by Lorenzo Ghiberti seven years later, following a competition in which his proposed design was selected over those of Brunelleschi and Jacopo della Quercia. It took 21 years to complete this work, which was executed with the participation of other great artists such as Masolino, Donatello, Paolo Uccello and Michelozzo. The **East Door**, or **Gate of Paradise**, which faces the cathedral, is Ghiberti's masterpiece. He started it in 1425 and took 27 years to complete it. "It was executed with great patience and effort. Of all my works it is the most remarkable . . . it was executed with great skill, in the right proportions and with understanding," he himself said of it. In fact, these relief panels depicting scenes from the Old Testament, with rich architectural

and natural backgrounds, demonstrate both exact perspective and a truly lifelike quality. In his work the artist included a portrait of himself to be preserved for posterity (left-hand door, right-hand side, fourth head from the top). The panels containing the reliefs are gradually being restored and replaced by copies. The originals are in the Cathedral Museum.

The **Cathedral Museum** is at the rear of the Duomo, across from the apse. It contains works of art from the Duomo, Baptistry and Campanile that have been stored here to save them from erosion. Highlights include the two choir lofts by Luca della Robbia and Donatello; the *Pietà* by Michelangelo, which he started when he was quite old and was completed by his student Calcagni; and Donatello's wood carving of Mary Magdalene.

From Piazza Duomo to Piazza della Signoria

Via de' Calzaioli, lined with elegant stores, leads from Piazza Duomo to Pi-azza della Signoria. Halfway to the square, Via degli Speziali turns off to the right towards **Piazza della Repubblica**, a large square that occupies the site of the Roman forum. The Mercato Vecchio and countless historical buildings were ruth-lessly demolished towards the end of the 19th century in order to make room for this square, and only the attractive old cafés that surround it are really worth vis-iting.

A bit further on you will come to the building known as **Orsanmichele** ❹ (the abbreviation for *San Michele in Orto*). Originally a granary instead of an oratory for Saint Michael, this peculiar church was was built in the 13th century by Arnolfo di Cambio. However, a painting alleged to work miracles attracted so many worshipers that the grain had to be moved, initially to be stored on one of the upper floors, and finally the entire build-ing was converted into a church. Its inte-rior includes Andrea Orcagna's famous marble tabernacle of the *Madonna delle Grazie*, on which lovely reliefs illustrate

his life, and death). The Palazzo Vecchio was originally the residence of the city's councils and administrative offices. Later it was the residence of Duke Cosimo I Medici. And from 1865 to 1971 it was first the Parliament and then the Foreign Ministry of the Kingdom of Italy. Today it is the seat of the municipal government and residence of the city's mayor.

The different names the palace has been given over the years reflect the course of the city's history. Originally it was called the Palazzo dei Priori. At the time of the oligarchy it was called the Palazzo della Signoria. While Cosimo I resided there, it was known as the Palazzo Ducale. And finally, after the duke moved to the Palazzo Pitti, it assumed the name **Palazzo Vecchio**, the Old Palace.

It is the largest communal palace in Florence (designed by Arnolfo di Cambio in 1298), a forbidding, fortress-like building of irregular blocks of rough-hewn, light brown ashlar, crowned by the rectangular battlements of the Guelphs. The 94-meter-high tower, with the swallowtail crenellations of the Ghibellines and a steep bronze roof, rises high above the Palazzo. It is no accident that the city hall resembles a fortress. Its original purpose was to protect the civil servants and defend their independence and autonomy.

the life of Mary. Of particular interest on the outside of the building are the pilasters with canopied niches containing the statues of the patron saints of the guilds. Fourteen niches or tabernacles are distributed around the building like a kind of outdoor museum of first-rate Renaissance sculptures, some of which have been replaced by newer works over the course of the years.

*Piazza della Signoria

Signoria means rule or power, and the ***Piazza della Signoria ❺** was and still is the political center of the city. It was the site of the first public assemblies, and it was here that the Dominican monk Savonarola was hanged, then burned at the stake (a small granite plaque next to the fountain of Neptune commemorates

For the same, defensive reasons, the entrance gate on the west side was kept small. It leads into the courtyard, which is surrounded by high porticoes. In the center is a fountain with putti and dolphin by Verrocchio. Not all sections of the palazzo's interior are open to the public. Most of the rooms date back to the 16th century and are decorated with numerous frescoes, paintings and statues.

Piazza della Signoria resembles an open-air sculpture museum. A copy of Michelangelo's *David* (the original, created between 1501 and 1504, is in the Galleria dell'Accademia) takes pride of place in front of the main entrance to city hall. Florentines claim that this work rep-

Above and Right: Ammanati's Neptune on the Piazza della Signoria wasn't, and isn't, to everyone's taste – but everyone seems to agree on Michelangelo's David.

resents the victory of democracy over tyranny. Opposite Michelangelo's masterpiece stands the marble group *Hercules and Cacus* by Bandinelli (1533), which Cellini is said to have referred to as a sack full of pumpkins.

The *Marzocco* Lion (which derives its name from the fact that it is said to once have stood at the plinth of a column of Mars), with Florence's coat-of-arms, is the emblem of the city. It is modeled on a sandstone original by Donatello (now in the Bargello). Defeated enemies of the Florentines were supposedly forced to kiss the lion's hindquarters. In 1980 a copy of Donatello's bronze sculpture of *Judith and Holofernes* was placed alongside it.

In front of the southwest corner of the Palazzo is the Neptune Fountain, with its sea god, by Ammanati, which is said to have inspired the following remark from his contemporaries, *"Ammanato, Ammanato, che bel marmo hai rovinato!"* ("What beautiful marble you have ruined!"). The equestrian statue to the left

of the fountain is by Giambologna and represents Cosimo I (1594-1598). The reliefs in the plinth depict him being crowned archduke by Pope Pius V.

The **Loggia dei Lanzi** is on the southern edge of the piazza. Built between 1376 and 1382 by Benci di Cione and Simone Talenti, probably based on a design by Orcagna. It was named after the German mercenaries (*Landsknechte* or *lanzichenecchi*) who acted as guards for Duke Alessandro I de' Medici. Today it houses a collection of statues, including the famous sculpture *Perseus and the Head of Medusa* by Benvenuto Cellini (ca. 1550), which is currently being restored.

The ****Uffizi**

To the left of the Loggia dei Lanzi, which served as an architectural model for the Feldherrnhalle in Munich, we continue on to the ****Uffizi ⑥**, the former "offices" of the archducal administration, located between the Palazzo Vecchio and

the Arno. Vasari built this edifice between 1560 and 1574, and it houses one of the richest museums in the world. Famous masterpieces include works by Botticelli (*Birth of Venus, Allegory of Spring, Adoration of the Magi*), Piero della Francesca (*Duke of Urbino*), Filippo Lippi (images of the Madonna), Michelangelo (*Holy Family*), Raphael (*Madonna of the Goldfinch*), Titian (*Venus of Urbino*), Andrea Mantegna (*Adoration of the Magi*), and so many others that it would take much more than just one visit to see them all.

The two parallel sections of the Uffizi building are connected by an open loggia on the south side. A corridor, built by Vasari in 1565, leads from the Uffizi across the Ponte Vecchio to the Palazzo Pitti, thus ensuring a private, safe and discreet connection between the two buildings. This has been open to visitors since 1997.

Above: Botticelli's "Spring" alone is worth a visit to the Uffizzi. Right: An open staircase in the inner courtyard of the Bargello.

Bargello and Santa Croce

If you pass the memorial to Cosimo I and continue along Via de' Gondi, you will come to Piazza San Firenze. At the far end of this piazza is the **Palazzo del Podestà** or **Bargello** ❼. Work on this plain battlemented castle, a symbol of the victory of Florence's bourgeoisie over the squabbling aristocracy, was begun in 1255, half a century before the Palazzo Vecchio, making it the oldest secular building in Florence. Initially it was the official residence of the city's leader. Later it housed the *podestà*, i.e., the city government. Next it became a courthouse and prison (*bargello* = police captain). Today it houses the National Museum, which makes it home to the best collection of Florentine Renaissance sculptures in existence.

The impressive inner courtyard (14th century) has a circular arcade and a magnificent flight of steps that lead up to a loggia. Next to the octagonal fountain in the courtyard was the arena for public executions, until Pietro Leopoldo abolished the death penalty in 1782.

Opposite the Bargello is the **Badia** ❽. The building's pointed tower is a memorable characteristic of Florence's skyline. This 10th-century church, which is part of the city's oldest and most important monastery, has frequently been expanded and renovated during the course of the centuries. Inside there are a number of works of art, including a masterpiece by Filippo Lippi and the tomb of the Tuscan margrave Ugo (died 1001) by Mino da Fiesole. Its atmospheric cloister is known as *Chiostro degli Aranci* (of the orange trees).

Directly next to the Badia is Via Dante Alighieri and **Casa di Dante**, the house where Dante is said to have been born. Various mementoes that commemorate Italy's greatest poet are displayed within the building.

Via dell'Anguillara leads to the Franciscan church of Santa Croce and **Piazza Santa Croce**, one of the most attractive squares in all of Florence. Lined with old mansions and palaces, it is in this square that the traditional *Calcio in Costume*, a historical soccer match between the city's different *quartieri*, is held every year in June.

Santa Croce ❾ is the largest and most beautiful of the Franciscan churches. Its construction most likely began in 1294, under Arnolfo di Cambio. It was finally completed and consecrated in 1443. The polychrome marble facade and the Neo-Gothic campanile were added to this Gothic church during the 19th century. The cruciform interior is a kind of pantheon of Florentine notables. The mendicant monks required financial support for its construction, and the return for a pious contribution was a final resting-place within the church itself. There are tombs and monuments to men of genius such as Michelangelo, Cherubini, Machiavelli, Foscolo, Rossini, Alberti, Dante, Galileo Galilei, and many more.

Even more striking than the tombs themselves are the works of art that were donated by the families and friends of the dead. Standing out in particular are Donatello's relief of the Annunciation and his famous wooden crucifix, of which Brunelleschi said that the artist had nailed a peasant to the cross. Then there are Rosselino's *Madonna and Child*, the octagonal marble pulpit by Benedetto da Maiano, and frescoes by Maso, Taddeo Gaddi and Giotto. In passing, one may note that Santa Croce houses the largest organ in Italy.

To the right of the church, in Santa Croce's first cloister, Brunelleschi created one of the very first Renaissance buildings, the **Pazzi Chapel**. The church museum is located in the monastery's former refectory and the adjacent rooms. It contains a collection of masterpieces of Florentine art.

South of the monastery of Santa Croce is a huge complex that extends down to the Arno, the **Biblioteca Nazionale** ❿. Built at the beginning of the 20th century,

the library houses a vast collection of manuscripts, incunabula, drawings and prints from the collections of the Medici, the Palatine Electors, and the Lorraines. Since 1885 a copy of every book published in Italy has been deposited here.

The catastrophic flood of 1966 severely damaged innumerable objects in both the National Library and in Santa Croce.

*San Marco

San Marco, another of Florence's Dominican monasteries, is located on the piazza of the same name, which you can reach by following Via Cavour or Via Ricasoli from the cathedral square. If you follow Via Ricasoli you will see, to the right, just before Piazza San Marco, the ***Galleria dell'Accademia** ⑪, the city's Academy of Fine Arts, which has housed

Above: Santa Maria Novella. Right: The Galleria dell'Accademia offers plenty of material for aspiring artists.

the original sculpture of David since 1910, as well as a number of other works by Michelangelo.

The monastery of ***San Marco** ⑫ was built by Michelozzo for Cosimo the Elder between 1437 and 1452. Today the former monks' cells on the upper floor are a Fra Angelico museum. This is where the "Blessed" Fra Angelico painted frescoes on the walls of his fellow monks' cells to inspire them to meditate. The most famous fresco, the **Annunciation**, can be seen at the staircase leading to the second floor.

At the far end of the right corridor are the cells that belonged to Savonarola when he was the prior of the monastery. A large bell by Donatello, the *Piagnona* or Bell of Lamentation, is set up in the cloister. It was rung to assemble the followers of this hyper-moral monk, whose aim was to turn all of Florence into a monastery. After his execution the bell was temporarily removed so that its sound would no longer remind people of this unpopular reformer.

Besides the frescoes in the cells, San Marco contains other famous paintings by the blessed Fra Angelico, such as the *Descent from the Cross* and the famous *Tabernacle of the Linaioli* (the flax-workers) in the pilgrims' hospice. It also displays a *Last Supper* by Ghirlandaio in the refectory, as well as works by Fra Bartolomeo. The library, which was also built by Michelozzo, contains precious manuscripts, missals and bibles, some of which are on display.

A painting of the Last Supper with great artistic value can be seen in the monastery of ***Sant'Apollonia** ⑬ at Via XXVII Aprile No. 1, to the west of Piazza San Marco. In the refectory of this former Benedictine monastery there is a museum containing works by the Renaissance painter Andrea del Castagno, including the aforementioned Last Supper. It is so captivating because of its realism, exact perspectives and powerful presentation.

Around Florence

Santissima Annunziata and ** San Lorenzo

Continuing along Via Battisti, you soon arrive at **Piazza della Santissima Annunziata** ⓮, a broad square surrounded by stately loggias. The equestrian statue of Ferdinando I in the center of the piazza is Giambologna's last work and was completed by Tacca, who also created the square's two curious fountains. But the most impressive part of this harmonious piazza, which resembles a huge cloister, is Brunelleschi's 15th-century facade of the **Ospedale degli Innocenti** (Foundlings' Hospital), with its resplendent loggia and charming majolica reliefs of terra-cotta babes in swaddling clothes by the great Andrea della Robbia.

One hundred years later, Antonio da Sangallo and Baccio d'Agnolo created the portico for the Servite Order on the opposite side of the square, and at the end of the 16th century the piazza was completed by the addition of the portico of the **Basilica of Santissima Annunziata** on the north side. A few steps beyond the Piazza Santissima Annunziata, on Via della Colonna, is the entrance to the Archeological Museum in the Palazzo Crocetta. The museum, which is unjustly neglected by most visitors to Florence, contains Greek and Etruscan masterpieces that can provide good insight into ancient art.

Continue along Via dei Servi in the direction of the Duomo, to Via dei Pucci, the extension of which is Via de Gori, which leads right to Piazza San Lorenzo. At the corner of the square opposite the San Lorenzo Church, is the **Palazzo Medici-Riccardi** ⓯, which Michelozzo built for Cosimo the Elder in the 15th century. This great palace, built of solid blocks of ashlar and with iron grilles over the ground-floor windows, looks more like a fortress than the city residence of a wealthy family. Today it houses a Medici museum. In the house chapel on the upper floor, you can see precious frescoes by Benozzo Gozzoli.

The church of **San Lorenzo** ⓰, commissioned by the Medici family, was

built by Brunelleschi on top of a building from the 4th century that had been destroyed by fire. Michelangelo's design for the facing of the brick facade was never carried out. The interior of this triple-naved church projects an air of harmony, calmness and serenity. The rich decor, of great artistic note, includes two bronze pulpits by Donatello as well as one of the most important works of Filippo Lippi, the *Annunciation* (over the altar).

The **Old Sacristy** (enter from the left-hand transept) is by Brunelleschi. In its architectural perfection, it became a model for the ideals of European architecture. The interior was decorated by Donatello and contains a tomb and a sarcophagus for members of the Medici family, both the work of Verrocchio (1472). The cloister is a picturesque garden court that leads to Michelangelo's renowned **Biblioteca Laurenziana**, which

Above: Images of foundlings on the loggia of the Ospedale degli Innocenti. Right: The market hall of San Lorenzo.

contains one of the most comprehensive collections of manuscripts in the world.

You can reach both the Medici Chapel and the New Sacristy from Piazza Madonna degli Aldobrandini. The octagonal **Medici Chapel** (1604) serves as a funerary chapel for six Medici princes. It is imposing, austere and cold, unlike the **New Sacristy**, a funerary chapel built for the Medici family by Michelangelo, which also contains his famous tombs. This masterpiece of the High Renaissance manages to ingeniously combine sculpture and architecture. The two tombs that were actually realized – Michelangelo originally projected six – rise up from the wall that, with its strict lines and clear geometric divisions, has an almost three-dimensional effect. Interred within the tombs are Lorenzo II, grandson of Lorenzo the Magnificent, and Giuliano, one of his sons. In niches above the tombs stand statues of the dead, while resting atop the sarcophagi themselves are the allegorical figures of Dawn and Dusk, Day and Night.

On Piazza San Lorenzo, and spilling over into the alleys around it, there is a colorful street market. It is, unfortunately, rather heavily geared towards tourists, so locals frequent the **Mercato Centrale di San Lorenzo** ⓱, the great market hall whose two floors are also a Mecca for Florentine gourmets. The ironwork construction of this 19th-century building is reminiscent of Parisian train stations, and definitely worth a look. The colorful stalls are a feast for the eyes and the unbelievably varied selection will make your mouth water.

And speaking of food, try one of the simple restaurants behind the market halls if you want to have a really good lunch. These eateries have small kitchens, staffed by perspiring cooks and rather limited menus offering only one or two simple dishes, but what you get is likely to represent the very best of plain Florentine fare. These places tend to be crowded, and you may have to wait a while for a table, but your patience will generally be rewarded.

Art connoisseurs will find a treat near San Lorenzo at Via Faenza 42, in the refectory of the former Franciscan monastery **★San Onofrio** ⓲. This is where Perugino's *Last Supper*, painted in 1445-1450 and one of the most famous depictions of the Last Supper in all of Florence, can be seen.

★Santa Maria Novella

The second church belonging to a mendicant order in Florence is **★Santa Maria Novella** ⓳, located near the train station, which bears its name. The mighty building dominates the Piazza Santa Maria Novella, to clear space for which the city bought and demolished several old buildings. The church was completed in 1279. The facade, the lower part of which is Romanesque-Gothic, was completed, in the Renaissance style, during the 15th century, by Leon Battisti Alberti.

The triple-naved interior is a masterpiece of the Florentine Gothic style. The side altars accommodate the graves of

notable Florentines, and are decorated with paintings and frescoes. Massaccio's famous fresco the *Trinity*, in the left nave, was discovered in the 19th century behind an altar with a painting by Vasari. It is organized according to strictly applied rules of perspective and reflects the new concept of the importance of man that was central to the philosophy of the early Renaissance. The portraits of donors on the fresco's edges are on the same scale as the holy figures, not on a smaller scale, as they would have been in the Middle Ages to reflect their lesser importance.

The frescoes in the choir, the work of Domenico Ghirlandaio, represent the people, customs and taste of the period in a precise and yet carefree manner. This makes them an invaluable document allowing insights into, for example, life in

Above: Please touch – the bronze boar is a symbol of good luck. Right: From shoemaker to millionaire – a shoe museum in the Palazzo Feroni (Piazza Santa Trinità) is dedicated to Salvatore Ferragamo.

the home of an aristocratic family at the time of Lorenzo the Magnificent (fresco of the *Birth of Mary* on the left wall).

The celebrated crucifix that was carved by Brunelleschi stands on the altar of the Gondi Chapel, which Donatello unselfishly praised as being much more beautiful than his own crucifix in Santa Croce. Another masterpiece is the painted crucifix by Giotto in the sacristy.

To the right of the church is an old cemetery where members of leading Florentine families are buried. To the left of this is the entrance to the cloisters of the former Dominican monastery. The first one, known as the Green Cloister, derives its name from the green tinge to the frescoes on its walls. Paolo Uccello's depictions of the Creation were damaged in the 1966 flood, but you can still make out the striking images of *The Deluge* and *Noah's Sacrifice*.

In the Spanish Chapel there are impressive 14th-century frescoes by Andrea da Firenze depicting the missionary works and triumphs of the Dominican Order.

People are represented by sheep, guarded by black and white dogs – *domini canes*, "dogs of God," or Dominicans – while the wolves that being torn apart by the dogs represent the heretics (Cathars and Waldensians) who enjoyed a considerable following in Florence at that time.

The Right Bank of the Arno

From Piazza della Signoria, continue heading west along Via Vacchereccia to the **Loggia del Mercato Nuovo** ⑳ (16th century) where gold and silk merchants once met. Today it is a great place for anyone looking to purchase samples of Florentine artisanship. On the south side of the loggia is the famous **Fontana del Porcellino** by Tacca (early 17th century). The "piglet" is a bronze copy of the original marble sculpture of a life-size, adult wild boar, now in the Uffizi. Touching it and throwing a coin into the fountain are supposed to bring good luck, a superstition that, based on his brightly polished nose, many find difficult to resist.

Not far from here, on Via Porta Rossa, is the **Palazzo Davanzati** ㉑, where the museum of the Old Florentine House has been located since 1956. This collection of furniture and objects for everyday use from the Middle Ages, Renaissance and Baroque period provide an interesting look into the highly civilized life of Florence's middle classes, and the precious furnishings of their homes.

Continue on to Via Tornabuoni, one of Florence's most attractive and elegant streets, and **Piazza Santa Trinità** ㉒, with a church of the same name. The column that supports the statue of Justice by Tadda (16th century) is a granite monolith that originally stood in the Baths of Caracalla in Rome.

The Gothic church of **Santa Trinità**, which dates back to the 11th century, was expanded in the 13th and 14th centuries, and in 1593-1594 it was given a Baroque facade by Buontalenti. The fine interior was financed by aristocratic families who had palaces nearby. Two of these *palazzi*, in fact, are directly on the piazza.

Better-known than either of these small palazzi, however, is **Palazzo Strozzi** ㉓, which stands a short distance away, on the corner of Via Tornabuoni and Via Strozzo. Filippo Strozzi had it built by Benedetto da Maiano in 1489, and it was completed in 1536 by Cronaca. Legend has it that Strozzi, a wealthy merchant, did not want to upset the most powerful man in Florence, Lorenzo the Magnificent, by building this opulent city palace. He therefore had a rumor spread to the effect that he was putting stores in on the ground floor to help finance the expensive building with the rents. Lorenzo was dismayed at the idea of his beautiful city being thus disfigured, and quickly granted Strozzi a free hand in building his palace. The result was one of the loveliest Renaissance palaces in Florence. Today it is home to various scientific institutions, and sometimes hosts major exhibitions.

Above and Right: The Ponte Vecchio, Florence's most famous bridge, where only goldsmiths are allowed to have their shops.

If you continue walking towards the Arno along Via Tornabuoni, you will come across one of Florence's most attractive bridges, **Ponte Santa Trinità** ㉔. In 1944, the retreating German Army blew up the the bridge (1567-70), but it was later rebuilt from the rubble that the locals had been able to retrieve from the Arno. Thus, Ammanati's masterpiece, which was based on a design by Michelangelo, was preserved.

If you continue to stroll further along the banks of the Arno, you will pass the **Palazzo Corsini** ㉕ with its splendid private collection of paintings (the entrance is on Via del Parione) and come to Piazza Goldoni. Here Via della Vigna Nuova turns off sharply to the right. On the left side of the street is the palace and the chapel belonging to the Rucellai family, both of which were designed by Leon Battista Alberti.

Also starting at Piazza Goldoni is Borgo Ognissanti, which will lead you to the square of the same name and the church **Ognissanti** ㉖ (the Church of All

Saints). Built during the 13th century, it was remodeled in 1627 by Bartolomeo Pettirossi, becoming Florence's first Baroque church. It houses a number of important works of art, such as the *Madonna* by Domenico and Davide Ghirlandaio, the *Last Supper* by Domenico Ghirlandaio (in the refectory), *Saint Augustine in his Study* by Botticelli, and a *Saint Jerome* by Ghirlandaio.

The nearby Ospedale San Giovanni di Dio probably dates back to the 14th century.

Across *Ponte Vecchio to the Left Bank of the Arno

*Ponte Vecchio ㉗ is the oldest and most famous bridge in Florence. It is very likely that the Etruscans built a bridge at this point over the Arno, and it is certain that the Romans did. When the defeated German Army was retreating from the city in 1944, Hitler ordered that all bridges across the Arno be blown up. Yet Ponte Vecchio was spared, thanks to a brave officer who dared to disobey orders and, rather than blowing up the bridge, simply blew up the houses at either end to block access. Thus, this masterpiece was saved for posterity.

During the Middle Ages butchers and tanners had their shops on the bridge, and they threw their waste directly into the river. In 1593, Grand Duke Ferdinando I passed an ordinance allowing only goldsmiths to operate shops on the bridge – and so it's remained to this day.

In the center of the bridge, between the two rows of shops, there is an open terrace from which you have a beautiful view of the Arno, Florence and the surrounding hills. On the right side of the bridge there is a bust of Benvenuto Cellini (1900), one of Florence's most celebrated goldsmiths.

Above the left-hand row of shops is the enclosed walkway that Vasari built for Cosimo I. It allowed him and his family to move freely between the Palazzo Vecchio and the Uffizi and their residence in the Palazzo Pitti, unobserved.

Before heading directly to the palace itself, turn right and walk along to the river until you come to **Piazza Santo Spirito** ㉘ and the church of Santo Spirito. In 1428, Brunelleschi designed it for rich Florentine families, but during the course of its construction, which continued throughout the century, his original design underwent a significant number of changes.

From outside, the church is misleadingly plain. In fact, the current facade wasn't added until the 18th century. Despite its simple exterior, the interior, with its semicircular side chapels and Corinthian columns, makes Santo Spirito one of the most brilliant creations of the Florentine Renaissance. This church, like most of the city's major churches, is also home to a number of famous works of art, including pieces by Filippino Lippi (*Madonna and Child with Saints and Donors*), Perugino (rose window on the facade) and Giuliano da Sangallo (entry hall and sacristy).

A bit further on, along Via Sant'Agostino and Via Santa Monaca, you will come to the church of **Santa Maria del Carmine** ㉙, which was leveled by fire in 1771 and rebuilt in the late-Baroque style. Luckily, the ****Brancacci Chapel**, in the right transept, was spared by the flames, preserving the sublime frescoes by Masaccio (*The Tribute Money*) and his teacher Masolino. The frescoes were started during the 15th century and completed by Filippino Lippi.

The neighborhoods of Santo Spirito and San Frediano, where these two churches are located, are two old, homey quarters where there are still plenty of artisan workshops that produce and restore paintings, furniture, and musical instruments, as well as executing a number of other typical Florentine crafts.

*Palazzo Pitti and the *Boboli Gardens

Via de Serragli, which divides these two neighborhoods, leads south from the Arno, past the Giardino Torrigiano, to the **Porta Romana**, one of Florence's medieval gates, through which you leave Florence to reach Siena and Rome. From here you can walk back to Ponte Vecchio along Via Romana, which is lined with magnificent palaces.

Opening out after Piazza Santa Felice is the gradual upward incline of the Piazza Pitti, which is dominated by the imposing ***Palazzo Pitti** ㉚. The palace is 200 meters long and is built entirely of ashlar blocks. Brunelleschi designed it, and construction began in the mid-15th century. His original client was the wealthy merchant Luca Pitti, but eventually Cosimo I chose it as his residence. Later, when Italy had become a kingdom, Victor Emmanuel II moved in and in 1919, Victor Emmanuel III bequeathed it

Above: He is popular with photographers – Bacchus in the Boboli Gardens. Right: The interior of San Miniato al Monte.

and the entirety of its valuable contents to the state.

The Palazzo Pitti contains one of the most famous collections of paintings in the world, the Galleria Palatina, as well as the Museo degli Argenti, the Museum of Crafts, a collection of costumes from various epochs, magnificently decorated apartments with paintings, tapestries and precious furniture, and the Galleria d'Arte Moderna, which contains art and objects from the 18th and 19th centuries. Ammanati's great courtyard behind the palace was originally used as an impressive open-air stage. Performances are still occasionally put on here today.

On the hill behind his palazzo, Cosimo I had the grandiose *Boboli Gardens ㉛ laid out. Winding, shaded paths lead up to terraces, from which one has a beautiful view of Florence. Fountains, grottoes, statues and a coffee house (from 1776) make the gardens into a kind of open-air museum. Logically enough, therefore, an admission charge of 4000 lire has recently been introduced for (foreign) visitors. (However, you can still walk in the large popular park of **Le Cascine** on the other side of the Arno, west of the train station, free of charge).

On the other side of the Boboli Gardens is **Forte di Belvedere** ㉜, a beautifully renovated fortress that was built by Buontalenti for Ferdinando I during the 16th century. From the fortress walls, which themselves regularly house major exhibitions, you can also enjoy a stunning panoramic view of Florence and the hills behind the city.

**San Miniato al Monte

The Romanesque marble facade of **San Miniato al Monte ㉝ has a classic beauty that can be seen from all over the city. Saint Minias's first church was built here during the reign of Charlemagne, and the monarch bequeathed vast estates to it. Eventually, however, it fell into a

state of disrepair, and had to be built anew in the 11th century.

San Miniato and its baptistry are the most precious examples of Romanesque architecture in Florence. The interior, like the facade, is also decorated with colorful marble, and geometric patterns predominate in this beautifully clear space. The raised presbytery with its beautiful choir screens stands on a crypt where, in an altar dating from the 11th century, the bones of Saint Minias are kept.

In front of the presbytery is a tabernacle that is the work of Michelozzo.

While you are here, be sure to note the church's wonderful inlaid marble floor as well as the exquisite marble pulpit from the 13th century.

To the right of the church is the Episcopal Palace, which formerly served as the summer residence of Florence's bishops. There is a beautiful view of the city from the square in front of the church, with the added bonus that it is much quieter and calmer than the crowded Piazzale Michelangelo.

*FIESOLE

One of the most popular excursions for visitors to Florence has always been *Fiesole ❷ to the north of the city. As the Roman settlement *Faesulae*, it once overshadowed Florence on account of its favorable defensive location high above the Arno and Mugnone valleys. Even before Roman times it was one of the twelve cities of the Etruscan League – remains of the city walls near the Roman amphitheater date from this period. Under the Romans, the city also boasted, in addition to the theater, a forum, a capitol, temples and baths. Fiesole was the center of the region, and it was wealthy and powerful. The era of the great barbarian migrations came and went without leaving any major traces. But then, in 1125, Fiesole was conquered and destroyed by its strengthened rival, Florence. It never managed to recover fully from this blow.

After the 15th century, wealthy Florentine families, notably the Medici, started having summer residences built on the hills of Fiesole. These villas are situated amid beautiful surroundings on a steep, terraced slope just below the town, and they command a spectacular view of Florence and the Arno valley. If you follow the winding Via Vecchia Fiesolana, it will lead you up to the church and monastery of the little village of **San Domenico**, where the painter monk Fra Angelico was a novice before he moved to San Marco in Florence. The *Altar of the Madonna* in the church, in the first chapel on your left, is his work.

Not far from San Domenico is the **Badia Fiesolana ❸**, which was the cathedral church of Fiesole until the 11th century, after which its monastery was turned over to the Benedictines. During the Renaissance, the abbey was enlarged and rebuilt. In the facade of the church,

Left: The steep streets of Fiesole require you to be in good shape.

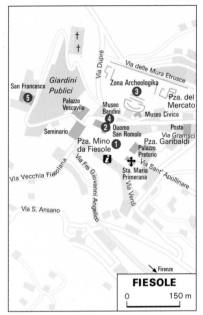

Around Florence

which was never quite completed, you can still see the light and dark stones of the old Romanesque facade. The interior is appointed in the style of Brunelleschi. To the right of the church is the entrance to the former convent.

Between the Badia and the city center is the **Villa Medici**, which is also known as *Belcanto* or *Il Palagio di Fiesole*. This villa was built by Michelozzo for Cosimo the Elder between 1458 and 1461. It was here that Lorenzo the Magnificent entertained his literary friends, like Poliziano, Pico della Mirandola and Landino. Today, the villa is privately owned, and it is not open to the public.

The center of Fiesole is **Piazza Mino da Fiesole ❶**, located on the site of the old Roman forum. To the north of the piazza is the Romanesque cathedral **San Romolo ❷**, with its high crenellated campanile. A few steps further is the entrance to the **Roman Theater ❸** and the archeological excavation site. The theater, which had a seating capacity of 3000, dates back to the first century B.C.,

as do the remains of bathing facilities and of a temple, which were discovered in a lower level. The north boundary of the excavation site is formed by remains of the Etruscan wall. Every year the *Estate Fiesolana* (Fiesole Summer) stages a number of theater performances and concerts here.

The **Museo Civico**, a building that resembles a temple, is immediately to the right of the theater entrance. It displays Etruscan and Roman finds, as well as medieval artifacts. Nearby, the small, but interesting **Museo Bandini** ❹ displays Florentine paintings from the 13th-15th centuries as well as Della Robbia terra cottas and woodcarvings.

The lovely 14th-century City Hall on the east side of the square is quite charming, and is adorned with numerous coats of arms. On the other side, adjacent to the 11th-century Bishop's Palace, the steep

Above: A 15th-century illustration from Boccaccio's Il Decameron (F. di Stefano). Right: La Petraia – the Medici summer palace.

Via di San Francesco leads up to the **Franciscan Monastery** ❺. The square in front of the monastery offers a beautiful view of Florence.

From Fiesole you reach **Poggio Gherardo** ❹ by way of Maiano. In 1348 Boccaccio and ten young Florentine aristocrats supposedly retreated to the **Villa di Poggio Gherardo** in the face of an outbreak of the plague in Florence. To pass the time, they exchanged ribald stories, which became the ostensible basis for Boccaccio's famous collection of novellas, *Il Decameron*.

Continuing on, you'll come to **Ponte a Mensola** and the church of **San Martino**, which contains a triptych by Taddeo Gaddi. Nearby is the **Villa I Tatti**, which today houses Harvard University's Center for Renaissance History, as well as a valuable art collection. The road leads on toward Settignano by way of Coverciano. Just past Coverciano come the villas of **Porziuncola** and **Capponcina**, where Eleanora Duse and her lover Gabriele d'Annunzio lived at the beginning of the 20th century.

Settignano ❺ was the hometown of such famous sculptors as Desiderio, the Rossellinos, and Bartolomeo Ammannati. Not far off, near Terenzano, is one of the most beautiful Renaissance villas in Italy, the **Villa Gamberaia**. Heavily damaged during World War II, it was restored according to the original plans. It is principally noted for its magnificent park, which contains statues, fountains and waterworks. You may be able to visit this park if you contact the owners (tel: 055 / 697 205).

THE MEDICI VILLAS

Some of the most famous villas built by the Medicis are on the northern outskirts of Florence. On the road that leads up to the slopes of Monte Morello and the Calvana Mountains, for example, you will find the **Villa Medicea di Careggi**.

Today, this is part of the huge hospital complex of the Florence Medical School. The villa, renovated by Michelozzo for Cosimo the Elder, is supposed to have been the Medici's favorite villa. It was here that Cosimo founded the Platonic Academy during the 15th century, which became a meeting-place for celebrated writers, philosophers and artists.

Within a radius of a few kilometers, there are three other famous villas. First, there is the **Villa Corsini** with its Baroque facade. To the left of this, Via della Petraia leads to the **Villa Medicea della Petraia**, a palace that had previously belonged to the Brunelleschi family and was purchased by the Medici in 1530. Later Ferdinando I had the building magnificently redesigned and renovated by Buontalenti.

The gardens were laid out by Niccolò Pericolo, known as Tribolo, who also created the elegant fountains of Venere-Fiorenza with a statue by Giambologna. The terraces of the hanging gardens command a beautiful view of the city.

From Villa Corsini, continue along Via di Castelloto to the **Villa Medicea di Castello**. During the 14th century a fortified castle stood upon this spot. Lorenzo and Giovanni di Pierfrancesco de' Medici acquired the estate in 1477, and Cosimo I later had it turned into an exquisite Renaissance villa. Here, too, it was Tribolo who was responsible for the layout of the villa's beautiful grounds and for the fountain, which depicts Hercules battling the giant Antaeus.

The renowned *Grotta degli Animali* (Grotto of the Beasts) at the end of the central path was also designed by Tribolo and was decorated with animal representations in different colors of marble by Ammannati and others (today, the bronze birds created by Giambologna can be seen in the Bargello Museum).

Since 1974 the **Villa di Castello** has been the headquarters of the *Accademia della Crusca*, the Italian language academy founded in 1583, which has been concerned with maintaining the purity of the Italian language ever since.

EXCURSION TO THE MUGELLO AND THE SIEVE VALLEY

If you want to see a part of Tuscany that is not overrun by tourists, venture into the Mugello and the Sieve valley, the area east of the Bologna-Florence expressway. For this trip, start out on the old road, the SS 65, which leads over the Apennines toward Bologna and runs through a landscape dotted with villas and gardens. The first town you will reach is **Pratolino ❻**, which is famous for its 16th-century **Villa Demidoff** (as it is called today). Grand Duke Francesco de' Medici had it built by Buontalenti for his mistress (later his wife), Bianca Cappello. It is surrounded by a wonderful park with numerous fountains, grottoes and statues, including the huge statue of Apennine, the mountain god, which is the work of Giambologna. During the summer the park is open to the public Thursday through Sunday, all day.

Continue on to **San Piero a Sieve ❼** in the Sieve valley, which is dominated by the impressive Medici fortress of San Martino. Immediately after San Piero a Sieve is the fortress-like edifice of the **Villa Medicea di Cafaggiolo**, which was built by Michelozzo for Cosimo I as a summer residence. Lorenzo the Magnificent later used it as a hunting lodge.

A few kilometers later a small road on the right leads to the Franciscan monastery of ★**Bosco ai Frati ❽**. Cosimo's architect, Michelozzo, who also designed the nearby **Castello di Trebbio**, practically rebuilt it from scratch. A precious wooden crucifix carved by Donatello is displayed in the diminutive *Museo d'Arte Sacra* in the monastery's chapter-room.

Continue past Barberino di Mugello and over the Futa Pass (903 meters), where one of Italy's largest cemeteries for German soldiers was laid out between 1962 and 1965. Eight kilometers further on, the road intersects with the SS 503, which returns to San Piero a Sieve via Firenzuola and the Giogo di Scarperia.

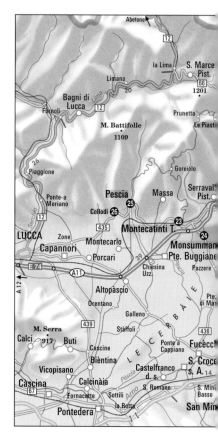

Firenzuola ❾ or Little Florence, a spa town and tourist center, 422 meters above sea level, was founded by the Florentines during the 12th century so they could control the road to Bologna. During World War II, it was almost completely destroyed, but later was rebuilt according to the original rectangular ground plan.

Scarperia ❿ is one of the more important towns in the Mugello. The medieval center of the town, which was founded by the Republic of Florence during the 12th century to control the pass road through the Apennines, is still very well preserved. The facade of the Palazzo Pretorio, with its high, turreted campanile, is adorned with coats-of-arms of stone and ceramic. A tabernacle ascribed to Andrea

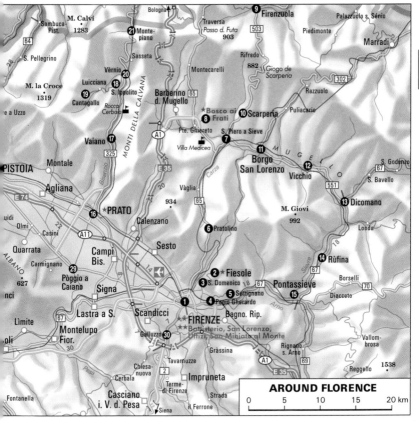

AROUND FLORENCE

| 0 | 5 | 10 | 15 | 20 km |

della Robbia is contained in the oratory of the Madonna di Piazza, where the curates once swore their oath of allegiance upon taking up office.

The Mugello race track (5.3 km long) is on the outskirts of Scarperia. It was built by Florence's Automobile Club in 1974 and was recently modernized to such an extent that Formula 1 races can now be held here.

Borgo San Lorenzo ⓫, the Mugello's capital, is a center of agriculture and industry, particularly brick making and artistic ceramics. Its church of San Lorenzo dates back to the 13th century. The hexagonal campanile, which is built entirely of brick, is from the same period. Its facade was severely damaged during an earthquake in 1919, but during the 1920s it was rebuilt, using the original materials.

From Borgo San Lorenzo, continue following the Sieve valley downstream for about seven kilometers to the village of **Vicchio** ⓬, birthplace of Fra Angelico (ca. 1387-1455). On the square named after the painter Giotto (who was born in the neighboring village of Vespignano) you will find the Palazzo Pretorio. The palazzo houses the Museo Beato Angelico, which displays sacred art from the Mugello.

The town of **Dicomano** ⓭, at the intersection with the SS 67, the *Tosco Romagnola*, was established in the days of the Romans. It has always served as a trans-

*PRATO

*Prato ⑯ lies on the plain between Florence and Pistoia, at the beginning of the Bisenzo valley. Excavations have shown that there were settlements here during the early Stone Age. Later, Prato fell under Roman rule and subsequently developed into a larger settlement during the Lombardian period. During the 12th century it became a free imperial city. This ushered in a burst of economic development, which wasn't even slowed down when the city came under the sway of the ubiquitous Florentines in 1350.

Since the Middle Ages Prato has had the weaving and cloth industry to thank for its exceptional prosperity. The development of a modern textile industry since the middle of 19th century has made this city – which after World War II even started recycling rags into cheap new garments – into a kind of "Manchester of Tuscany." All manner of wool and woolens are processed into finished products every day in the city's countless mills and factories. Today Prato, with approximately 170,000 inhabitants, is one of Italy's wealthiest cities.

Around 600 years ago, the local merchant Francesco di Marco Datini invented not only the bank draft as a means of making payments without cash, but also double-entry bookkeeping. Yet, despite their love of cash and commerce, the business-minded Pratese have by no means overlooked art and culture. The old city center demonstrates a wealth of old buildings, and modern Prato has managed to maintain a feeling for the arts.

The center of the hexagonal downtown area, encompassed by a 14th-century city wall, is Piazza Communale with its medieval city hall and **Palazzo Pretorio** ①, which houses the valuable art collection of the municipal museum.

From here Via Mazzoni leads to the cathedral square and the ***Cattedrale di Santo Stefano** ②, which is an excellent

portation hub, and therefore as a trade center, of the Sieve valley. It is for this reason that the little city was spared by the Florentines when they conquered all of the castles in the area during the 14th century. Dicomano suffered severe damages during several earthquakes, the last of which was in 1919. It was rebuilt during the 1940s, but unfortunately very little is left of the old town.

Rufina ⑭, which is renowned for its good wine, lies on the road to Pontassieve. There is a wine museum located in the cellars of the 16th-century Villa di Poggio Reale. To arrange visits and for general information, call tel: 055 / 836 9848.

From **Pontassieve** ⑮, an old trade center at the confluence of the Sieve and Arno rivers, you can drive the 18 kilometers back to Florence.

Above: The beautiful cathedral in Prato, and Michelozzo's famous outdoor pulpit (1434-1438), which is decorated with marvelous reliefs by Donatello.

example of Romanesque-Gothic architecture. From outside the cathedral displays a typically Tuscan exterior with stripes of pale white and green serpentine marble. Above the main portal is a relief by Andrea della Robbia, while projecting from the right side of the facade is the famous **outdoor pulpit**, which was built by Michelozzo in 1434-1438 and is decorated with Donatello's magnificent bas-reliefs of dancing children (the originals can be seen in the Cathedral Museum, located in the Bishop's Palace). It is from this pulpit, the *Pergamo del Sacro Cingolo* (Pulpit of the Holy Girdle), that several times a year the faithful are given a chance to glimpse a belt said to have belonged to the Virgin Mary, which was brought to Prato in 1141 by a local crusader when he returned home.

The interior of the cathedral consists of a Romanesque nave, flanked by massive columns of green serpentine marble, and a Gothic transept. The marble pulpit is by Mino da Fiesole and Rossellino, while the main altar bears a wooden crucifix by Ferdinando Tacca. Most impressive, however, are the choir frescoes by Fra Filippo Lippi, a masterpiece of the early Renaissance. Particularly beautiful is the Dance of Salome (on the right), one of the series of frescoes illustrating scenes from the life of John the Baptist. Legend has it that the painter monk, who was not at all indifferent to the pleasures of the flesh, depicted in Salome his mistress, the nun Lucrezia Buti, who bore him two children. Their son, Filippino, later followed in his father's footsteps and became a famous artist.

Another church worth seeing is **Santa Maria delle Carceri** ❸ on Via Cairoli, a beautiful domed building that was built by Sangallo between 1485 and 1492. The church stands on the remains of an old prison (*carceri*), on the wall of which was painted an image of Mary that is said to have miraculous properties. The marble exterior of the church has never been

completed, but the building's architectural proportions are magnificent. The interior contains a beautiful majolica frieze by Andrea della Robbia.

Across from the church is the **Castello dell'Imperatore** ❹, the emperor's fortress, which Frederick II built in the 13th century on top of the old castle of the counts of Alberti. The mighty walls and towers, with their swallowtail merlons, are reminiscent of the Hohenstaufen castles in Apulia and Sicily. Because Frederick died in 1250, the courtyard was never completed, but today it is used as an open-air stage for plays and concerts.

Nearby is the **Palazzo Datini** ❺ on Via Rinaldesca, which Datini, the wealthy banker and merchant mentioned earlier, had built for himself. In 1870, 460 years after Datini's death, numerous accounts ledgers, insurance policies, partnership contracts and business letters were discovered in a hiding place beneath the staircase. Today, this valuable historical material is kept in the archives in the palace.

Info p. 93

Examples of modern art in Prato can be found in Piazza San Marco on the east side of the old town center, where there is an impressive white marble sculpture by Henry Moore.

If you leave the square and head south, you will pass through the modern sections of the city (the Institute for Textile Technology and the Textile Museum, which was founded in 1886, are both located on Viale della Repubblica) before arriving at the ***Museo d'Arte Contemporanea Luigi Pecci ❻** (1988). This isn't just home to a museum of modern art, but also houses a research center and the Center for Information and Documentation (CID).

Leave the old city center in a northerly direction by way of the Piazza Mercatale, and you will come to a bridge that spans the Bisenzio. This is an excellent point of departure for an excursion into the countryside around Prato.

Above: The cathedral in Pistoia and its 67-meter-high campanile.

The Bisenzio Valley

From Prato, the highway SS 325 heads north to Bologna, parallel to the expressway and railway tracks. It follows the **Bisenzio valley** to the border between Tuscany and Emilia, between the karstenite slopes of the Monti della Calvana and the wooded ridge of the Apennines. Ever since the age of industrialization, the valley has been densely settled, because the Bisenzio River supplied the countless textile factories, mills, paper factories and copper plants with water.

In a green hollow full of olive groves lies the town of **Vaiano ⓱**, center of Italy's modern textile industry. During the Middle Ages, this town was an important military outpost for Prato.

The 11th century saw construction of the Badia di San Salvatore. Only the church, with its impressive 13th-century campanile, remains standing today. Its triple-naved interior is reminiscent of Prato's cathedral. The 18th-century sacristy, with wooden inlays, is of particular interest, as is the 14th-century cloister with its colonnaded portico and loggia.

Further north are the ruins of **Rocca Cerbaia**, a castle that belonged to the Alberti family in the 12th century, perched on a steep cliff. To get there you have to walk up a small path that begins just past the little medieval bridge and ends at Montecuccoli, a village on the ridge of the Calvana, 633 meters high.

From Mercatale di Vernio, at the confluence of the Fiumenta and Bisenzio rivers, a steep road leads up to the climatic health resort of **San Ippolito** ⓲ (415 meters), a town that is famous for its *carnevalino* (carnival and fair), which is held on Ash Wednesday. Another road leads across the Bisenzio and through the lofty town of Lucciana to **Cantagallo** ⓳, where you can depart on a lovely hike to the Pacini hut on the Pian della Rasa (1001 meters).

After Mercatale, you come to the mouth of the 18-kilometer-long train tunnel that cuts through the Apennines. Once you get past this you will arrive in **San Quirico di Vernio** ⓴ in the Fiumenta valley, above which looms a fortress with remnants of the old castle. On the first Sunday in Lent the traditional Sagra della Polenta is held here (the polenta is made using chestnut flour).

After a steep climb you will reach one of the less difficult Apennine passes. This brings you over into Emilia and onto a sunny plateau where the pretty little climatic health resort of **Montepiano** ㉑ is located. Like many mountain towns, this is a good departure point for a number of different hikes along well-marked trails.

*PISTOIA

*Pistoia ㉒, like Prato, also stands in the cultural and political shadow of the region's more important cities, i.e., Florence, Lucca and Pisa. However, there is one very good reason to visit Pistoia: its old town center has a number of impor-

tant works of art that can easily match the magnificence of some of Tuscany's other, more renowned works of art.

During the Roman era Pistoia was a fortified village on the Via Cassia, but it had its heyday was during the 12th and 13th centuries, when it declared itself a free municipality. This was when the buildings that still grace the historic old town center were erected.

The old town, which is based on a rectangular ground plan, is surrounded by the remains of a 14th-century city wall. The picturesque **Piazza del Duomo** ❶, which is lined with a number of important buildings, is the best starting point for a walk through this historical district.

On the southeast side of the piazza is the ***Cattedrale di San Zeno**, whose 67-meter-high campanile, the lower part of which resembles the tower of a fortress, is the city's trademark. This Romanesque-Pisan church (12th/13th centuries) was built on the site of another 5th-century church. Its well-proportioned marble facade, with a porch supported on slender

columns, is decorated with a relief of the Madonna and majolica coffers by Andrea della Robbia. Among the number of notable art works inside, the most famous is the **Silver Altar of St. Jacob**, a masterpiece of Italian silversmithing that took almost 200 years to complete (from 1287 to 1456).

The south side of the square, next to the cathedral, is formed by the medieval Palazzo Vescovile, the **Bishop's Palace**. Adjoining it is the octagonal **baptistry**, which was built in the 14th century according to designs by Andrea Pisano.

Nextdoor is then 14th-century **Palazzo Pretorio**, decorated with armorial bearings and with an attractive interior courtyard, which today serves as a courthouse.

On the northeast side of the piazza and to the left of the cathedral is the **Palazzo Comunale**, a massive sandstone building that was begun during the 13th century

Above: The "Seven Works of Mercy" on the majolica frieze of the Ospedale del Ceppo.
Right: The pulpit in Sant'Andrea by G. Pisano.

and finally, after many interruptions, was completed in the 14th century. A 17th-century wing joins it to the cathedral. On the ground floor, the facade is divided into five loggias, while arched window openings create the division in the three upper stories. Above this, the facade sports the Medici coat-of-arms and the papal keys in honor of the Medici Popes, Leo X and Clemens VII. Next to the central window, you can make out a head carved in black marble, but no one is quite sure of its significance. The palace houses the **Museo Civico**, which has an attractive collection of paintings.

If you leave the Piazza del Duomo and head northeast, Via Pacini will take you to the **Ospedale del Ceppo ❷,** named for the hollow tree-stump (*ceppo*) where alms were collected. Built in the 13th or 14th centuries, the hospital, which is still in use today, was adorned with a beautiful portico in the 16th century. The facade sports a magnificent majolica frieze from the school of Della Robbia, depicting the Seven Works of Mercy.

The church of ***Sant'Andrea** ❸, an architecturally interesting building in the Pisan style, contains a special treasure: the **Pulpit by Giovanni Pisano**, which was built between 1298 and 1301, or, in other words, before he began work on the pulpit in Pisa's cathedral. The relief panels depict scenes from the life of Christ, and Pisano's dramatic representation of the Massacre of the Innocents is particularly impressive.

Another architectural masterpiece just south of the Piazza del Duomo, on Via Cavour, is the church of **San Giovanni Fuorcivitas** ❹. A particularly notable feature is its exterior side wall, which is beautifully decorated with stripes of light and dark marble and geometrical patterns. Above the entrance is a terra-cotta relief by Gruamonte from Como, while the church's interior contains a stoup by Giovanni Pisano and a terra-cotta relief of the *Visitation*, which is ascribed to either Luca or Andrea della Robbia.

Things are more modern in the **Pallazo Tau** on Via Garibaldi, which devoted to modern art. Displayed here is a collection of sculptures and drawings by Marino Marini, who was born in Pistoia.

Ice Machines and Snow Cannons

Pistoia's convenient location between Florence, Pisa and Lucca is not the only reason one might want to choose to stay longer in this area. Another enticement is the beautiful countryside around Pistoia, which is ideal for long excursions, by foot or on horseback. An attractive wooded landscape, medieval villages, old traditions and festivals are all reasons to get to know the Pistoian Apennines and their nature parks. One specialty of the region are the so-called *ghiaccai*, devices that were used in the 19th and early 20th centuries to keep ice that had been "mined" in the mountains cold enough to transport down to the cities on the plain. Until the availability of artificial ice, this was the

sole source of income for many families in the Reno valley. A few of these devices are displayed in Le Piastre, about 20 kilometers from Pistoia.

And Pistoia's backcountry isn't only popular during the summer. During the winter the area around **Abetone** is a winter sports paradise, and the recent introduction of snow cannons has only helped to improve the snow conditions.

Pools, Flowers, and a Little Wooden Scamp

The world-renowned health resort of **Montecatini Terme** ㉓ is one of the most elegant thermal spas in Italy, and its waters were probably known and valued even in antiquity. Since the late 18th century, palazzo-like edifices have been built above its eleven springs, which are said to be especially good for people suffering from liver disorders and rheumatism. With it beautiful parks, large hotels, and tidy organization, this town is an ideal place for anyone looking for a way to

combine the necessity of a "cure" with pleasant and relaxing surroundings. It is not, however, very interesting for anyone who has come with hopes of finding the "real Tuscany." The same holds true for nearby **Monsummano** ㉔, which offers natural steam baths in caves. Its hot and healing steam, which comes from the bowels of the earth, can be enjoyed in the natural Grotta Giusti or in the artificial Grotta Parlanti.

To liven things up a bit, there are a number of different excursions that could invigorate a "cure." Among them, trips to the medieval villages of **Monsummano Alto** and **Montecatini Alto**, or north to Valdinievole, with its old mountain villages and villas, or to the nearby town of **Pescia** ㉕, famous for its flower market.

A few kilometers past Pescia is the village of **Collodi** ㉖, a name that Carlo Lorenzini, the Florentine author of the

Above: The healing waters of Montecatini Therme. Right: The monks' litte cell-houses in Certosa del Galluzzo.

beloved story of *Pinocchio*, adopted as his *nom de plume*. In addition to the **Pinocchio Park**, which boasts life-sized wooden figures from the tales of the long-nosed puppet, this medieval village along the slope of a hill is home to the **Villa Garzoni** and its truly beautiful gardens.

LOWER ARNO VALLEY AND MONTALBANO

The drive from Monsummano along the SS 436 leads through the marshy areas of Fucecchio, with its unusual flora and fauna, to the Arno valley, where the town of **San Miniato** ㉗ extends along a mountain ridge to the south. Because of its strategic location high above the valleys of the Arno, the Elsa and the Egola, San Miniato was of military significance even during the Roman era. During the reign of the German emperor Otto I it became the seat of the imperial palatinate in Tuscany. Today, this sleepy little town only awakens in the fall, when it hosts a popular truffle festival (the third Saturday in October), and its market for white truffles is held every weekend in November.

One noteworthy sight is the **tower**, the last remnant of a castle that Frederick II had built high above San Miniato. Below this, on the tree-shaded Prato del Duomo, stands the town's 13th-century **cathedral** with its proud campanile.

Between San Miniato and Empoli, on the highway leading from Livorno to Florence, a small road turns off to the left, where it takes you across the Montalbano ridge to Pistoia. This winding, yet beautiful scenic road passes through dense olive groves on its way to **Vinci** ㉘, birthplace of none other than Leonardo. There is a museum devoted to him in the old castle, while the house where he is supposed to have been born is actually a bit outside town, near Achiano, almost hidden behind olive trees and cypresses. Here, too, you can see exhibits and reproductions of some of his works.

Above the town, the road continues through lovely forests, and over the hill a view opens out over the densely populated valley that extends from Pistoia through Prato to Florence. At Casalguidi, a road leading off to the right will take you via Quarrata and Olmi, to the straight road from Pistoia to Florence, the SS 66. The famous wine town of Carmignano is situated on the slopes of Montalbano to your right. At about the latitude of Prato, is **Poggio a Caiano** ㉙ with its beautiful **Medici villa**, which Lorenzo the Magnificent had Guiliano da Sangallo redesign in the Renaissance style. Especially attractive is its facade with its majestic entrance loggia and majolica relief by Andrea Sansovino. The villa contains a museum and is surrounded by a beautiful park.

A brief detour from Poggio a Caiano leads you to another Medici villa, the **Ferdinanda**, near the town of **Artimino**. Ferdinando I had it built by Buontalenti in 1594 as a hunting lodge. The roof of this castle-like villa, with its lovely open-air staircase and a loggia, is adorned with countless chimneys of various shapes.

Certosa del Galluzzo

South of Florence, high above the road to Siena and surrounded by a wall, is the **Carthusian monastery** of **Galluzzo** ㉚. It was founded for the Carthusian order during the 14th century by the Florentine statesman Niccolò Accaiuoli. Patrons gave generous donations, and over the years the monastery was expanded and furnished with precious works of art, many of which can be seen today in the gallery in the Palazzo Accaiuoli. Unfortunately, Napoleon's armies stole a large part of the original collection in 1810.

The monastery consists of little individual cell-houses for the monks, who live in strict seclusion, and common rooms for prayers and church services. The only way to see inside the monastery is with a guided tour conducted by a Cistercian monk. These are offered several times a day.

FLORENCE (☎ 055)

ℹ Tourist Information Office (APT), Via A. Manzoni, 16, tel: 23 320, fax: 234 6286, www.firenze.turismo.toscana.it, e-mail: apt@firenze.turismo.toscana.it. **Tourist Information at Amerigo Vespucci Airport** tel: 315 874, fax: 318 609. **City and Province of Florence**: Via Cavour 1/R, tel: 290 832/3.

RENTAL CARS: **Avis**, Lungarno Torrigiani 33B, tel: 241 145; weekends: Borgo Ognissanti 128, tel: 213 629. **Europca**r, Borgo Ognissanti 53, tel: 236 0072. **Hertz**, Via Maso Finguerra 23, tel: 239 8205.

TRAINS: **Central Station Santa Maria Novella**, Piazza Stazione, tel: 147 888 088 (9:00 am- 5:00 pm), 24-hour information tel: 166 105 050.

BUS COMPANIES: **A.T.A.F.** (City bus routes, good services to central train station and cathedral, tickets from machines at news stands and in many bars, 24-hour tourist ticket,) tel: 565 0222. **SITA**, Via Santa Caterina da Siena 15. Regional bus routes tel: 214 721, 483 651; long distance routes tel: 294 955, 24-hour service tel: 166 845 010. **CAP**, Largo Fratelli Alinari 9, tel: 214 637. **Tourist buses** (reservations, tours), tourist buses arrive at the parking lots Olmatello Palazzeschi and Strozzi Montelungo according to a "bus pass system" between 8:00-9:00 am and 8:00 pm.

BICYCLE RENTALS: **Alinari**, Via Guelfa 85, tel: 280 500.

AIRPORT: **Amerigo Vespucci**, Peretola, Via del Termine 11, tel: 373 498. Domestic flight info, tel: 306 1700; international flight info, tel: 306 1702.

RADIO TAXIS: **CO.TA.FI.** tel: 4390, 4499. **SO.CO.TA.** tel: 4242, 4798.

ATTENDED PARKING LOTS: **Fortezza da Basso**, large parking lot near central station. **Central Statio / Station S.M.N.**, underground parking.

ADDITIONAL PARKING: Mercato Centrale, Lungarno Torrigiani, Lungarno Zecca Vecchia, Piazza della Libertà, and off the main roads outside the city center.

▣ ⑤⑤⑤ Annalena, Via Romana 34, tel: 222 402, fax: 222 403; some rooms with view of the gardens, near the Pitti Palace, fairly low wooden ceilings everywhere. Breakfast is extra. **Excelsior**, Piazza Ognissanti 3, tel: 264 201, fax: 210 278. **Regency**, Piazza M. d'Azeglio 3, tel: 245 247, fax: 234 6735. **Brunelleschi**, Piazza S. Elisabetta 3, tel: 27 370, fax: 219 653. **Minerva**, Piazza S. M. Novella 16, tel: 284 555, fax: 268 281.

⑤⑤ Beacci Tornabuoni, Via Tornabuoni 3, tel: 212 645, fax: 283 594; in the upper floors of a medieval city palace, attractive interior decoration, roof garden for houseguests. **Galileo**, Via Nazionale 22/A, tel: 496 645, fax: 496 447. **Golf**, Viale Fratelli Rosselli 56, tel:

281 818, fax: 268 432; often full, even during the off-season, parking in the courtyard. **David**, Viale Michelangiolo 1, tel: 681 1695, fax: 680 602. **La Noce**, Borgo La Noce 8, tel: 292 346, fax: 291035; in an old building, but the rooms on the second floor have been refurbished and have TVs; very close to the market. **Pendini**, Via Strozzi 2, tel: 211 170, fax: 281 807; upper floors of a 19th-century building, rooms decorated in imitation baroque style, large rooms with view over the Piazza della Repubblica or the neglected inner courtyard. **Porta Rossa**, Via Porta Rossa 19, tel: 287 551, fax: 282 179; 14th-century building, renovations over many centuries were made in the various styles and continue; pleasant atmosphere but not always modern comfort for sleeping, reasonably quiet location on a side street. **Select**, Via Galliano 24, tel: 330 342, fax: 351 506; air-conditioned rooms with bath, mini-bar and TV; has its own parking garage. **Vasari**, Via B. Cennini 9-11, tel: 212 753, fax: 294 246; well cared-for inn near the train station, has limited parking in courtyard.

⑤ Alessandra, Borgo SS. Apostoli 17, tel: 283 438, fax: 210 619; fairly central location, near the Ponte Vecchio; clean rooms with wooden furniture. **Casci**, near the cathedral, tel: 211 686, fax: 239 646; Swiss management, most rooms face the main road. **Firenze**, Piazza Donati 4, tel: 214 203, fax: 212 370, in the house where Gemma Donati, wife of Dante Alighieri, was born. Modern rooms, not far from cathedral. **Grazia e Griselda**, Via L. Alamanni, tel: 211 145, fax: 284 617; clean, but not all rooms have a shower. **Il Cestello**, Piazza di Cestello 9, tel: 280 632, fax: 280 631; quiet location, large, refurbished rooms, some have a view of the Arno. **La Scaletta,**Via Guicciardini 13, tel: 283 028, fax: 289 562; just a stone's throw from the Ponte Vecchio, rooms of varying sizes in deliberately old fashioned style, lovely view from the roof garden of the Boboli Gardens to the south. **La Sorelle Bandini**, Piazza Santo Spirito 9, tel: 215 308, fax: 282 761; early reservations are essential because it is often full. The top floors of a 15th-century palace building in historical surroundings; the view over the city's roofs is particularly nostalgic. **Monica**, Via Faenza 66, tel: 283 804, fax: 281 706; a small inn with a large air conditioning system, refurbished, roof garden on second floor. **Porta Faenza**, Via Faenza 77, tel: 284 119, fax: 210 101. **Santa Croce**, Via Bentaccordi 3, tel: 217 000; relatively quiet location in an area that is very medieval, very small rooms.

HOTEL RESERVATION CENTERS: **Consorzio Finestre Sull'Arno**, c/o Hotel Augustus, Vicolo dell'Oro 5, tel: 571 740. **Coopal**, Via Il Prato 2/R, tel: 219 525, fax: 292 192. **Florence Promhotels**, Viale Volta 72, tel: 570 481, fax: 587 189, www.promhotels.it, e-mail:

info@promhotels.it. **Top Quark** Family Hotels/Sun Rays Hotels/Hotel Italiano, Via Trieste 5, tel: 462 0080, fax: 482 288, www.emmeti.it/topquark, e-mail: topquark.fi@mbox.it.net. **Associazione Gestori Alloggi Privati** (private rooms), Via dei Neri 9, tel/fax: 284 100. **Agriturismo** (farm vacations) Mugello Alto Mugello Val die Sieve, tel/fax: 571 948, e-mail: info.sottobosco @flashnet.it.

AGRITURISMO (farm vacations): **La Fattoressa**, Via Volterrana 58, tel: 204 8418. **Le Macine**, Viuzzo del Pozzetto 1, tel: 653 1089. **Il Milione**, Via di Giogoli 12-14 and Via della Greve 7-9, tel: 204 8713. **Poggio Gaio**, Via San Michele a Monteripaldi 4, tel: 228 0348, fax: 225 327.

YOUTH HOSTELS: **Archi Rossi**, Via Faenza 94, tel: 290 804, fax: 230 2601; near the main station, approx. 80 beds. **Santa Monaca**, Via Santa Monaca 6, tel: 268 338, fax: 280 185; privately run, fairly busy due to central location, cooking facilities. **Villa Camerata**, Viale A. Righi 2-4, tel: 601 451; quite far from the city center on the outskirts, in a park with historical surroundings; rooms with 10-20 beds, not ideal for active nightlife.

ROOM RENTAL / EXCHANGE: Via Orti Oricellari 10, tel: 287 530, fax: 295 253; Mon-Fri 10:00 am-6:00 pm.

 Campeggio Michelangelo (Campeggio Italiani e Stranieri), Viale Michelangelo 80, tel: 681 1977, fax: 689 348; open all year. **Villa Camerata**, Viale A. Righi 2-4, tel: 601 451, 600 315, fax: 610 300; open all year.

 Antico Ristoro di' Cambi, Via S. Onofrio 1, tel: 217 134; closed Sun. Simple home-style cooking, middle price range. **La Baraonda**, Via Ghibellina 67/R, tel: 234 1171; closed Sun and Mon lunch. Friendly trattoria, light, typical Florentine cuisine, fair prices for quality offered. **Burde**, Via Pistoiese 6/R, tel: 317 206; closed evenings and holidays. One of the last old trattorias in Tuscany, excellent simple fare. **La Carabaccia**, Via Palazzuolo 190; closed Sun and Mon lunch. For less well-off gourmets, selected fine main courses, exquisite wines. **Cibreo**, Via dei Macci 118/R, tel: 234 1100; closed Sun and Mon. Typical Tuscan dishes, prices right for the quality. **Dino**, Via Ghibellina 51/R, tel: 241 452; closed Sun evenings and Mon. **Enoteca Pinchiorri**, Via Ghibellina 87, tel: 242 777; closed Sun and Mon, and Wed lunch. One of the city's top Italian restaurants, its high prices reflect the quality offered. **Le Fonticine**, Via Nazionale 79/R. tel: 282 106; closed Sun and Mon. Good, reasonably priced cuisine, most food made on the premises. **Alle Murate**, Via Ghibellina 52/R, tel: 240 618; closed Mon. Dishes from various Italian regions. **Pallottino**, Via Isola delle Stinche 1, tel: 289 573; closed Mon. Tuscan cuisine, reasonable prices. **Ruggero**, Via Senese 89/R, tel: 220 542; closed Tue and Wed. Typical Florentine trattoria, fair

prices. **Sabatini**, Via de Panzani 9, near the central station, wickedly expensive gourmet shrine. **Alla Vecchia Bettola**, Viale Ariosto 32-34, tel: 224 158; closed Sun and Mon. Tuscan cuisine, fairly expensive.

 Antico Caffe Torino, Viale Matteotti 2, tel: 588 247. **Caffetteria Gilli**, Piazza d. Repubblica, 1/R, tel: 213 896. A "must" in Florence. **Chez Moi**, Via di Porta Rossa 15, tel: 27 232. Night club. **Genesi**, Piazza del Duomo 20, directly opposite the cathedral. Popular drinking establishment with bar. **Moulin Rouge**, Via Baccio Bandinelli, tel: 208 608. Night club. **Paszkowski**, Piazza d. Repubblica 6/R, tel: 210 236. Attractive street café, serves excellent ice cream. **Pozzo di Beatrice**, Piazza di S. Trinita 5, tel: 270 804. Night club. **Rivoire**, Piazza d. Signoria, 5/R, tel: 214 412. Chocolate specialties. **Roof Garden Baglioni**, Piazza dell'Unita d' Italia, tel: 23 846. Night club.

 Cotton Pub, Via delle Terme 20, tel: 264 140. **Kneype**, Viale Gramsci 1, tel: 234 3890. **Spaziouno**, Via del Sole 10. Pub with movie theater, drinks at good prices; a one-time membership fee is charged at the entrance to the theater.

 Jaragua, near Piazzale Michelangelo; closed Mon. South American Music. **Jazz Club**, Via Nuova de'Caccini 3, tel: 247 9700. **Pongo**, Via Verdi 59. Popular rock music café. **Red Garter**, Via dei Benci 33. Rock music pub; live shows Thu, Fri and Sat. **Tenax**, Via Pratese 46, tel: 308 160, fax: 308 160. **Villa Kasar**, Lungarno Colombo 23, tel: 676 901, 676 912, fax: 332 348.

 MUSEUMS: **Uffizi Gallery**, Piazzale degli Uffizi; Tue-Sat 8:30 am-10:00 pm (summer), 8:30 am-6:50 pm (winter), Sun 8:30 am-8:00 pm (summer), 8:30 am-1:50 pm (winter), closed Mon. **Palazzo Pitti**: Galleria Palatina and Appartamenti Monumentali; Tue-Sat 8:30 am-10:00 pm (summer), 8:30 am-6:50 pm (winter), Sun and holidays 8:30 am-8:00 pm (summer), 8:30 am-1:50 pm (winter), closed Mon. Museo delle Porcellane and Museo degli Argenti; 2nd and 4th Mon and 1st, 3rd and 5th Sun 9:00 am-2:00 pm; currently closed for restoration work. Galleria dell'Arte Moderna and Galleria del Costume; Tue-Sat 8:00 am-1:50 pm, closed Sun and Mon. **Galleria dell' Accademia**, Via Ricasoli 60; Tue-Sat 8:30 am-10:00 pm (summer), 8:30 am-6:50 pm (winter), Sun 8:30 am-8:00 pm (summer), 8:30 am-1:50 pm(winter), closed Mon. **Museo Nationale Bargello**, Via del Proconsolo 4; Tue-Sat 8:30 am-1:50 pm, 2nd and 4th Sun 8:30 am-1:50 pm, and 1st, 3rd and 5th Mon 8:30 am-1:50 pm. **Museo San Marco**, Piazza San Marco 1; Tue-Sat and 2nd and 4th Sun 8:30 am-1:50 pm, and 1st, 3rd and 5th Mon 8:30 am-1:50 pm. **Museo Palazzo Davanzati**, Via Porta Rossa 13, temporarily closed. **Archeological Museum**, Via della Colonna 36; Tue-Sat 9:00 am-2:00 pm, Sun 9:00 am-1:00 pm,

Around Florence

closed Mon. **Medici Chapel**, Piazza Madonna degli Aldobrandini, Tue-Sat 8:30 am-4:50 pm, 1st, 3rd and 5th Sun 8:30 am-1:50 pm, and 2nd and 4th Mon. **Palazzo Vecchio** and **Quartieri Monumentali**, Piazza della Signoria; Mon-Wed and Fri 9:00 am-7:00 pm, Thur 9:00 am-2:00 pm, Sun and holidays 8:00 am-1:00 pm, closed Sat. **Palazzo Medici Riccardi**, Via Cavour 1; Mon, Tue and Thu-Sat 9:00 am-1:00 pm and 3:00-6:00 pm, Sun and holidays 9:00 am-1:00 pm, closed Wed. **Museo dell'Opera del Duomo** (Cathedral Museum), Piazza Duomo 9; Mon-Sat 9:00 am-6:50 pm (Feb 1-Oct 31), 9:00 am-6:20 pm (Nov 1-Jan 31), Sun 9:00 am-1:20 pm. **Museo dell'Opera di S. Croce**, Piazza S. Croce 16; Thu-Tue 10:00 am-12:30 pm and 2:30-6:30 pm (March 1-Oct 31), 10:00 am-12:30 pm and 3:00-5:00 pm (Nov 1-Feb 28), closed Wed. **Museo di Storia della Scienza** (Science History Museum), Piazza dei Giudici 1; Mon-Sat 9:30 am-1:00 pm and Mon, Wed, Fri also 2:00-5:00 pm, closed Sun and holidays. **Museo Marino Marini**, Piazza San Pancrazio; Mon and Wed-Sat 10:00 am-5:00 pm, Thu 10:00 am-11:00 pm (summer), Sun 10:00 am-1:00 pm, closed Tue and all of August. **Museo Stibber**, Via Stibbert 26; Mon-Wed and Fri 10:00 am-1:00 pm and 3:00-6:00 pm (summer), 10:00 am-2:00 pm (winter), Sat and Sun 10:00 am-6:00 pm, closed Thu. Guided tours every half hour. **Pinacoteca della Certosa**, Certosa del Galluzzo; Tue-Sun 9:00 am-noon and 3:00-6:00 pm (summer), 9:00 am-noon and 3:00-5:00 pm (winter), closed Mon. **Museo San Ferragamo**, Via del Tornabuoni 2; Mon-Fri 9:00 am-1:00 pm and 2:00-6:00 pm, closed Sat and Sun. Designer shoe collection of Hollywood's maker of "dream shoes," Ferragamo (died 1960).

CHURCHES: Most churches are open in the morning and late afternoon and close from noon-4:00 pm. The **Duomo**, Mon-Sat 10:00 am-5:00 pm, Sun 1:00-5:00 pm. **Cathedral Dome**, Mon-Fri 8:30 am-6:20 pm, Sat 8:30 am-5:00 pm (1st Sat 8:30 am-3:20 pm), closed Sun and holidays. **Baptistry**, daily noon-6:30 pm, holidays 8:30 am-1:30 pm. Ascent of the **Campanile**, daily 9:00 am-6:50 pm (summer), 9:00 am-4:20 pm (winter).

MEDICI VILLAS: **Villa di Castello** and **Villa della Petraia**, Nov-Feb 9:00 am-4:30 pm, March and Oct 9:00 am-5:30 pm, April, May and Sept 9:00 am-6:30 pm, June-Aug 9:00 am-7:30 pm, closed 2nd and 3rd Mon. **Cerreto Guidi**, 9:00 am-6:30 pm, closed 2nd and 3rd Mon. **Poggio a Caiano**, 9:00 am-5:30 pm (summer), 9:00 am-3:30 pm (winter), closed 2nd and 3rd Mon.

OFFICE FOR MUSEUM RESERVATIONS: **Musei Statali Firenze**, tel: 294 883.

GUIDED TOURS: **Guide Turistiche Della Toscana**, Via Calimala 2, tel/fax: 230 2283. **Centro Guide Turis**

mo Firenze e Provincia, Via Ghibellina 110, tel: 288 448, fax: 288 476. **Guide Turistiche Fiorentine**, Via Ugo Corsi 25, tel/fax: 422 0901.

✚ **ACI** (Italian Automobile Club), tel: 116. **Pharmacies** (open all day): **Comunale**, in the central train station, tel: 289435; **Insegna del Moro**, near the cathedral. **Arcispedale di S. M. Nuova**, Pz. S. M. Nuova 1, tel: 27 581. **Careggi**, Viale Morgagni 85, tel: 427 7111.

🎇 **Easter Sunday** (scoppio del carro), fireworks display at the cathedral, in which a mass is celebrated, during which two oxen draw a wooden cart (carro) in front of the portal; a flame from the portal sets off the fireworks on the cart. **June 24** (calcio in costume), festival of the patron saint S. Giovanni (St. John), traditional soccer game on the Piazza della Signoria in remembrance of Charles V's unsuccessful siege of the city in the 16th century; procession in historical costumes.

🛍 **Via Tornabuoni**, everything that money can buy for an elegant appearance can be found on this exclusive shopping street, including *Gucci*. **Ponte Vecchio**, on this historic bridge over the Arno, you will find one tiny jewelry shop after another. **Mercato Cascine**, every Tuesday morning there is market on the bank of the Arno (near the Ponte della Vittoria), where you can find everything from cooking pots to chandeliers, and if you are good at bargaining, you can get them at quite low prices. **Straw Market**, Via Calimala, near the Piazza della Repubblica; mostly typical tourist goods, incl. hats, handbags and leather goods. More valuable goods, including gold and silk, were traditionally traded in this historical loggia.

🚔 *SAFETY:* Florence is an Eldorado for pickpockets who involve you in a harmless conversation and at the same time relieve you of your valuables! You should even beware of wide-eyed children: gangs of children practice a variety of clever methods of stealing. Use secure parking lots, where possible. Don't leave valuables visible in the car, and it's best to leave the glove compartment open, to show that nothing is in it. Should you lose something or be robbed, here are the most useful addresses: **Railway Police Dept.**, tel: 212 296. **Theft** (cars, property), tel: 49 771. **Fire Department**, tel: 115 and 241 841. **Lost and Found Office**, Via Circondaria 19 (9:00-noon), tel: 328 3942. **Consulates**, USA: Lungarno Vespucci 38, tel: 239 8276; United Kingdom: Lungarno Corsini 2, tel: 284 133 and 212 594. **Ambulance Services:** Misericordia, tel: 212 222; Fratellanza Militare, tel: 215 555; Association of Doctors, tel: 475 411; Coronary Illness, tel: 283 394, 244 444 and 4976; 24-Hour Ambulance, tel: 111 8394. **Emergency Services**, tel: 113 and 318 000. **Police (Carabinieri)**, tel: 112. **Traffic Police**, tel: 32 831 and 577 777.

FIESOLE (☎ 055)

ℹ **Tourist Information Office (APT)**, Piazza Mino 36, tel: 598 720, fax: 598 822.

⬛ **ⓈⓈⓈ Villa San Michele**, Via Doccia 4, tel: 59 451, fax: 598 734. **Villa Aurora**, Piazza Mino 39, tel: 59 100, fax: 59 587.

ⓈⓈ Villa Bonelli, Via F. Poeti 1A, tel: 59 513, fax: 598 942. **Bencistà**, Via B. da Maiano 4, tel/fax: 59 163. **Dino**, Via Faentina 329, tel: 548 932. **Villa Fiesole**, Via Fra' Giovanni Angelico 35, tel: 597 252, fax: 599 133.

Ⓢ Villa Baccano, Via Bosconi 4, tel/fax: 59 341. **Villa Sorriso**, Via Gramsci 21, tel/fax: 59 027.

AGRITURISMO (farm vacations): **Azienda Agricola Terenzano**, Via della Rosa 15, tel: 659 3021. **Fattoria di Poggiopiano**, Via dei Bassi 13, tel: 659 3020.

⬛ **Campeggio Panoramico**, Via Peramonda 1, tel: 599 069, fax: 59 186.

✖ **Le Cave di Maiano**, Via delle Cave 16, tel: 59 133; closed Mon lunch. Traditional cuisine, country-style environment; prices are acceptable. **Pizzeria San Domenico**, San Domenico, tel: 59 182; closed Mon.

🏛 *MUSEUMS:* **Civic Museum** and **Roman Theater**, Via Portigiani 1; Wed-Mon 9:00 am-7:00 pm (summer), 9:00 am-5:00 pm (winter), closed Tue. **Museo Bandini**, Via Duprè 1; daily 9:00 am-7:00 pm (summer), 9:00 am-4:30 pm (winter), closed 1st Tue. **Antiquarium Costantini**, Via Portigiani 1, daily 9:00 am-7:00 pm (summer), 9:00 am-5:30 pm (winter), closed 1st Tue. Valuable collection of antique ceramics.

🔭 *SIGHTS:* Viewpoint **Parco della Rimembranza**. **Church** and **Museum of S. Francesco**, Via S. Francesco; daily 10:00 am-noon and 3:00-6:00 pm (summer), 10:00 am-noon and 3:00-5:00 pm (winter). **Villa Gamberaia**, 8:00 am to sunset.

PRATO (☎ 0574)

ℹ **Tourist Information Office (APT)**, Piazza S. Maria delle Carceri 15, tel: 24 112.

🚗 *CAR RENTAL:* **Avis**, Via della Repubblica 289, tel: 596 619. **Hertz**, Viale Vittorio Veneto 57, tel: 21 055. *TAXI:* **Radiotaxi**, tel: 5656. **Eurotaxi**, tel: 564 061 and 571 676.

⬛ **ⓈⓈⓈ Art Hotel Museo**, Viale della Repubblica 289, tel: 5787, fax: 578 880. **Palace**, Via Piero della Francesca 71, tel: 5671, fax: 567 267. **President**, Via A. Simintendi 20, tel: 30 251, 30 252 and 30 253.

ⓈⓈ Flora, Via Cairoli, 31, tel: 33 521, fax: 40 289. **Giardino**, Via G. Magnolfi 2, tel: 606 588 and 26189. **San Marco**, Piazza S. Marco, tel: 21 321, 21 322 and 21 323. **Villa S. Cristina**, Via Poggio Secco 58, tel: 595 951, fax: 572 623.

Ⓢ Stella d'Italia, P.za Duomo, 8, tel: 27 910, fax: 40 289. **Il Giglio**, P.za S. Marco 14, tel: 37 049, fax: 604 351. **Roma**, Via G. Carradori 1, tel: 31 777. **La Toscana**, Piazza G. Ciardi 3, tel: 28 096.

✖ **Art Restaurant**, Viale della Repubblica 289, tel: 578 888; closed Sun. **Barbarossa**, Via Tiziano 15, tel: 27 331 and 23 371; closed Sun. **La Cucina di Paola**, Via Banchelli 16, tel: 24 353; closed Mon. **Le Mura**, S. Antonio 24, tel: 24 320; closed Mon. **Tonio**, Piazza Mercatale 161, tel: 21 266, closed Sun and Mon. **Il Piraña**, Via Tobia Bertini, tel: 25 746; closed Sat lunch and Sun. Very modern design, high prices, but excellent fish dishes. **Trattoria Lapo**, Piazza Mercatale 141, tel: 23 745; closed Sun. Initially uninviting, but has a very folkloric character. **La Vecchia Cucina di Soldano**, Via Pomeria 23, tel: 34 665; closed Sun. Trattoria.

🏛 **Palazzo Datini**, Via Ser Lapo Mazzei, Mon-Fri 9:00 am-noon and 3:00-6:30 pm, in July and Aug also Sat 9:00 am-noon, closed Sun and holidays. **Luigi Pecci** (Museum of Contemporary Art), Wed-Mon 10:00 am-7:00pm, closed Tue. **Medici Museum** in **Poggio a Caiano**, daily 9:00 am-5:30 pm (summer), 9:00 am-3:30 pm (winter), closed 2nd and 3rd Mon.

➕ **Ospedale Misericordia e Dolce**, Piazza dell'Ospedale, tel: 6011.

PISTOIA (☎ 0573)

ℹ **Tourist Information Office (APT)**, Via Roma 1, Palazzo dei Vescovi, tel: 21 622, fax: 34 327.

⬛ **ⓈⓈ Leon Bianco**, Via Panciatichi 2, tel: 26 675, fax: 26 704. **Milano**, Viale Pacinotti 10, tel: 975 700, fax: 32 657. **Patria**, Via F. Crispi 6, tel: 25 187, fax: 368 168. **Piccolo Ritz**, Via A. Vannucci 67, tel: 26 775, fax: 27 798. **Hotel Le Rose**, Viale Adua 89, tel: 20 785, fax: 976 161. **Signorino**, Il Signorino, Via Bolognese 207, tel: 475 162/070, fax: 475 162. **Il Convento**, Via S. Quirico 33, Loc. Ponte Nuovo, tel: 452 651, fax: 453 578.

Ⓢ Autisti, Viale Pacinotti 89, tel: 21 771. **Il Boschetto**, Viale Adua 467, tel: 401 336. **Firenze**, Via Curtatone e Montanara 42, tel: 21 660, fax: 23 141.

✖ **Leon Rosso**, Via Panciatichi 4, tel: 29230; closed Sun. **La Vela**, P.za dell'Ortaggio 12, tel: 33 658; closed Sun night and Mon. Good cuisine, low prices.

🏛 **Museo Civico**, Tue-Sat 9:00 am-6:00 pm, Sun 9:00 am-12:30 pm, closed Mon. **Palazzo Tau**, Tue-Sat am-1:00 pm and 3:00-7:00 pm, closed Mon. **Villa Garzoni Gardens** in Collodi, Mon-Fri 9:00 am-sunset (April-Oct), 9:00-1:00 pm and 2:30 pm-sunset (Nov 1-Feb 28), Sat and Sun 9:00 am-sunset. **Pinocchio Park**, 9:00 am-sunset. **Museo Vinciano** (in the Vinci castle), daily 9:30 am-6:00 pm (summer till 7:00 pm).

CHIANTI

CHIANTI

WINE COUNTRY

VIA CHIANTIGIANI

VIA CASSIA

SAN GIMIGNANO

VOLTERRA

WINE COUNTRY

The word Chianti is familiar to many, many people, even those who have never been to Tuscany. It conjures up images of rolling hills, silvery olive groves, cypresses and, of course, vineyards. And nearly everyone has tasted Chianti wine at one time or another. During the 1960s and 70s, you could buy it the grocery store, in the famous *fiaschi*, for next to nothing. Today, those straw-wrapped bottles are largely obsolete, and quality and prices have increased substantially.

Glossy photographs in magnificent coffee-table books and large-format, full-color, glossy calendars show a Tuscany that is mostly limited to Chianti, as if Tuscany's beautiful countryside were best represented by this small region, which is true.

The landscape between Florence and Siena, between the upper Arno valley and the valley of the Elsa, is breathtakingly beautiful. In addition to its famous wine, it boasts historic towns that are rich in history and art, monasteries and villas, castles and fortified villages, and beautifully solitary farmsteads standing amidst vineyards and olive groves.

Left: In May, irises transform the area around San Polo into a sea of flowers.

No other part of Tuscany can boast such a variety of attractions, and no other part is visited by as many tourists. Unfortunately, the down side of this is inevitable as well. It is more expensive and more crowded here, especially in the towns that everyone wants to be able to say they have seen. Because of the crowds, the "real" Tuscany frequently loses out and what the tourist gets to see is an artificial preparation of *Toscanità*, which is only there to bleed him for as much money as it possibly can.

It is well worth your time, then, to deviate from the well-traveled roads, and explore the narrow valleys and bumpy country lanes, winding and difficult as they may be. You will be rewarded with splendid views, majestic solitude and, sometimes, unforeseen encounters.

Geography and History

Geographically, Chianti lies within the triangle that is formed by the Arno valley between Florence and Arezzo, the road between Arezzo and Siena, and the Siena-Florence expressway. The Chianti region, home to the famous "Gallo Nero," however, is limited to the townships of Radda, Castellina and Gaiole.

The Etruscans inhabited this area as early as the 7th and 8th centuries B.C.,

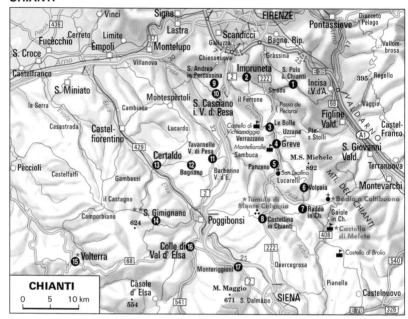

and it is they who are thought to have first brought viticulture to Tuscany.

For many years, the rival cities of Florence and Siena fought over this fertile region, until it was finally won by Florence in the 13th century. According to an old legend, this came to pass in a rather unusual manner. Both cities were to send out a rider at the first crowing of the cock. At the point where the two riders met up, the new border would be drawn. The clever Florentines, however, starved their black cock, which was so hungry that he started to crow well before dawn. Naturally, the Florentine rider was able to cover a much greater distance than his Sienese colleague, and thus the Chianti region was won for Florence. The black cock was incorporated into the coat-of-arms of what came to be known as the *Lega del Chianti* (League of Chianti), which was formed by the three cities of

Radda, Gaiole and Castellina, and fell under Florentine jurisdiction.

In addition to its "historic" center, the name Chianti also applies to the wine region of Chianti, which is divided into seven zones, plus the Chianti Classico, which, in accordance with a 1929 law, is made up of ca. 70,000 hectares of vineyards. Only wines that are made within this region can bear the name *Vino Chianti Classico Gallo Nero*.

To get to know Chianti, we recommend you take one of two routes. The first follows the Via Chiantigiana (SS 222), from Florence, via Greve, to Siena. The other, the Via Cassia (SS 2), runs a little further west, parallel to the Florence-Siena expressway.

★VIA CHIANTIGIANA

As you leave Florence, follow the historic main road into Chianti by taking the Via di Ripoli toward Grassina. Grassina is a small town of little importance, where the mountain river of the same name

Right: The wine festival in Greve, in Chianti's wine country, takes on something of the character of Thanksgiving and a harvest festival.

 Info p. 107

Chianti

flows into the river Ema. However, if you are traveling during the month of May, you might, want to consider an excursion to San Polo in Chianti.

A Sea of Blue Blossoms

In Grassina, turn left into Via Tizzano. You will pass a number of scattered estates and churches, through the village of Capannucia, and, after about ten kilometers, you will reach the town of **San Polo in Chianti** ❶, one of Tuscany's iris-growing centers. In May, the hills around San Polo are covered with purple-blue blossoms, and the air is filled with the intensive aroma of spring violets, which some say you can detect in the bouquet of some Chianti wines.

The medicinal and cosmetic values of these flowers were appreciated as early as the days of Hippocrates, and even today they are planted, harvested and processed by hand. The roots are powdered and used as a basis for perfume production on the international cosmetic market. Unfor-

tunately, the irises bloom for only one short week in May. If you are lucky enough to be nearby during that week, you should do everything you can to experience this singularly enchanting sight.

Impruneta

If it doesn't happen to be iris season, take the main road out of Grassina, past the *Golf dell'Ugolino*, which is considered to be one of the most beautiful golf courses in Italy. Coming over a range of gently rolling hills that separates the Ema valley from the Greve valley, you reach Strada in Chianti, a village of little charm. At a junction just before Strada, turn right to **Impruneta** ❷ (six kilometers), a town that is renowned for its ceramics, which are shipped all over the world. As early as the 14th century, the town began to produce its famous Cotto tiles. Most of the workshops are family-owned, even today, although a few of them have gone into a more industrial kind of production. In any event, it is well worth your time to visit

the various workshops. Everyone is friendly and perfectly happy to let you observe the craftsmen at work. And if you feel the urge to adorn your balcony with some particularly well-formed ceramic pots, don't hesitate to make the investment. The prices for hand-made pottery here are high, but they are still cheaper than they would be back home.

From a historical perspective, Impruneta is also of cultural interest for its image of the Madonna, which is believed to perform miracles, and hangs in the **Basilica di Santa Maria**. During the Middle Ages the Florentines had such a profound veneration for the *Madonna dell'Impruneta*, which was carried to Florence in solemn religious processions during times of war, plague, drought and other catastrophes, that Impruneta became the religious center of the entire Northern Chianti region. Also dating from the Mid-

Above: For centuries Impruneta has been a center for ceramics. Right: Under the arcades of the main square in Greve.

dle Ages is the festival of San Luca, celebrated annually, in mid-October, with horse races, a fair, and general festivities.

From Impruneta you can return to Via Chiantigiana by way of Il Ferrone, either by driving to Strada and continuing on through Chiocchio, or by opting for the somewhat longer route over the Passo dei Pecorai to **Le Bolle ❸**, where both roads converge. Just beyond the "Shepherd's Pass," the SP 3 leads to the 10th-century **Castello di Vichiomaggio**, atop a hill overlooking Le Bolle. Only one tower, dating from the 13th century, remains of the original structure. The rest was converted into a villa in the 16th century.

Via Chiantigiana continues on toward Greve, past the castles of Verrazzano and Uzzano. The **Castello di Verrazzano** once belonged to the family of the seafaring Giovanni di Verrazzano, the first person to explore the Atlantic Coast of North America in 1524. Of the old 13th-century mansion, only a turreted tower remains. Today Verrazzano is one of Chianti's most prized vineyards.

The same is true of the vineyards of **Castello di Uzzano**, which sits like a crown atop the mountain, overlooking the terraced vineyards that produce the "Niccolò di Uzzano." This castle, too, belonged to an aristocratic family, one scion of which was the eponymous Niccolò. The Uzzani played an important role during the days of the Republic in Florence.

Greve in Chianti

Greve ❹ is not a particularly attractive town. In fact, the only thing worth seeing is its arcaded marketplace, the Piazza Giovanni da Verrazzano, which lies at the center of town like an extended triangle. Located at the point where the road from Florence intersects with the one connecting the Greve valley with the upper Arno valley, Greve has been an important center of trade from the very beginning. It is particularly well-known for its wild boar

delicacies, which you can buy in pretty shops beneath the arcades. At one end of the marketplace stands **Santa Croce**, a church that was rebuilt in neoclassical style in the middle of the 19th century. It contains a triptych by Bicci di Lorenzo and a 14th-century *Annunciation* of the Florentine School.

A small road leads from Greve to the castle **Montefioralle** (1.5 kilometers), which is nestled amidst cypresses, vineyards ands olive trees. If you wish to end your tour of Chianti here, you can take the road from Greve to Figline Valdarno (19 kilometers), and drive through the Arno valley back to Florence.

From Greve to Radda

Two roads lead from Greve to Radda in Chianti. One follows Via Chiantigiani through oak forests, olive groves, and vineyards to **Panzano** ❺ (6 kilometers). This little town has its roots in the days of the Etruscans, and it was later an arena for the contests and strife between Guelphs and Ghibellines. During the 1950s, it developed into a favorite home away-from-home for British ex-patriots who fell in love with Panzano's dream location high above the valley and its truly magnificent surroundings. Today, however, you will find that there are more Germans and Swiss in town.

Just past Panzano, the road to the **Pieve di San Leolino** branches off to the left. This beautiful Romanesque church was first mentioned in a manuscript in A.D. 982. At some point during the 12th or 13th century it was enlarged, but retained its Romanesque style. In the 16th century it was further decorated with the beautiful portico, which rests on five sandstone pillars. The church's interior is decorated with the works of Sienese painters.

Just past Panzano, the SP 2 turns left and leads past Lucarelli and the Castello di Monterinaldi to Radda (10 kilometers).

The other way to get from Greve to Radda is certainly longer, but it is particularly attractive because of its beautiful scenery. To take this route, turn left (to-

ward Lamole) just outside of Greve, and follow the road past vineyards, olive groves and beautiful estates until you get to the **Villa di Vignamaggio** (16th century). It is said that this was once the home of Mona Lisa del Giocondo, whose mysterious smile Leonardo da Vinci made famous. Through pine avenues and chestnut groves, the road continues on to the pretty village of Lamole, and from there to **Volpaia ❻**, once a fortified medieval town with a castle that is believed to have been built around the year 1000.

For many centuries, this town had to suffer the fighting between Florence and Siena, both of which valued it for its strategic location atop a hill directly on the border of the two city-states. However, when the Republic of Siena fell in 1555, Volpaia lost its military importance.

Today, Volpaia still boasts some of its old city walls and several beautifully restored medieval buildings. The most im-

Above: A vineyard in Chianti. Today many vintners also offer tourist accommodations.

portant of these is the 15th-century **Commenda di San Eufrosino**, which is now used for exhibitions and other cultural events.

Radda in Chianti

From Volpaia, it is six kilometers to **Radda in Chianti ❼**, which lies on a hill 533 meters above the Pesa and Arbia valleys. Today, it is home to the headquarters of the *Consorzio del Gallo Nero*. The town is quite small and lives from viticulture and the wine trade, as well as the tourist trade that has been spurred by its incredibly beautiful surroundings.

Radda has managed to maintain much of its medieval character. As the seat of the Chianti League's *Podestà* (since 1415) it attracted aristocracy from the surrounding area, who built their elegant homes around the dignified **Palazzo del Podestà**. The palace, which was built early in the 15th century and was later expanded, is adorned with the coats-of-arms of the various city fathers.

From Radda to Siena

From Radda it is just ten kilometers to ★**Badia a Coltibuono**. Formerly a Benedictine monastery, this site is endowed with a beautiful, albeit heavily restored, Romanesque church. Today, the adjacent monastery hosts cultural events, as well as furnishing a home for the winery. Right next to it, you can find a fine restaurant with a magnificent view of the surrounding forests.

At the junction of the road to Montevarchi, follow the SS 408, the so-called "Castle Road of Chianti," to the right and you will come to Gaiole in Chianti, a little wine-producing village surrounded by hills that are covered with grapevines. Long ago, ★**Castello di Meleto** (3 kilometers) controlled the access roads to Gaiole from its lofty vantage point. Of all of the fortifications in the Chianti League, these are the best-preserved original structures.

Just past Meleto, a left turn onto a small road leads to the **Castello di Brolio**. Built in its present form in the latter part of the 15th century, this edifice belongs to the well-known family of Ricasoli Firidolfi, who ruled this region after the 12th century. One of their ancestors, Bettino Ricasoli, created the original formula for Chianti wine. Near Brolio, in the little village of San Regolo, there is a charming *trattoria* that serves good local cuisine. A connecting road leads in a westerly direction back to the SS 408, which will bring you to Siena (about 30 kilometers).

Castellina in Chianti

Another road from Radda to Siena leads through **Castellina in Chianti ❽**, which is situated atop a hill high above the Arbia, Elsa and Pesa valleys. The town was once part of the defensive fortifications that Florence had erected in a line from the Elsa to the Arno valley. After a turbulent history against a backdrop of power struggles between Florence and Siena, Castellina lost its strategic importance when the Republic of Siena fell and the fortifications were gradually turned into residential buildings.

Today, like most of Chianti's mountain villages, it suffers from a decline in population due to migration into the cities. Although it hasn't been altogether spared architectural modifications, it retained at least parts of its original structures.

In the center of town stands a medieval castle, which today houses the city's administration. Just outside town you will find a large Etruscan gravesite, ★**Tumulo di Monte Calvario**, which is thought to date back to the 7th century B.C. and is among the most interesting excavation sites in the Chianti region. It is testimony to the former importance of the spot due to its geographical location between the Arno valley and Volterra.

VIA CASSIA

Via Cassia (SS 2) runs parallel to the Florence-Siena expressway, and, since it has exits to a larger number of towns than the Chiantigiana, traffic tends to be fairly heavy. This old Roman road follows the mountain crests and offers one magnificent panoramic view after the other.

Leave Florence on Via Senese, towards Poggibonsi. Between Certosa del Galluzzo and San Casciano in Val di Pesa, just past the "Florence American Cemetery and Memorial" (built by American architects in 1959), a side road to the right leads to **Sant'Andrea in Percussina ❾**. This is where Niccolò Machiavelli sat, in 1513, in the Villa Albergaccio, and brooded over his great treatise, *Il Principe* (*The Prince*). The Osteria, which the great political author frequented, serves commendable cuisine to this day.

The little town of **San Casciano Val di Pesa ❿** owes its importance to its location at the junction of two important thoroughfares. One connects Florence with

Rome, the other connects the Pesa and the Greve valleys. As well as the ruins of a medieval fortress, there are also remnants of the old city walls. While here, you should see the collegiate church of San Francesco and the Chiesa della Misericordia. Built in the 14th century and restored in the 16th, the latter houses the **Museo della Misericordia**, which displays works by Ugolino di Neri, Simone Martini, Taddeo Gaddi and other masters.

Leave town on the SS 2, and you can continue to **Tavarnelle Val di Pesa** ⓫ (15 kilometers), which was a postal station on the old consular road during Roman times. From here, you might want to take a detour to **Badia di Passignano**. Exit to the left and drive towards Sambuca until you see, amidst the vineyards, wheat fields and forests, the turreted towers of the abbey, which was founded by Vallombrosian monks in the 11th century.

Above: Fifteen of San Gimignano's 72 dynastic towers have survived.

Only a few kilometers past Tavernelle is Barberino Val d'Elsa, with the remains of medieval fortresses and the Palazzo of the Barberini. Just beyond that, turn right onto one of several roads leading to Certaldo. One route that can be recommended leads through **Bagnano** ⓬, where you can visit the octagonal chapel of **San Michele**. Its cupola is a replica of that atop the Duomo in Florence, scaled down at a ratio of 1:8.

The picturesque old town center of **Certaldo** ⓭ is located on a hill above the modern city and is built entirely of red brick. The author of the *Decameron*, Giovanni Boccaccio, once lived here. His home now houses a center for Boccaccio studies and a library of his works. The main street, which is also paved with red stones, ends at the **Palazzo Pretorio**, also known as the **Palazzo dei Vicari**. Its facade is adorned with a wealth of armorial bearings in both terra cotta and stone. The church of **Santi Michele e Jacopo** (Saints Michael and Jacob) contains the grave of Boccaccio, as well as the remains of Beata Giulia. Legend has it that for thirty years she had herself walled in, in a cell next to the church.

The SS 429 leads from Certaldo, through the Elsa valley and on to Siena. Around Poggibonsi and Colle Val d'Elsa, a number of roads from various directions converge to intersect, ultimately, in San Gimignano. The shortest and fastest way to San Gimignano is through Poggibonsi, but the smaller roads are more attractive.

**SAN GIMIGNANO

The skyline of **San Gimignano ⑭** is probably the most-photographed in all of Tuscany. Correspondingly, tourist traffic in and around the town is heavy, particularly on weekends and holidays, when even Italians swarm up the hill like locusts. One bit of advice: rather than spend hours sitting in traffic, hoping to get a place in the overcrowded parking lots near the old city walls, park below the city and take a beautiful walk across the fields toward the towers. They serve as great landmarks so you can't get lost.

San Gimignano is a medieval town *par excellence*. Its 13th- and 14th-century structures have remained practically untouched. During the 10th century, this former Etruscan settlement took the name of the canonized Bishop of Modena, San Gimignano, who reportedly saved it from a barbarian invasion. In 1199, it became a *libero commune*, a city with an independent government. As a free republic, it competed with other nearby cities, Volterra in particular. Eventually, internal power struggles divided the population into two camps, followers of either the Guelph Ardinghelli or the Ghibellinese Salvucci, and in 1348 the plague devastated the city to such an extent that in 1354 it finally succumbed to Florence.

San Gimignano developed into a trade center along the old Frankish Road, which was used by pilgrims on their way to Rome, as early as the 8th century. The

SAN GIMIGNANO
0   200 m

Chianti

cultivation of saffron, used to color valuable silks, ensured the city's considerable wealth. The majority of its important public buildings were constructed during the period of the republic, as were the residential dynastic towers of the town's leading families, which served, in effect, as miniature fortresses. During the 14th century, there were 72 such residential towers – today there are 15. Great artists from Florence, Pisa, Lucca, and Siena were commissioned to decorate churches and homes. During the 13th century a double ring of city walls, much of which still stands, was erected to protect the fortified town center and the districts of San Matteo and San Giovanni.

San Gimignano (pop. 8000) hasn't grown much since the Middle Ages, and it can easily be explored in a day. The center of town is the **Piazza della Cisterna ①**, with a magnificent fountain that was built in 1273, and Cathedral Square with its **cathedral** and **Palazzo del Podestà**, both built in the 12th century. Arnolfo di Cambio is thought to

have been responsible for the **Palazzo del Popolo** ❷, decorated with armorial bearings, at the south end of the square. It was completed in 1288, it now houses the municipal administration and civic museums. The tallest tower is the City Hall, the *Torre Grossa* – after it was built, no one was allowed to construct anything taller. Most of the surviving towers surround these two squares.

Worth seeing is the interior of the Romanesque cathedral **★Collegiata Santa Maria Assunta** ❸ (remodeled and expanded by Guiliano da Maiano in the 15th century) with its works by Benozzo Gozzoli, Taddeo di Bartolo, Jacopo della Quercia and Barna da Siena. There are also two frescoes by Ghirlandaio in the chapel of Saint Fina.

Via San Matteo leads from Cathedral Square to the Porta San Matteo. Not far from here is the church of a mendicant order **★Sant'Agostino** ❹, where Benozzi

Above: A Fresco by Benozzo Fozzoli in San Gimignano's cathedral.

Gozzoli's 15th-century frescoes show, with glowing colors and great attention to detail, scenes from the life of the church's father Augustine. **Via San Giovanni** ❺, which connects the Piazza della Cisterna with the Porta San Giovanni, will bring you into the main flow of tourist traffic – it is lined with souvenir shops and restaurants that cater to tourists.

If you don't care for these supermarkets of mass-produced "typical Tuscan products" and seek more meaningful impressions, you need only go a few steps further to experience the real, living San Gimignano, which actually does still exist. And at night, after the busloads of tourists have left, quiet descends. If you then stand on the city walls, or on the ruins of the old fortress, and take a look at the breathtakingly beautiful surroundings, you will have to agree that this town has earned its reputation as one of the most beautiful sites in all of Tuscany.

VOLTERRA

Just ten kilometers south of San Gimignano, rejoin the main road, No. 68. Twenty kilometers further west, you reach **★Volterra** ⓯ (16,000 residents), located atop a bare hill between the Cecina and the Era valleys. The landscape here is starker, not planted with vineyards or olive groves, but divided up as wheat fields or sheep pastures. The hill consists of clay and sandstone from the Pliocene period (five - two million years ago), and is subject to severe erosion. Landslides and mudslides are responsible for the phenomenon known as *balze*, deep crevasses that have already swallowed up entire Etruscan necropolises. The ancient settlement of Badia, just outside of town, is also in danger of being swallowed.

The first settlements on this hill date back to the New Stone Age. After the Villanova period, they united to form a single town that became a member of the Etruscan League. Today, remnants of a

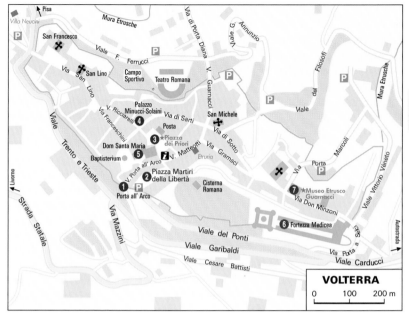

city wall, the 4th-century B.C. **Porta all'Arco** ❶, adorned with mysterious heads, and the **acropolis**, testify to the importance of this early settlement, known as *Velathris*.

Take the time to visit one or two of the **★alabaster workshops** that are clustered along **Via Porta all'Arco** ❷, to watch the modern techniques of this ancient Etruscan craft. Of course, much of what is produced from this semi-transparent gypsum today is tourist-oriented kitsch, but you can occasionally find a pretty piece that makes a nice souvenir.

During the 3rd century B.C., the Etruscan city was incorporated into the Roman Empire. Its residents quickly adopted the Christian faith, and by the time the Roman Empire fell, Volterra had a Bishop and was a substantial diocese. After the 12th century, it was a free commune with an independent government and laws. It fell under Florentine rule in 1472.

Today, Volterra is a quiet, contemplative town that has maintained much of its medieval character.

The **Piazza dei Priori** ❸, considered to be one of the best-preserved medieval squares in all of Italy, is at the towns historical center. Nearby, the monumental **Palazzo dei Priori** proudly shows off the armorial bearings of its Florentine governors. Construction on this building began in 1208, making this the oldest City Hall in Tuscany. On the other side of the piazza stands the 13th-century **Palazzo Pretorio** with its battlemented *Torre del Porcellino*, or Piglets' Tower.

The medieval **tower houses**, such as those on Via Buonparenti, west of the piazza, which belonged to the Buonparenti and Bonaguidi families, contribute to the city's architecturally homogeneous appearance. Amazingly, the old city still has a distinctly medieval flair that managed to withstand even the widespread architectural improvements and additions of the Renaissance. For example, the **Palazzo Minucci Solaini** ❹ (northwest of the piazza), still stands harmoniously between two medieval tower residences, just as it did centuries ago.

The Romanesque **cathedral** ❺ and baptistry are on Piazza San Giovanni, just a few steps further on. Far more interesting than the exterior of the cathedral are the works of art inside, including the marble ciborium on the altar, the angels supporting the candelabra at either side of Mino da Fiesole's high altar, the Romanesque pulpit, and a 13th-century wooden sculpture showing Christ being taken off the cross. A fresco by Benozzo Gozzoli in the Cappella dell'Addolorata depicts the Adoration of the Magi. The octagonal green-and-white striped **baptistry**, dating from 1284, has been restored and is once again open to the public.

In Volterra, you can also see ruins from the ancient world, such as the remains of the **Roman theater** and the **Roman baths**. The highest point of the city is dominated by the mighty **citadel** ❻, the so-called *Maschio*, which Lorenzo the Magnificent had built for defense pur-

poses. Today, this gigantic Renaissance building serves as a prison and can only be viewed from a distance. From the lovely park in front of the castle, however, you can take in the full effect of this impressive edifice.

While you are here, don't miss the Etruscan **Museo Etrusco Guarnacci** ❼, which has grown out of the substantial private collection that Mario Guarnacci, a local prelate and scholar, donated to the city in 1761. The museum displays several of the most significant Etruscan artifacts found in the Volterra region.

From Volterra, you can return to San Gimignano and then head to **Colle di Val d'Elsa** ⓰ with its pretty medieval Upper City. From here, it is only ten kilometers to **Monteriggioni** ⓱. This town's well-preserved city wall crowns a ridge of hills. Unfortunately, Monteriggioni is far more charming from outside its fortified wall than it is from within – the entire town has succumbed to tourism. From here, you can travel the last few miles to Siena along the superstrada.

Above: Today, as in the days of the Etruscans, craftsmen tool alabaster in Volterra.

CHIANTI

CASTELLINA IN CHIANTI (☎ 0577)

Tenuta di Ricavo, Loc. Ricavo, tel: 740 221, fax: 741 014. Quiet, beautiful surroundings. **Villa Casafrassi**, approx. 8 km south of Castellina, towards Siena, tel: 740 621, fax: 740 805. Restored country house with a large garden.

Salivolpi, on the road to San Donato, tel: 740 484, fax: 740 998. Friendly and comfortable, good rates. **Belvedere di San Leonino**, Loc. di San Leonino, 8 km south of Castellina on the Chiantigiana, tel/fax: 740 887. Attractive house, beautiful location, swimming pool.

Albergaccio di Castellina, Via Fiorentina 35, tel: 741 042; closed Sun. Cozy atmosphere, traditional cuisine. **Pestello**, 7 km toward Poggibonsi, tel: 740 215; closed Wed. Country cuisine.

CERTALDO (☎ 0571)

Osteria del Vicario, Via Rivellino 3, tel: 668 228; closed Wed. Hotel-restaurant in a former monastery.

GREVE (☎ 055)

Ufficio del Turismo, Via Lucacini 1, tel: 854 5243.

Albergo del Chianti, Piazza Matteotti 86, tel/fax: 853 763. **Verrazzano**, Piazza Matteotti 28, tel: 853 189, fax: 853 648.

Borgo Antico, Via Case Sparse15, Lucolena, tel: 851 024; closed Tue. Old-style Chianti cuisine. **Casprini**, Via Chiantigiana 40, Loc. Passo dei Pecorai, tel: 850 716; closed Wed. Steaks from charcoal grill. **La Novella**, Via Musignano 1, Loc. Pian del Quarto, San Polo, tel: 855 195; closed Wed. Farmhouse trattoria.

IMPRUNETA (☎ 055)

Il Cavallacci, Via Aldo Moro 3, tel: 231 3863; Mon-Sat evenings only, Sun lunch and dinner. Pretty country house, good regional dishes.

PANZANO (☎ 055)

Villa le Barone, Via S. Leolino 19, tel: 852 621, fax: 852 277. Renaissance villa in top location.

Trattoria Montagliari, 2 km outside town, tel: 852 184; closed Mon. Very popular, reservations a must!

RADDA (☎ 0577)

Associazione Pro Loco, tel: 738 494, fax: 738 783.

Relais Fattoria Vignale, Via Pianigiani 8, tel: 738 300, fax: 738 592. Elegant 18th-century mansion, famous vineyard. Often full.

Residence San Sano, Loc. San Sano, Lecchi in Chianti, tel: 746 130, fax: 746 156. Tastefully converted old fortress. **Podere Terreno**, Via della Volpaia, tel/fax: 738 212. Good food.

Le Vigne, follow the signs on SS 408, tel: 738 640; closed Tue (Oct-Apri)l. Tuscan cuisine and worth the trip on unpaved road. **La Bottega di Volpaia**, Loc. Volpaia, tel: 738 001; closed Tue (Nov-April). Small bar-trattoria opposite Castello, offers homemade salami.

SAN CASCIANO VAL DI PESA (☎ 055)

AGRITURISMO (farm vacations): **Azienda Agricola Poggio Borgoni,** Via Borromeo 134, tel: 822 8119, fax: 828 089.

Trattoria di' Sor Paolo, Via Cassia towards Florence, tel: 828 402; closed Mon. Rustic Trattoria with plain fare. **La Tenda Rossa**, Piazza Monumento 9/14, Cerbaia Val di Pesa, tel: 826 132; closed Sun and Mon lunch. One of Italy's leading restaurants.

SAN GIMIGNANO (☎ 0577)

Associazione Pro Loco, Piazza del Duomo 1, tel: 940 008, fax: 940 903.

La Cisterna, Piazza della Cisterna 24, tel: 940 328, fax: 942 080. Converted monastery in town center, attractive rooms, 18th-century Florentine style. **Bel Soggiorno**, Via San Giovanni 91, tel: 940 375, fax: 943 149. Beatiful 13th-century building, attractive, cozy rooms; restaurant with country views. **Villa Baciolo**, Loc. San Donato, 4 km south of S. Gimignano, tel: 942 233, fax: 942 233. Medieval country house amid vineyards and olive groves. **Le Renaie**, Loc. Pancole, tel: 955 044, fax: 955 126. Simple country hotel with pool and tennis courts.

YOUTH HOSTEL: **Ostello della Gioventù**, Via delle Fonti 1, tel: 941 991, fax: 805 0104. No youth hostel card required, no age limit.

Il Boschetto, Loc. S. Lucia 2 km south of town, tel: 940 352, fax: 941 982. Pretty location.

Osteria del Carcere, Via del Castello 13, tel: 941 905; closed Wed. Tuscan cuisine.

VOLTERRA (☎ 0588)

APT, Via Turazza 2 (left at the Palazzo dei Priori), tel/fax: 86 150.

Villa Nencini, Borgo S. Stefano 55, tel: 86 386, fax: 80 601. **Etruria**, Via G. Matteotti 32, tel/fax: 87 377.

Trattoria del Sacco Fiorentino, Piazza XX Sett. 18, tel: 88 537; closed Wed. Classical Tuscan cuisine in tasteful surroundings. **La Tavernetta**, Via Guarnacci 14, tel: 87630; closed Thu. Good food, low prices.

Museo etrusco Guarnacci, daily 9:00 am-7:00 pm (March 1-Nov 30), 9:00 am-2:00 pm (Dec 1-Feb 28).

BETWEEN SIENA AND AREZZO

SIENA
CRETE
VALDICHIANA
AREZZO
CASENTINO

★★SIENA – CITY OF THE PALIO

Since time immemorial, the Sienese have been known for their collective pride. Dante described them as a "proud people" as early as the 14th century. And they have reason to be proud. **★★ Siena ❶** has preserved its medieval appearance in a marvelous fashion, keeping up its traditions and barring the damaging inroads of modernity from its city center, which was made a pedestrian zone in 1956. All of this helps keep Siena one of the most fascinating cities in Tuscany, despite the hordes of tourists that continually stream through. Wandering through the narrow streets between the old brick facades, you sense that you are in a living Italian city that, for all of its art treasures, has a vibrant, rather than museum-like, air.

Siena's residents have always set special store by the beauty of their city. And because of this, the city itself is truly a work of art. It was built according to careful plan, following exact regulations and restrictions that had to be strictly upheld. In the 14th century, for example, the city government ruled that all of the windows on the Piazza del Campo had to match

Preceding Pages: The Crete – a landscape of arid beauty. Left: A flag-waver at the Palio in Siena.

those of the town hall. No one was to be allowed to ruin the city's image by following his own whim. And this, like so many Sienese traditions, has been upheld to the present day.

Little is known of Siena's beginnings. Legend has it that Ascius and Senius, the sons of Remus, were forced to flee their uncle Romulus, the founder of Rome, and subsequently founded the city on three hills in Etruria. But this story, which dates back to the Renaissance, is just a charming piece of fiction that was invented by the Sienese themselves. It does, however, explain why you can see the symbol of the Roman she-wolf throughout the city.

Siena didn't become truly important until the Middle Ages, when, located on the old trade route of the Frankish Road, it became a center of finance and trade. Silver from the surrounding hills also helped Siena gain wealth and power. In 1472, one of the first great banks, Monte dei Paschi, was founded, and today it is still going strong.

During the 13th century, the Republic of Siena had some 20,000 inhabitants, making it a major urban center for that period. It continued to flourish until the 16th century, although it engaged in constant skirmishes and power struggles with its bitter rival, Florence. In 1260, Siena managed to defeat Florence in the Battle

of Montaperti, but just nine years later they were in turn defeated at Colle Val d'Elsa. Under the Guelph regime of the "Council of Nine" that followed (1292-1355), important artists were brought to the city, including Duccio di Buonisegna, Simone Martini, Pietro and Ambrogio Lorenzetti, and the sculptor and architect Nicola and Giovanni Pisano. Their work helped shape the appearance of Siena today, and made it a true city of the arts.

Decline set in with the plague in 1348, and Siena never fully recovered. For the next 150 years, the city was torn by internal strife. It was only through the efforts of Siena's great, and later canonized, heroes, Saint Catherine and Saint Bernard, and those of Pope Pius II, a scion of the Sienese Piccolomini family, that the tensions finally eased altogether. Eventually, Emperor Charles V, an ally of Florence, stepped in, and in 1555 the city was

Right: Siena's large, shell-shaped Piazza del Campo is one of the most beautiful squares in the world.

incorporated into the Medici Duchy of Tuscany. Although Siena has been forced into the secondary position of a provincial town ever since, you can still sense traces of its former enmity toward Florence, its onetime rival.

The city's silhouette is visible from a distance: It crowns the three hills across which Siena has spread in a roughly Y-shaped form, and is dominated by the towers of its town hall and mighty, black-and-white striped cathedral. Narrow medieval streets wind crookedly between houses of red-brown brick (artists use a pigment of this shade called "siena"), and lead up hill and down, making it difficult to keep your sense of direction. At every corner in the Old Town, however, there are signs indicating the direction of the Campo as well as a number of the city's other major sights.

★★Piazza del Campo

The secular center of the Siena is a piazza that is one of the most beautiful in all

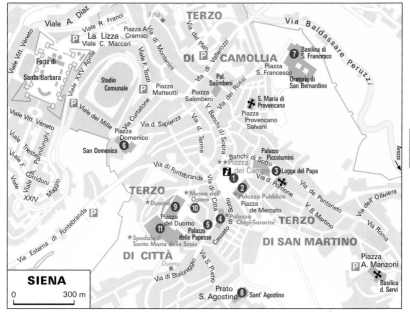

of Italy, if not the entire world. The **★★Piazza del Campo ❶** lies like a great seashell in the hollow between the town's three hills and its red brick cobbles divide it into nine clear sections. Arranged in a semicircle around the piazza are the lovely, neatly ordered palaces. In some of the facades there are groups of three pointed-arched windows, separated by little columns, that reflect the prescriptions of the medieval building codes. At the upper edge of the piazza, roughly in the middle, is the **Fonte Gaia** (Spring of Joy). The fountain's original reliefs by Jacopo della Quercia are displayed in the Palazzo Pubblico.

The **Palazzo Pubblico**, or Town Hall, with ist slightly crooked walls, forms the lower edge of the Campo. This gorgeous Gothic building, which was built between 1297 and 1310, perfectly reflects the pride and the indefatigable desire for independence that has always character-ized the people of Siena. Today, the pal-ace continues to serve as the headquarters of the city administration.

In front of the palace's left wing is the **Cappella di Piazza**, built in 1352 after the plague had run its course. Above it, the town hall's brick-red and travertine-white tower, standing 88 meters high, (102 meters, if you count its lightning rod), thrusts into the deep blue Sienese sky. The work of eight different archi-tects, the **Torre del Mangia** was named after the sexton Mangiaguadagni, mean-ing money-eater. It was Lippo Memmi who supposedly designed the tower's broad travertine platform, which affords a marvelous view of the city's red rooftops and the surrounding hilly countryside. To the right of the Capella di Piazza there is a bust of the aforementioned money-hun-gry sexton, complete with coats of arms, as you enter the Cortile del Podestà. From here, you can climb the 332 steps to the top of the tower – a laborious climb, but one that is not to be missed.

Inside the **★Palazzo Pubblico ❷**, a tour of the second floor (the ground floor belongs to the city administration, and is not open to the public) takes you through

a series of marvelously decorated rooms that are filled with some remarkable works of art.

The Sala del Mappamondo contains two famous frescoes: Simone Martini's **Maestà** (1315), restored and visible in all of its former glory since January 1994, as well as a depiction of the knight Guido Riccio da Fogliano riding to the Siege of Montemassi (1328), which is attributed to the same artist. This fresco is the first known large-scale landscape in European art.

In the Sala della Pace, you can see Ambrogio Lorenzetti's famous allegorical frescoes depicting Just and Unjust Government and the effects of both on the city and the country. Created between 1338 and 1340, under the regime of and dedicated to the Council of Nine, these marvelous images are also interesting depictions of 14th-century daily life.

Above: Participating in the Palio is an honor for every Sienese. Right: The race itself is a test of endurance for the horses and the riders.

The Palazzo's other rooms contain countless other highlights of Sienese art and it would be impossible to list them all here. Just take your time, stroll through the rooms at your own pace, and enjoy fine works of art by Sodoma, Taddeo di Bartolo, Jacopo della Quercia, and Sano di Pietro – to name only a few.

The *Palio

When you leave the Palazzo Pubblico and come back out onto the broad Piazza del Campo, where you are likely to encounter a couple of idlers loafing around, tired tourists sitting in the sun and resting their feet, or a couple of children splashing each other in the fountain, you may have trouble imagining that, twice a year, thousands of people crowd onto this square and overrun it completely. Every year since the 17th century, July 2 and August 16 have seen the *Palio delle contrade*, a horse race in honor of the Virgin Mary in which the city's 17 historic quarters compete with one another for a

trophy. The Palio, or victory trophy, is a flag with the image of the Virgin, and every year a different artist designs it anew.

The Palio is the most fascinating festival in all of Tuscany. It plays an important part in the city's life throughout the year, and the weeks before it see the preparations for this great event rising to an ever-increasing level of intensity.

Every Sienese citizen is born into a *contrada*, or city neighborhood, and remains a member for the rest of his life. A marked self-confidence and interaction according to certain fixed rules are characteristic of the individual contrada, whose members are bound into a fixed social unit. Siena's notably low crime rate may well be a result of the special sense of community that this system engenders.

Practice races begin in the days leading up to the festival, during which the members of the different contrade start to heat up the competition with mocking songs and insults. By the time the big day rolls around, the tension in the city is palpable everywhere. Since there isn't enough

room for all 17 contrade to run at once, ten contrade participate in each palio. Each group of ten includes the seven who didn't take part in to the last race, as well as three who are chosen by lot. The horses, too, are chosen by lot, and the jockeys are professionals brought in from all over Italy, who have to compete the breakneck race around the square bareback. Not surprisingly, there are quite often spectacular falls, and because of the hard, packed sand surface that is brought in especially for the race, these often result in serious injuries.

Just in case, before the race begins, the horses and riders are blessed in the churches of whichever contrada they are riding for. In addition, the Archbishop of Siena blesses the individual teams, riding past his palace in a blaze of colorful historic costumes. And the Madonna, in whose honor this all takes place, certainly extends a protecting hand...

After a number of practice runs and a historic, festival parade, the race, which hardly lasts more than a minute, begins.

Even if you have to sweat it out for a couple of hours on the Campo, in the broiling noonday sun, in order to secure a good view of this colorful spectacle, the experience is truly worth the effort. Of course, you can always try to buy one of the extremely expensive seats on the grandstand, in the windows or on one of the overcrowded balconies that surround the square, but these prime positions are usually sold out far in advance.

After the race, there is a rush of relief that finds expression in cries of joy, enthusiastic embraces, or even tears. The victorious contrada marches through the city in triumph and gives thanks to the Mother of God in the church of the Madonna di Provanzano. And then the celebrations begin in earnest. There is one festive dinner after another, and even the victorious horse takes part, sitting at a place of honor. Unfortunately, all of this is only open to the Sienese.

Above: A side street in Siena. Right: Siena's cathedral towers above the city's rooftops.

The Palaces

The gorgeous old palaces of Siena, which are testimony to the city's past wealth, can easily be reached and explored on foot. On Banchi di Sotto, near the Campo, you will come to the **Renaissance Palace of the Piccolomini**. Built in 1469, it was most likely constructed according to plans by Rossellino. Since 1885, this building has housed the city archives, including certificates and documents designed and executed by famous Sienese artists. Opposite is the entrance to the university, one of the oldest in Italy, which is documented as early as the year 1240. Today, it is housed in the former monastery of San Vigilio, dating from the 16th century. A bit further on is the **Logge del Papa ❸**, which the Renaissance Pope Pius II commissioned for his family from the architect Antonio Federighi.

At the intersection of Banchi di Sotto, Banchi di Sopra and Via del Città is the three-arched **Loggia della Mercanzia**, a

15th-century Renaissance building that has been lightened up with Late Gothic elements. Banchi di Sopra leads to the Piazza Salimbeni, where you can see the Gothic palace of the same name. To the right and left of it are the Renaissance palaces Spanocchi (built in 1470 according to designs by Giuliano da Maiano) and Tantucci (1548). Today, these three palaces house the venerable bank Monte dei Paschi.

On Via di Città, you can see the slightly crooked facade and the lovely inner courtyard of the Gothic **Palazzo Chigi-Saracini** ❹. Today this palace is the seat of the Accademia Musicale Chigiana, which was founded in 1923 by Count Guido Saracini. In the summer, classical concerts are performed here. Inside, the palace houses a wonderful art gallery, but you can only visit it with special permission. Somewhat further on, at Via di Città 126, you arrive at another Piccolomini palace, which is known as **Palazzo delle Papesse** ❺ because it was commissioned by the sister of Pope Pius II. Built in the style of the Florentine Renaissance, it was constructed between 1460 and 1465.

Siena's Churches

Siena has produced a number of great saints over the years, including the patron saint of Italy, Catarina di Siena. There is a small sanctuary in her honor at Vicolo del Tiratoio 15, a few steps away from the church of **San Domenico** ❻. This powerful Gothic brick building, begun in 1226, is a Dominican church even today. Inside, a reliquary contains the head of Saint Catherine. The chapel that is dedicated to her also contains two noteworthy frescoes by Sodoma, depicting the Faint and the Ecstasy of Saint Catherine. Other art treasures that can be found in this chapel include the ciborium on the main altar and two marble angels.

Like the Dominicans, the Franciscans and the Augustines also built their churches and monasteries on what was then the edge of the city, probably because it gave them more room to construct and expand their large building complexes. You will find the Gothic **Basilica di San Francesco ❼**, which contains wonderful frescoes by Ambrogio and Pietro Lorenzotti, on the Piazza di San Francesco. Today, its crypt houses the law school's library.

Near the church, the upper floor of the **Oratorio di San Bernardino** (a saint who is particularly beloved in Italy) shelters paintings by Sodoma. The church of the Augustine order, **Sant'Agostino ❽**, on Prato Sant'Agostino, is also home to a number of marvelous works by Perugino, Matteo di Giovanni, Simone Martini and Sodoma.

The *Cathedral

Siena's famous cathedral is at the center of the city, only a few paces from the Campo. The ***Cathedral ❾** took some 200 years to build, and the mighty edifice you see today is only a portion of the building that was originally planned by the ambitious Sienese. It was, in fact, to be merely the transept of a huge new cathedral. However, of this mammoth edifice, all that was actually realized are the walls that you see to the right of the present cathedral. The devastating outbreak of the plague of 1348, high costs and political developments gradually led to the end of its construction. What remains of this great undertaking is a masterpiece of Italian Gothic that is certainly impressive enough in its own right.

Giovanni Pisano was responsible for the cathedral's signature green-and-white striped, ornate facade (1284-1296). Today, the original monumental statues and busts are displayed in the cathedral's museum. The central bronze portal, added in 1958, is the work of the contemporary artist Enrico Manfrini. The mosaics at the top of the facade were completed in the

Right: Duccio di Buoninsegna's "Maestà" can be seen in Siena's Cathedral Museum.

late 18th century. To the right of the cathedral is the campanile, the facade of which also has stripes of contrasting marble. The width of the tower's window openings increase as they get closer to the top.

Inside, the cathedral, with its three naves, is veiled in a mystical twilight, and there are echoes of an oriental mosque in its 26 two-colored columns, blue ceiling with gold stars, and multicolored walls. The ornate floor, which occupied 40 artists for two centuries, is executed in a number of different techniques, from mosaic to sgraffito to marble inlay. The most valuable sections are protected by a wooden floor, and are only unveiled between August 15 and September 15. Looking down from a molding above the columns are the busts of Christ, 172 popes and, below them, 36 emperors from the 15th and 16th centuries. The stoup by the main entrance is the work of Antonio Federighi.

The cathedral's most important work of art, however, is the famous octagonal marble pulpit by Nicola Pisano and his son Giovanni (with some collaboration from other artists such as Donato and Arnolfo di Cambio). A light, which is coin-operated, illuminates the masterfully sculpted reliefs of Biblical scenes for 60 seconds a time. The expressively sculpted figures are full of life, their faces carved with individuality – you can see their descendants on the streets of modern-day Siena.

Other noteworthy works of art include the main altar by Baldassarre Peruzzi, the bronze statue of John the Baptist by Donatello (on the left side of the transept, in the Cappella di Giovanni Battista), the Piccolomini Tomb in the right-hand aisle, near the entrance to the campanile, and, above all, the Libreria Piccolomini (left-hand aisle), a library with decorative frescoes by Pinturicchio (1505-1507) that beautifully depict scenes from the life of Pope Pius II.

Between Siena and Arezzo

The **Baptistry** lies below the apse of the cathedral, where the "Sabatelli Steps" (1451) lead down to the Piazza San Giovanni. The upper part of this baptismal church was never completed, and its neatly organized facade includes parts of the cathedral's apse. Mighty columns, which also carry the weight of the cathedral choir, support the frescoed ceiling. The font is a 15th-century masterpiece, and displays reliefs by Ghiberti, Jacopo della Quercia, Donatello and others.

The ★**Cathedral Museum** ⑩ (Museo dell'Opera) is housed within a portion of the walls of the never-completed "New Cathedral." This is also the entrance to the unfinished facade of the cathedral, which commands a wonderful view of Siena and the surrounding countryside. On the museum's ground floor, you can see the originals of Pisano's sculptures for the cathedral, but the showpiece is on the upper floor: the *Maestà* by Duccio di Buoninsegna. Painted on both front and back, upon its completion, this beautiful altarpiece (1308-1311) was celebrated

with three days of festivities. For the next 200 years it adorned the cathedral's main altar. It represents, in fact, the first masterpiece of the great age of Sienese painting during the 14th century. While the main image is still locked in the conventions of tradition, depicting a rigid figure of an enthroned Madonna against a background of gold and strictly symmetrical figures of saints, the smaller side panels depict scenes from the life of Christ with minute exactitude.

On the top floor of the museum you will find the painting of the *Madonna with the Big Eyes* (first half of the 13th century). Sienese troops swore a vow before this image before marching into the Battle of Montaperti, where they defeated the Florentines.

Back on Piazza del Duomo, to the left of the cathedral, is the 18th-century neo-Gothic, Archbishop's Palace. Opposite the palace is the facade of the ★**Spedale di Santa Maria delle Scale** ⑪, a hospital that was constructed as a hospice for pilgrims in the days of the Frankish Road,

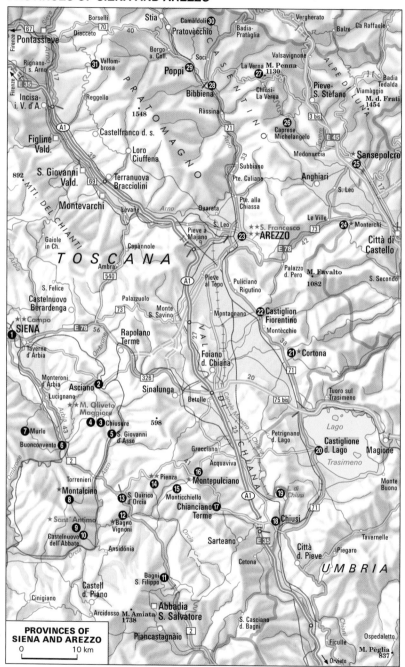

perhaps as early as the 9th century. In the "Pilgrims' Room," the magnificently restored frescoes by Domenico di Bartolo (ca. 1440) give us an impression of what medieval "welfare services" were like.

In addition to the particularly important buildings discussed here, Siena contains a wealth of other churches, palazzi, and museums. Anyone who comes prepared to spend a little more time will soon discover that the city, which may initially appear a little forbidding, only begins to unfold its charms to those who first spend a few hours wandering around. Furthermore, the shopping here is good, whether you are in the market for handicrafts or culinary specialties like wild boar salami, wine, olive oil or the famous Sienese panforte, a kind of hard fruitcake with almonds, all of which make excellent gifts as well as souvenirs. If you want to sample these delicacies yourself, visit the Piazza del Mercato, below the Campo, where a food market is held every morning, except Sundays and Mondays.

THE *CRETE

South of Siena, the character of the landscape changes. The fertile, wooded hills of Chianti give way to barren, arid mounds of earth that stretch across the horizon like the waves of a frozen sea. *Crete Senesi is the name of this region, an area of heavy, clayey, and often eroded earth that is only good for growing grain or grazing sheep. Naked, bitter country, but marvelous for its breadth and the way you can see, without any obstacles, for kilometers into the distance. Lone farmhouses stand atop hills, a few solitary cypresses or pines set as if to underline the junction of two roads or mark the summit of a rise of land – graphic accents like these make this a veritable El Dorado for photographers with a good eye.

The Crete has a different face for every season, determined by the rhythm of sowing and harvesting. In the spring, the broad wheat fields are a tender green. In the summer they are a rich yellow gold. And in the fall, when the fields are shorn by harvesters and plowed anew, there is a spectrum of earth tones ranging from rust-red, through every shade of brown, to a tired gray. Interspersed with these are lush fields that are covered with spring flowers or, later in the year, with a thin veil of grass that is fodder for herds of grazing sheep.

Long ago, the small, mostly fortified towns that are visible across the hills from afar, began to appear on this barren landscape. The best-known of these are described below, but any excursion in this region, especially along the scenic routes that promise particularly beautiful landscapes (marked with green signs), can be very rewarding.

Truffles and Monastic Spirits

The first tour starts in **Asciano ❷**, some 25 kilometers southeast of Siena, which can be reached by taking the scenic SS 438. At the center of this picturesque medieval village, set high above the Ombrone valley, there is an interesting museum that house works by Ambrogio Lorenzetti, Matteo di Giovanni and Duccio. There is also a little anecdote about Asciano that Dante mentioned in his *Inferno*. It is about a certain Caccia d'Asciano who ran through his vast fortune in a very short time due to his predilection for having his meals decorated with gold coins, which he then spit out as if they were olive pits. While Asciano's inhabitants have less eccentric eating habits today, there is one very special, and almost equally costly, specialty that dominates their menus: truffles, which will are discussed in more depth in a later chapter.

From Asciano, head to **Chiusure ❸**, a small fortified town of red brick, with a magnificent view of the surrounding hills and the nearby monastery complex of

Between Siena and Arezzo

Monte Oliveto Maggiore. As you proceed toward the monastery, you will have the opportunity to see the small landslides, triggered by erosion, that are typical of the Crete and are particularly prevalent around Monte Oliveto.

Surrounded by a grove of centuries-old cypresses, the Benedictine monastery of ****Monte Oliveto Maggiore** ❹ was founded in 1319, by the Sienese lawyer Giovanni Tolomei, who, at the age of 40, withdrew from the world and retired to his estate south of Siena in order to live the rest of his life in reflective prayer and atonement. Following the rules of the Benedictine order, the monks here busied themselves with cultivating the surrounding countryside, while at the same time elevating their monastery into a center for religious, scientific and artistic study. A number of famous scholars were trained here and several major artists received en-

Above: A wonderful fresco in the cloister of Monte Oliveto Maggiore. Right: In Murlo's Etruscan Museum.

couragement. As a result, the walls of the main cloister bear frescoes by Luca Signorelli and Sodoma depicting scenes from the life of Saint Benedict.

The abbey is rich in other art treasures, as well. There are choir pews with inlays by Fra Giovanni da Verona, richly illuminated music books, a huge old library, and other paintings and frescoes that are everywhere. In one room near the exit from the cloister, the monks sell their own goods that are produced at the monastery, including olive oil, honey, herbal liquors, posters, books and ceramics. The former stables are now a hotel with more than 50 beds. If you enter the abbey across the drawbridge of the turreted tower, the first thing you will see is a relief of the Madonna from the school of Della Robbia. And when you leave this lovely Renaissance complex, you will be sent on your way with a blessing from a relief of Saint Benedict, which is by Della Robbia himself.

Not far from Monte Oliveto Maggiore is **San Giovanni D'Asso** ❺, a village that is famous for its truffles. Every year, on the third Sunday in November, there is a sales exposition of these rare white fungi, and every year the community donates a particularly fine specimen to someone who has made notable efforts toward world peace during the previous twelve months.

It is only nine kilometers from Monte Oliveto Maggiore to **Buonconvento** ❻, which lies at the point where the Arbia flows into the Ombrone. The village's medieval center is well preserved, and a person strolling through its narrow streets could easily imagine that he had traveled back in time to the Middle Ages.

The Etruscans of Murlo

If you follow Via Cassia for about 12 kilometers, back toward Siena, you will come, at Lucignano d'Arbia, to a small road that leads to the left toward the old

Etruscan settlement of **Murlo** ❼. It is said of this tiny, beautifully restored village that its residents bear a remarkable resemblance to their Etruscan forefathers, and DNA tests on bones that have been unearthed at nearby excavation sites have supposedly proven that, in the people of Murlo, the genetic makeup of this long-vanished people has been amazingly well preserved through the millennia. The local media, of course, wasn't going to overlook this sensation, and photographs of the local pizzeria owner, his mother and other villagers that have been placed next to sculpted heads of Etruscan statues and frescoes, demonstrate quite convincingly that there is a certain similarity. However, more interesting on the whole, is the town's very informative, well-laid-out, and justifiably renowned **museum**. Not only does it display finds from excavations in the surrounding hills, but it also explores and presents antique techniques of tool and jewelry manufacturing.

In the Land of Fine Wine

From Murlo, an unpaved dirt road leads some 25 kilometers through wonderful oak, beech and chestnut woods, and past fine views, to ***Montalcino** ❽. You can also reach this village, which is perched on a hilltop 560 meters high and is surrounded by vineyards, via a less spectacular route by taking the SS 2 and joining, just past Buonconvento, the SP 45, which leads up to Montalcino.

This is where the famous – and expensive – *Brunello di Montalcino* is produced, and you can sample it to your heart's content in the town's restored fortress. However, the wine isn't the only reason to visit this village. There is also the Palazzo dei Priori, a remarkably narrow building from the late-13th century, with an exaggeratedly high tower; the Diocesan Museum with its 14th-century wooden sculptures; and beautiful fres-

Between Siena and Arezzo

coes in the church of San Agostino. It is also nice just to stroll through the medieval streets, past stores selling wine, oil, honey, or ceramics, and take in the marvelous view of the surrounding countryside. In the summer (second half of July) there is a theater festival, and in October the *Sagra del Tordo*, with archery competitions and parades in historic costumes.

South of Montalcino rises the Amiata massif. As you drive toward it, after about ten kilometers, you will arrive at one of Tuscany's loveliest Romanesque monastery churches. Standing in a spacious meadow near Castelnuovo dell'Abate, tucked away in the hilly countryside, is ***Sant'Antimo** ❾, a beautiful church built with simple, strong lines out of travertine and alabaster. A nearby cypress echoes the lines of its mighty campanile in a most photogenic manner. Inside, this three-nave church from the 12th century is light and airy. Pillars and rafters bear the weight of the galleries, and their capitals are adorned with remarkable representations of animal heads, plants, and

geometric figures. Especially in the fall, when the stark noonday sun comes through the windows, the interior is bathed in a feeling of mystic warmth.

Lunch in **Castelnuovo dell'Abbate** ❿ means a stop at the bar and trattoria *del Bassomondo*, where you can buy home-made cheese, sausage, and a freshly filled bottle of *Rosso di Montalcino*, to take with you, or simply enjoy on the spot.

From here, a winding road leads on to Ansidónia, where you can choose to either continue your trip by heading south into the Amiata region or by returning to Siena by way of the Cassia. In the heat of summer, the best bet is to detour into the cooler mountain air. Here, you can spend a night or two in the villages of Abbadia di San Salvadore, Piancastagnaio, San Fiora or Arcidosso, all of which lie on the road that follows the base of the Amiata massif, and all of which are worth a visit

Above: San Antimo is one of Tuscany's most beautiful monastery churches. Right: Taking a break to enjoy the sun and read the paper.

(see the section on Grosseto for more details). The center of this area is the 1738-meter-high extinct volcano, which has countless springs that deliver water all the way to Siena and Grosseto. Around it, particularly to the northeast, the region is rich in minerals and large geothermic fields that are increasingly being used for technical purposes. In places, stinking drilling rigs and steam springs interfere with the lovely landscape, but overall the mountains still offer plenty of beautiful spots where you can hike through an intact natural landscape for hours on end.

Another result of the area's volcanic roots is evident in **Bagni San Filippo** ⓫, where warm, sulfurous water flows over a kind of frozen waterfall of calcium into shallow, natural pools. It is marvelous to sit in one of these pools and get a natural massage from the powerful streams of water. Unfortunately, they are closed to protect their fragile fossilizations. There is, however, an old-fashioned hotel with a thermal swimming pool, but the strong smell of sulfur is not to everyone's taste.

Between Siena and Arezzo

There is another thermal spring to the north, near Via Cassia, just before you get to San Quircio d'Orcia. A large stone pool filled with 52°C spring water takes the place of the usual piazza in the center of ★**Bagno Vignoni** ⑫. It is said that the Romans soaked in its sulfurous waters – an inscription states that they dedicated the healing waters to the nymphs. The juxtaposition of the still waters and the old houses that surround it creates a strange atmosphere that inspired the Russian director Tarkowski to film parts of his classic movie *Nostalghia* here. Today, however, swimming in the old stone pool is forbidden. Those suffering from rheumatism, arthritis, or nerve infections can pay the admission fee to soak in Hotel Posta's thermal pool.

San Quircio d'Orcia ⑬ is a pretty little town above the valleys of the Orcia and Asso. Home to the beautiful Romanesque church of **Collegiata**, with a beautiful portal attributed to Giovanni Pisano, the Palazzi Chigi and Pretorio are also worth visiting.

From here, the SS 146 heads in an easterly direction. Ten kilometers later, you will reach ★★**Pienza** ⑭, named for Pope Pius II Piccolomini, who was born at the beginning of the 15th century in the town that was then known as Corsignano. With an in-depth humanistic education and a broad range of interests, the pope wanted to transform the place of his birth into an "ideal city," in the Renaissance sense, based on the plans of the architect Rossellino. Unfortunately, he died before his plan could be completed. However, the central Piazza Pio II – its clever trapezoidal shape makes it appear much larger than it is – with its cathedral, the Palazzi Piccolomini and Vescovile, and the Palazzo Communale, with its open loggia, can be described as a successful and unified work of art. The apse of the city's cathedral **Santa Maria Assunta** was built out over a slope, and although its supports were replaced during the last century, they could still be more stable.

The Casa dei Canonici, to the left of the cathedral, is home to the **Museo della**

Pienza, in fact, is generally a shopper's paradise for any one looking to buy local products such as oil, wine, herbs, or goat cheese.

Halfway along the road to Montepulciano is **Monticchiello** ⓯, a small village that is almost too perfectly renovated, and has become known for its *Teatro Povera* (Poor Theater). Since 1967, the village residents have presented pieces they have written and staged themselves, generally with a touch of social criticism, in the second half of July.

Like nearly every city in this area, **★Montepulciano** ⓰ was long a bone of contention between Siena and Florence until it finally fell to Florence in 1390. If you approach the city from the west, the first thing you will see, in a lonely field at the foot of the hill of Montepulciano, at the end of an avenue of cypress trees, is the Renaissance church of **San Biagio**. The temple-like travertine building, built in the form of a Greek cross topped with a dome, was the greatest work of Antonio da Sangallo the Elder (1455-1531).

Cattedrale, which displays an excellent collection of liturgical objects.

A true masterpiece is the **★Piccolomini Palace**, modeled on the Palazzo Rucellai in Florence. The square interior courtyard is surrounded by a portico, and while the hanging gardens on the palace's south side command a marvelous view out over the Orcia valley. Another, more modest palace, was commissioned by Cardinal Ammanati at the behest of his friend, Pope Pius himself.

By an unfortunate coincidence, Pius II and his architect died in the same year, 1464. After their deaths, the *città ideale* gradually returned to the sleepy insignificance of a small country town. But visitors may want to take note of the Emporio delle Fattorie, a kind of mail-order service offering the very best Italian culinary delicacies (store: *La Cornucopia*, Piazza Martiri della Liberta 2, tel: 748 150).

Climbing a steep hill, you come to the medieval village, where the larger buildings demonstrate the style of the Florentine Renaissance. The best place to see this is on the broad, red-paved **Piazza Grande**, the highest point of the city, which is surrounded by lovely old palaces. The turreted **Pallazzo Communale** dates from the second half of the 14th century. Its facade is believed to have been designed by Michelozzo in 1424, and is reminiscent of the Palazzo Vecchio in Florence, and its tower commands a breathtaking panoramic view of the surrounding area. To the left of the town hall, some steps lead up to the **Cathedral**, which was built in the 17th century on the site of the former parish church. The most notable works here are the triptych above the high altar, by Taddeo di Bartolo (ca. 1403), which depict the Ascension of the Virgin, and the reclining figures on the tomb of Bartolomeo Aragazzi, secretary

Above: A rainy day in the "ideal city" of Pienza.
Right: Montepulciano with a dusting of snow – an unusual view of the city.

to Pope Martin V, which have also been ascribed to Michelozzo.

Opposite the town hall, Sangallo the Elder built the **Palazzo Contucci**, the top floor of which was completed by Baldassarre Peruzzi. The palace stands atop the oldest wine cellar in the city, which are open to the public. The vats of the famous *Vino Nobile di Montepulciano* were once reserved solely for the city's richest aristocratic families, who were evidently able to afford to employ the most important architects of their time. The Tarugi family, for instance, commissioned Sangallo the Elder with the building of their **Palazzo Nobili Tarugi**. The elegant fountain in front of it, which has two griffons and two lions holding the Medici coat-of-arms, is also the work of this master. Other families also commissioned marvelous Renaissance palaces, including the Cervini, Avignonesi, Neri, Orselli (whose former home is today the town's Museo Civico), and others. In addition to the palaces, there are also a number of interesting churches, such as Sant'Agnese, on the

site of a church that was built in 1306 by the saint herself; the 14th-century Santa Maria dei Servi, with a Gothic facade and Baroque interior by Andrea Pozzo; and Sant'Agostino, with a facade and a group of terra-cotta sculptures by Michelozzo.

The house at Via Poliziano 5 was the birthplace of the Renaissance poet and philosopher Poliziano.

The Poliziani, what the locals call themselves, after the city's original, early medieval name, Mons Politianus, like a good celebration. Montepulciano, like Siena, has contrade, and on the last Sunday in August they vie with each other in the *Bravio delle Botti*, which involves rolling heavy vats of wine up the town's steep streets. August 15th sees a costume festival called the *Bruscello*. And Hans Werner Henze, a German composer, has held a summer music festival here, the *Cantiere Internazionale dell'Arte* (July/ August), since 1976.

From Montepulciano, it isn't far to **Chianciano Terme** ⑰, one of Tuscany's largest thermal baths, which is supposed

to be particularly effective for those with liver complaints. The selection of hotels here is impressive, and since 1915, they have all been under the same private management. Research labs, clinics, swimming facilities – the town has everything a spa guest could desire, but little to offer the average tourist. However, a museum that will display Etruscan artifacts from the area is under construction.

A similar museum is the main attraction in **Chiusi** ⓲, located on a hill past the Chiana valley, a few miles from the Autostrada del Sole. It was a member of the Etruscan League and numerous artifacts from this period are preserved in archeological museums across Tuscany. One of the most famous of these is the **Museo Archeologico Nazionale** (National Archeological Museum) in Chiusi. It exhibits Etruscan art objects and tools, as well

Above: Valdechiana – many of the cows here spend all of their days in the barn. Right: The extensive grounds of the Convento delle Celle in Cortona.

as some Greek vases. (The main building is currently being reorganized and modernized.) A great many Etruscan graves have been found in the surrounding area – the best known are Tomba del Granduca, della Scimmia and della Pellegrina – and the museum offers guided tours of these sites. Not far from the Tomba del Granduca is the **Lago di Chiusi** ⓳, where you can opt to take a more or less refreshing swim in its warm waters.

THE VALDICHIANA

As it was in the days of the Etruscans, the Chiana valley is still the breadbasket of Tuscany. It is also this area that produces the white Chianina cattle, with their marvelous meat, that is used in the renowned *bistecca fiorentina*. In Arezzo, the Chiana valley branches off from the Arno valley and to the south. The valley itself is fairly densely populated and traversed by the Autostrada del Sole, the Milan-Rome railway line, and a whole network of roads. But clinging to the hill-

sides on either side of the valley, which has been repeatedly flooded and infested with malaria over thousands of years, are old villages that are well worth exploring.

The SS 71 leads along the east side of the Chiana valley, from Chiusi to Arezzo, which takes you on a brief detour through Umbria. At **Castiglione del Lago ⑳**, it takes you along the banks of the Lake Trasimeno, which is lovely to look at, but a swim here isn't likely to yield much in the way of refreshment because it is fairly shallow and warm.

★Cortona

Some 25 kilometers from Castiglione del Lago is the town of **★Cortona ㉑** (population 22,000), perched on a rock ledge high above the Chiana valley. The road leads steeply up the olive-tree-covered slopes of Monte Sant'Egidio, to one of the parking lots just below the city itself, where you have to leave your car. From here, it is a bit of a hike to the medieval city center, but the effort is amply re-warded by the fabulous view of the valley. On a nice day, you can see all the way to the Amiata massif.

The medieval city of Cortona was built upon the ancient Etruscan settlement of Curtuns, to which the old city walls still bear witness. In 1538, the town was incorporated into the Duchy of Tuscany.

Cortona is a provincial town full of atmosphere. The best way to explore it is by wandering aimlessly through its narrow streets. The center of town is the **Piazza della Repubblica**, from which a huge outdoor staircase leads up to the **Palazzo Communale** (13th century), which is an ideal place from which to observe the activity on the piazza. The streets here are either uphill or downhill, and the old side streets date back to the days of the Etruscans. The only level street is the short Via Nazionale, which leads to the wide viewing terrace on the Piazza Garibaldi.

To the right of the Palazzo Communale is the Piazza Signorelli and the 13th-century Palazzo Pretoria, home to the **Museo dell'Accademia Etrusca** and its collec-

tion of Roman, Etruscan and Egyptian artifacts. Particularly notable is a 16-armed bronze candelabra from the 5th century B.C. Nearby, on the piazza in front of the cathedral, the diocesan museum displays works by Fra Angelica, Luca Signorelli, Pietro Lorenzetti and Sassetta.

The city's most important building, the Renaissance church of the **Madonna dei Calicinaio** (15th/16th centuries), is about three kilometers away, on the southeastern edge of town.

A little off the main road is the Capuchin monastery delle Celle, which Saint Francis himself founded between 1211 and 1221. The *Tanella di Pitagora* or Grave of Pythagoras is nearby. Dating from somewhere between the 4th and 1st centuries B.C., it is the most famous of the area's many Etruscan graves.

The painters Luca Signorelli and Pietro da Cortona were both from Cortona.

Above Left: The Corso Italia is one of Arezzo's busiest shopping streets. Above Right: Arezzo is a treasure-trove for lovers of antiques.

****AREZZO**

Just 40 kilometers separate Cortona from Arezzo. Traveling between the two, you pass **Castiglion Fiorentino** ㉒, a fortified town of Roman origin. Its 16th-century town hall houses a museum with paintings from the 13th-16th centuries, as well as valuable objects of gold working.

Because was conveniently located on main transportation routes, at the confluence of the Arno and Chiana valleys and near the Tiber valley, ****Arezzo** ㉓ was already an important center of trade in the days of the Etruscans and the Romans, famous for the excellence of its craftsmen.

At first a free city-state, Arezzo was sold to Florence in 1384, for the sum of 40,000 gold florins. This ushered in a period of decline, brought about in part by the increasing swampiness of the Chiana valley. Since the 19th century, the city has seen a second flowering as an economic center that, because of its internationally known clothing and gold industries, doesn't have to rely on tourism.

Today, Arezzo (pop. 92,000) is a lively and pleasant little city. In particular, it draws admirers of the painter Piero della Francesca, whose cycle of frescoes in the church of San Francesco is indubitably among the high points of Renaissance painting. But the city has many other sights that make it worth visiting. In addition, it is a perfect point of departure for trips through the upper Arno (Casetino) and upper Tiber valleys.

The cathedral **San Donato ❶**, started in the late 13th century and completed in the 15th, stands at the highest point of a city that snakes around the hill in a great semicircle. Notable here are Guillaume de Marillat's 16th-century stained-glass windows, and Piero della Francesca's painting of Mary Magdalene (1459). In front of the cathedral there is a large area of green park, called the Prato, that has lovely views out over the countryside. Behind the Prate is the Medici fortress that was commissioned during the 16th century by Cosimo I. Just below the cathedral, at Via dell'Orto 28, is the house where Petrarch was supposedly born on July 20, 1304. The house, however, dates from the 16th century. Today, it houses the Accademia Petrarca di Lettere and Arti e Scienze.

If you walk down the Corso Italia, the 13th-century **Palazzo Pretorio ❷**, its facade adorned with armorial bearings, is on your right. Today it is home to the city library. Diagonally across from it is the oldest church in Arezzo, the Romanesque **Pieve di Santa Maria ❸**. Its unusual facade is divided into three rows of blind arches, while its mighty campanile, with 80 windows in its five stories, is locally known as the "Tower of 100 Holes." Inside, the church is simple, even severe. Behind the high altar is a polyptych by Pietro Lorenzetti. At the cathedral's apse is the **★Piazza Grande ❹**, the city's asymmetric, slightly sloped main square, surrounded by beautifully restored medieval houses. At one end, the square is

bounded by Vasari's Palazzo delle Logge; while adjacent to Pieve's choir is the Palazzo del Tribunale with its tapering open-air staircase. Next to it is the Palazzo della Fraternità dei Laici. On the south side of the square there are a number of antique shops. Arezzo is a veritable Mecca for anyone interested in old furniture or gadgets. On the first weekend of every month, the city hosts one of the most important antique markets in Italy, and its stands spread throughout the entire Old City.

Below the Piazza Grande, Via Mazzini and Via Cavour will bring you to the Piazza San Francesco with the famous church of **★★San Francesco ❺**. Started in 1290, this building with the red brick facade has been continually expanded and renovated. Its spacious interior, however, is pure Gothic, so there is nothing to distract the eye from the wonderful frescoes. Most impressive are those by Piero della Francesca with the cycle of the *Legend of the Cross*. Unfortunately, these works are currently being restored, and until the res-

torations are finished, it is only possible to view certain sections.

Other testaments to the city's cultural significance through the ages include the church of **San Domenico** ⑥, with its painting by Cimabue; **Santa Maria delle Grazie**, with its Renaissance portico; a number of palaces; and the old city gates. The town's most important artists are represented in the **Museum for the Middle Ages and Modernity** ⑦. The former monastery of Sand Bernardo, built on the remains of a Roman amphitheater, now houses the Archeological Museum, which displays prehistoric finds as well as Etruscan and Roman artifacts. This is also where you can see the famous "Aretin Vases," which were highly esteemed as early as the days of the Roman Emperors. Incidentally, the Roman patron of the arts, Gaius Maecenas, a great

Above: The "Giostra del Saracino," a 14th-century equestrian tournament, in Arezzo. Right: Piero della Francesca's "Pregnant Madonna" (Madonna del Parto), in Monterchi.

friend of Emperor Augustus, whose name has entered many European languages as a synonym for "patron," was born in what was then known as Arretium. But, he and Petrarch aren't the only famous local sons. Others include the musician Guido Monaco, who invented musical notation (11th century); the painter, architect and art historian Giorgio Vasari (16th century); and the writer and satirist Pietro Aretino (16th century). Arezzo's university was founded as early as the 13th century, making this one of Europe's oldest university towns. The city's ★**Giostra dei Saracino**, a festive tournament that has been staged since the 14th century and probably dates back to the time of the Crusades, is held on the first Sunday in September, on the Piazza Grande. Two representatives of each of the city's four neighborhoods ride with lances towards the figure of a "Saracen," trying to hit it as precisely as possible. If they hit it, the Saracen spins around and hurls balls of lead and leather at its attacker. The winning team gets the Golden Lance.

THE CASENTINO

The Casentino region belongs to the "other," less well-known Tuscany. This mountainous, forested region extends north of Arezzo along the upper Arno valley. Anyone who likes solitude, nature, and tranquil little mountain villages along with his art and culture has come to the right place. Because it is away from the main travel routes, this area has always been preferred by hermits, namely, but also by wealthy families who had their summer residences built here. It is this solitude that has allowed the region to preserve its unspoiled nature and simple lifestyle. Locals still craft wood and ceramics according to traditional methods, and till their fields in accordance with the rhythm of the seasons.

From Arezzo, head east on the SS 73. Near Le Ville, a side road leads off to the little village of ***Monterchi ㉔**, which is known for Piero della Francesca's unusual *Madonna del Parto*. This fresco, the renovation of which was completed in 1993, can be found in a little museum on the edge of town. The extremely pregnant Madonna, flanked by an angel on either side, challenges the viewer with an inimitable Piero gaze, and, today, is shielded by a pane of protective glass. The work is impressive, even in these modest surroundings.

From Monterchi, the road leads past the medieval settlement of Anghiari to ***Sansepolcro ㉕** (Holy Sepulchre). The town gets its name from relics of Christ's tomb that were preserved here. Originally, it was under the administration of the Camaldolian order, which founded a monastery here. After being a free commune for a time during the mid-13th century, it came under a number of different rulers, until Pope Eugene IV finally sold it to Florence for 25,000 ducats.

Sansepolcro is a peaceful little place, but is also has a several fascinating art treasures. As the birthplace of Piero della

Francesca, the town's **Pinacoteca Communale** houses some of his most famous works, including the *Resurrection*, *Madonna della Misericordia* (Madonna of Mercy), and others. Other sights include the **Palazzo delle Laudi** (late-16th/early-17th centuries), today the town hall; the **Palazzo Pretorio**; and the **Cathedral**, which also contains valuable works of art. Along the central Via Mateotti, 14th- and 15th century **tower houses** convey a flavor of the Middle Ages – an appropriate background for the Palio della Balestra, a crossbow competition that is held on the second Sunday in September.

From Sansepolcro, the SS 3 leads through the upper Tiber valley to Pieve San Stefano, 15 kilometers away. From here, the winding and marvelously scenic SS 208 leads off to Bibbiena. A few kilometers after Pieve San Stefano, a little road leads the ten kilometers to the mountain village of **Caprese Michelangelo ㉖**, where Michelangelo Buonarotti was born on March 6, 1475, son of the town's mayor. A small museum in the 14th-cen-

tury Casa Communale houses objects relating to the artist, including copies and photographs of some of his works.

Another small road runs 13 kilometers from here and joins the SS 208 in Chiusi della Verna. Here, the Franciscan monastery of **La Verna** ㉗, perched atop Monte Penna, at an altitude of 1130 meters, has wonderful views. Parts of this monastery complex, in which Saint Francis supposedly received his stigmata, date as far back as the 13th century. The church is visited by countless pilgrims and displays terra-cotta reliefs by, among others, Andrea della Robbia, the most important ceramicist of the 15th century.

The mountain road S 208 leads on to **Bibbiena** ㉘ in the Arno valley, the most important center of industry and trade in the Casentino. Probably of Etruscan origin under the name Vipena, the city was hotly contested during the Middle Ages because of its strategic location. Its notable sights include the **Palazzo Dovizi** (early-16th century) and the church of **San Lorenzo** with its adjacent Renaissance monastery. From Bibbiena, you can proceed south, along the Arno valley and back to Arezzo (33 kilometers), or continue northward along the scenic SS 70, to Pontassieve and Florence.

If you choose the latter route, you will come, after a few kilometers, to the medieval town of **Poppi** ㉙, which sits high atop a solitary hill in the Casentino valley. The castle of the Counts of Guidi, begun in the 12th century and later known as the **Palazzo Pretorio**, is one of Tuscany's most significant medieval buildings. It is said that Dante wrote Canto XXIII of the *Inferno* here. There are also plenty of unhappy legends told about this castle. The square in front of the fortress, today a pretty garden, is said to have been the site of bloody duels, afterwhich the losers were thrown into a dungeon under the lawn. And it was in the so-called "Devil's Tower," that the lascivious widow of one Guidi was locked up and left to starve to

Above and Right: Pilgrims the world over are drawn to La Verna, a Franciscan monastery.

death, by villagers who were irate at her habit of luring local young men to the palace and, after having her pleasure with them, mercilessly and cruelly killing them.

In a way, even the small 17th-century church of Madonna del Morbo has a bloody history. It was designed by Francesco Folli da Poppi, the inventor of the blood transfusion, during an outbreak of the plague.

From Poppi, you can easily take a detour to the famous **Hermit's Monastery of Camaldoli ㉚** (13 kilometers), whence the order of the Camaldolians got its name. Founded by Saint Romuald in 1012, and standing in the middle of a thick forest at an altitude of 1100 meters, the monastery's distinctive feature is its cells, today 50 in number, which sit like a row of little huts, each of them being exactly the same distance from the other. Women were once forbidden to set foot on the grounds, but today, it is a popular spot for day-trips, and yet, it has managed to preserve its mystical air. A guesthouse is available for visitors who want to brush up on their meditation skills, and the monks sell their own products, including tea, honey, and cosmetics, in the old monastery apothecary.

On the way to Florence, you pass another famous monastery, the **Abbey of Vallombrosa ㉛**, located 961 meters up in the wooded mountains of Pratomagno, which form the Casentino's western border. This monastery was founded in the early 11th century by Florentine nobleman Giovanni Gualberto Visdomini, who retreated into the forest to lead the simple life of a hermit. Together with a few other like-minded souls, he founded the Vallombrosa order, which still exists today as a chapter of the Benedictines, and has spread throughout Italy. So powerful was this monastery that during the Middle Ages that its abbots bore the title of Count or even Marquis. The complex's present appearance is the result of extensive 17th-century renovations and reconstruction. The refectory and a mighty open fireplace in the kitchen are among its highlights.

PROVINCE OF SIENA

ASCIANO (☎ 0577)

Il Bersagliere, V. Roma 39/41, tel/fax: 718629.

Museo di Arte Sacra, Piazza F.lli Bandiera, tel: 719 510. **Museo Etrusco**, Corso Matteotti 46; Tue-Sun 10:00 am-noon and 4:30-6:30 pm (summer), 10:00 am-noon (winter), closed Mon.

BAGNI SAN FILIPPO (☎0577)

Terme S. Filippo, tel: 872 982, fax: 872 684.

Thermal Springs, the limestone falls are impressive, but swimming is currently forbidden because there is a danger of fragile fossilizations breaking off.

BAGNO VIGNONI (☎ 0577)

La Posta, tel: 887 112, fax: 887 119. **Le Terme**, tel: 887 150, fax: 887 497.

Osteria del Leone, tel: 887 300; closed Mon. Good, creative cooking, sevice is sometimes slow. Restaurant in **Hotel Terme** serves very good food.

CASTELNUOVO DELL'ABBATE (☎0577)

Bassomondo, tel: 835 619; closed Mon. Tasty snacks, homemade salami and cheese.

CHIANCIANO TERME (☎ 0578)

Ambasciatori, Viale della Libertà 512, tel/fax: 64 371. **Grand Hotel**, Piazza Italia 80, tel: 63 333, fax: 62 014. **Grand Hotel Terme**, Piazza Italia 8, tel: 63 254, fax: 63 524. **Astoria**, Via G. Roncacci 15, tel/fax: 64 044. **Conte**, Via Ugo Foscolo 26, tel: 60 205, fax: 60 600. **Firenze**, Via della Valle 52, tel: 63 706, fax: 63 700.

CHIUSI (☎ 0578)

Centrale, Piazza Dante 3, Loc. Chiusi Scalo, tel/fax: 20 118. **Il Patriarca**, SS 146, Loc. Querce al Pino, tel: 274 407, fax: 274 594. **La Sfinge**, Via Marconi 2, tel: 20 157, fax: 222 153.

Ristorante Zaira, Via Arunte 12, tel: 20 260; closed Mon, in the winter. Excellent cuisine.

Museo Nazionale Etrusco, Via Porsenna 17, tel: 20 177; Mon-Sat 9:00 am-2:00 pm, Sun and holidays 9:00 am-1:00 pm. Information on Etruscan tombs in the museum.

MONTALCINO (☎ 0577)

Al Brunello, Loc. Bellaria, Traversa Osticcio, tel: 849 304, fax: 849 430. **Il Giglio**, Via Soccorso Saloni 5, tel/fax: 848 167.

Al Brunello di Montalcino, Loc. Bellaria, tel: 849 304; closed Tue. Specialty is game. **Il Moro**, Via Mazzini 44, tel: 849 384; closed Sat in the winter. Regional cuisine. **Giardino da Alberto**, Piazza Cavour 1, tel: 849 076; closed Wed. Good food at decent prices. **La Cucina di Edgardo**, Via S. Saloni 21, tel: 848 232; closed Wed. Large, varied menu, moderate prices.

Fortezza in Montalcino, July-Sept: daily 9:00 am-1:00 pm and 2:30-8:00 pm; Oct-June: Tue-Sun 9:00-6:00 pm, closed Mon. The abbey church **Sant'Antimo** is open Mon-Sat 10:15 am-12:30 pm and 3:00-6:30 pm, Sun and holidays 9:00-10:30 am and 3:00-6:00 pm. Tel: 835 659

MONTEFOLLONICA (☎ 0577)

La Chiusa, Via della Madonnina 88, tel: 669 668; closed Tue. Montefollonica is on the N 327, which turns off to Torrita di Siena between Pienza and Montepulciano, and became famous for this restaurant, which is said to be one Tuscany's best. Very good food, atmosphere is not great, prices reflect quality of the food.

MONTE OLIVETO MAGGIORE (☎ 0577)

La Torre, at the entrance to the monastery, tel: 707 022; closed Tue. Simple cuisine, pleasant atmosphere.

Monastery, daily 9:15 am-noon and 3:15-6:00 pm (summer), 9:15 am-noon and 3:15-5:00 pm (winter).

MONTEPULCIANO (☎ 0578)

Duomo, Via S. Donato 14, tel/fax: 757 473. **La Terrazza**, Via Piè al Sasso 16, tel/fax: 757 440. **Museo Civico**, Via Ricci 11, tel: 716 935. **City Hall Tower**, daily 8:00 am-1:30 pm.

MURLO (☎ 0577)

L'Albergo di Murlo, Via Martiri di Rigo Secco 1, Vescovado, tel: 814 033, fax: 814 243. **Mirella**, Casa Chiavistrelli, Loc. Casciano, tel: 817 667, fax: 817 667.

Museum im Castello, daily 9:30 am-12:30 pm and 3:00-7:00 pm, 9:30 am-12:30 pm and 3:00-5:00 pm (March and Oct), in July and Aug also 9:00-11:00 pm, closed Mon (Oct-March).

PIENZA (☎ 0578)

Albergo Corsignano, tel: 748 501, fax: 748 166. **Hotel Il Chiostro**, tel: 748 400, fax: 748 440.

Museo Diocesano, Corso Rossellino 30; Wed-Mon 10:00 am-1:00 pm and 2:00-6:30 pm (summer), Sat and Sun 10:00 am-1:00 pm and 3:00-6:00 pm (winter), closed Tue. **Palazzo Piccolomini**, Tue-Sun 10:00 am-12:30 pm and 4:00-7:00 pm (June-Sept), Tue-Sun 10:00 am-12:30 pm and 3:00-6:00 pm (Oct-May), closed Mon.

SAN QUIRICO D'ORCIA (☎ 0577)

Palazzuolo, Via Santa Caterina 43, tel: 897 080, fax: 898 264. **Castello di Ripa d'Orcia**, in a fortress in the Orcia valley, tel: 897 376, fax: 898 038. *AGRITURISMO* (farm vacations): **Il Rigo**, Loc. Casabianca, tel: 897 575 and 897 291, fax: 898 236.

Horti Leonini (16th century), one of the first examples of the Italian-style of garden.

SIENA (☎ 0577)

Piazza del Campo 56, tel: 280 551, fax: 270 676.

Certosa di Maggiano, Via di Certosa 82, tel: 288 180, fax: 288189. **Park Hotel**, Via Marciano 18, tel: 44 803, fax: 49 020. **Villa Patrizia**, Via Fiorentina 58 tel: 50 431, fax: 50 442. 😊😊 **Hotel S. Caterina**, Via Piccolomini 7, tel: 221 105, fax: 271 087. **Antica Torre**, Via Fieravecchia 7, tel/fax: 222 255. **Duomo**, Via Stalloreggi 38, tel: 289 088, fax: 43 043. **Residence Fattoria di Catignano**, Loc. Catignano, tel: 356 744, fax: 356 755. 😊 **Piccolo Hotel Il Palio**, Piazza del Sale 19, tel: 281 131, fax: 281 142. **Bernini**, Via della Sapienza 15, tel/fax: 289 047.

YOUTH HOSTEL: **Guidoriccio**, Via Fiorentina 89, Loc. Stellino, tel: 52 212, fax: 055-805 0104.

🏕 **Colleverde**, Strada di Scacciapensieri 47, tel: 280 044, fax: 333 298. **Le Soline**, Casciano di Murlo, tel: 817 410, fax: 817 415.

❌ **Antica Trattoria Botteganova**, Chiantigiana road towards Gaiole 29, tel: 284 230; closed Mon. Classical Tuscan cuisine from local produce, reasonable prices. **Mariotti da Mu golone**, Via dei Pellegrini 6/8, tel: 283 235; closed Thu. In city center, good Sienese cuisine, delicious pastries for dessert. **Al Marsili**, Via del Castoro 3, tel: 47 154; closed Mon. In the old city. **La Torre**, Via Salicotti 7, tel: 287 548; closed Thu. Modest trattoria, reasonable prices.

🏛 *MUSEUMS:* **Cathedral Museum**, daily 9:00 am-7:30 pm (March 16-Sept 30), 9:00 am-6:00 pm (Oct), 9:00-am-1:30 pm (Nov 1-March 15). **Libreria Piccolomini** (in cathedral), daily 9:00 am-7:30 pm (summer), closed lunchtime (winter). **Pinacoteca Nazionale:** Palazzo Buonsignori, Via S. Pietro 29; Mon 8:30 am-1:30 pm, Tue-Sat 9:00 am-7:00 pm, Sun and holidays 8:00 am-1:30 pm (summer); Tue-Sat 8:30 am-1:30 pm and 2:30-5:30 pm, Sun 8:00 am-1:30 pm, closed Mon (winter) and Jan 1, May 1 and Dec 25.

📷 *SIGHTS:* **Palazzo Comunale** and **City Hall Tower**, Piazza del Campo; Mon-Sat 10:00 am-6:00 pm (summer), 10:00 am-11:00 pm (July, Aug), 10:00 am-4:00 pm (winter), Sun and holidays 9:30 am-1:30 pm, closed Jan 1, May 1 and Dec 25. **Cathedral**, 9:00 am-7:30 pm (summer), closed 1:00-2:30 pm (winter).

PROVINCE OF AREZZO

ANGHIARI (☎ 0575)

❌ **Locanda al Castello di Sorci**, 3 km south of Anghiari, tel: 789 066; closed Mon. Very original, busy.

AREZZO (☎ 0575)

ℹ️ **APT**, Piazza della Repubblica 28, tel: 377 678.

🛏 😊😊😊 **Etrusco**, Via Fleming, 39, tel: 984066, fax: 382 131. 😊😊 **Continentale**, Piazza Guido Monaco 7, tel: 20 251, fax: 350 485. **Europa**, Via Spinello 43, tel: 357 701, fax: 357 703. 😊 **Astoria**, Via Guido Monaco 54, tel: 24 361, fax: 24 362. **Cecco**, Corso Italia 215, tel: 20 986, fax: 356 730.

❌ **Il Cantuccio**, Via Madonna del Prato 76, tel: 26 830; closed Wed. Good, traditional Tuscan cuisine at good prices.

🏛 *MUSEUMS:* **Archeological Museum** Via Margaritone 10; Mon-Sat 9:00 am-2:00 pm, Sun 9:00 am-1 pm. **Cathedral Museum**, Thu-Sat 10:00 am-1:00 pm.

📷 *SIGHTS:* **Casa Petrarca**, Via dell'Orto; Mon-Fri 10:00 am-noon and 3:00-5:00 pm. **Basilica S. Francesco** is open daily, closed lunchtimes. Open all day on Sun and holidays during the summer.

BIBBIENA (☎ 0575)

🛏 😊😊 **Borgo Antico**, Via B. Dovizi 18, tel: 536 445, fax: 536 447.

CAPRESE MICHELANGELO (☎ 0575)

🛏 😊😊 **Il Faggetto**, Loc. Alpe della Faggeta, tel/fax: 793 925.

CORTONA (☎ 0575)

ℹ️ **APT**, Via Nazionale 42, tel: 630 352.

🛏 😊😊 **Albergo S. Michele**, Via Guelfa 15, tel: 604 348, fax: 630 147. **San Luca**, Piazza Garibaldi 2, tel: 630 460, fax: 630 105. **Sabrina**, Via Roma 37, tel: 630 397, fax: 630 564. *YOUTH HOSTEL:* **Ostello S. Marco**, Via Maffei 57, tel/fax: 601 392.

❌ **Cacciatore**, Via Roma 11, tel: 630 552; closed Wed. **Trattoria dell'Amico**, Via Dardano 12, tel: 604 192; closed Mon. Typical trattoria feeling. **Trattoria Dardano**, Via Dardano 24, tel: 601 944; closed Wed.

🏛 **Diocesan Museum**: Tue-Sun 9:30 am-1:00 pm and 3:30-7:00 pm (April 1-Sept. 30), 10:00 am-1:00 pm and 3:30-6:00 pm (Oct), 10:00 am-1:00 pm and 3:00-5:00 pm (Nov 1-March 31), closed Mon. **Etruscan Tomb Tanella di Pitagora**, daily 9:00 am-12:30 pm and 3:30-6:30 pm. **Museo dell'Accademia Etrusca** (in Palazzo Casali), Tue-Sun 10:00 am-7:00 pm (April 1-Sept 31), 9:00 am-1:00 pm and 3:00-5:00 pm (Oct 1-March 31), closed Mon.

POPPI (☎ 0575)

🛏 😊😊 **Parc Hotel**, Via Roma 214, tel. 529 994, fax 529 984. 😊 **Casentino**, Piazza Repubblica 6, tel: 529 090, fax: 529 067.

🏛 **Castello di Poppi**, daily 9:30 am-12:30 pm and 3:30-6:30 pm (summer), 9:30 am-12:30 pm and 2:30-5:30 pm (winter).

SANSEPOLCRO (☎ 0575)

🛏 😊😊 **Borgo Palace**, Via Senese Aretina 80, tel: 736 050, fax: 740 341. **Fiorentino**, Via L. Pacioli 60, tel: 740 350, fax: 740 370.

❌ **L'Oroscopo**, Via P. Togliatti 68, Loc. Pieve Vecchia, tel: 734 875, only servers dinner. Set menu only if pre-ordered. Hotel and Pizzeria in house.

🏛 **Museo Civico**, daily 9:00 am-1:30 pm and 2:30-7:30 pm (June-Sept), 9:30-1:00 pm and 2:30-6:00 pm (Oct-May).

Between Siena and Arezzo

THE MAREMMA AND
ITS HINTERLAND

MAREMMA
AROUND THE AMIATA
WEST OF THE AMIATA
GROSSETO / GREEN HILLS
SILVER COAST
ETRUSCAN TOUR
COLLINE METALLIFERE

THE MAREMMA

With the mighty Amiata Plateau to the east, the gentle hills of its interior, and the long stretch of coast that borders the Tyrrhenian Sea, the province of Grosseto is a region that has been blessed by both nature and by history. The Etruscans were the first to "discover," arriving in the 8th century B.C., and they stayed because of the area's wealth of natural resources. The Etruscans were also the first to drain the swampy coastal region of the Maremma, but 500 years later, they had to yield to the Romans, who proceeded to build their settlements atop the Etruscan ruins.

Christianity followed during the 5th century, and the old Etruscan centers of Populonia, Sovana and Roselle were early bishoprics. After a brief spell under the control of Lombards and the Franks – both of whom were also interested in the region's minerals – the Aldobrandeschi family took control of the area in the 8th century. Their process of *castellamento*, around 1200, lead to nearly every hilltop being crowned with a castle. Small wonder then that the Aldobrandeschi's pride eventually led to their downfall. In his *Di-*

Preceding Pages: Inside the church of Santa Maria, in Sovana. Left: Local social life is often played out on the street.

vine Comedy, Dante Alighieri made Umberto atone for his family's sins and had him appear with his neck bent under a heavy stone.

The rest of the story is quickly told. In the 14th century, the Republic of Siena gained control of the region. Yet, despite the ample supply of fortifications, they were forced to yield the coastal regions to the Spanish, who left the Maremma to its own devices, which meant, in effect, to malaria. It wasn't until the Congress of Vienna in 1815, that the region became part of the Grand Duchy of Tuscany.

The Hapsburgs, and after them the Italian government, drained the "bitter Maremma," as it is called in one song. After thus being freed from the plague of malaria, the region became a great producer of grains. Since its mineral resources were exhausted long ago, the province's wealth lies mainly in its varied landscape and its rich past.

The gateway to the Maremma – as the entire region is often called today – is a bridge on the SS 223 that leads across an inaccessible valley, near Bagno di Petriolo, about halfway between Siena and Grosseto (the rising stench of sulfur underlines the presence of a hot springs in the area). Just ten kilometers further on, you encounter the first testimony to the area's medieval past. The **Abbey of San**

PROVINCE OF GROSSETO

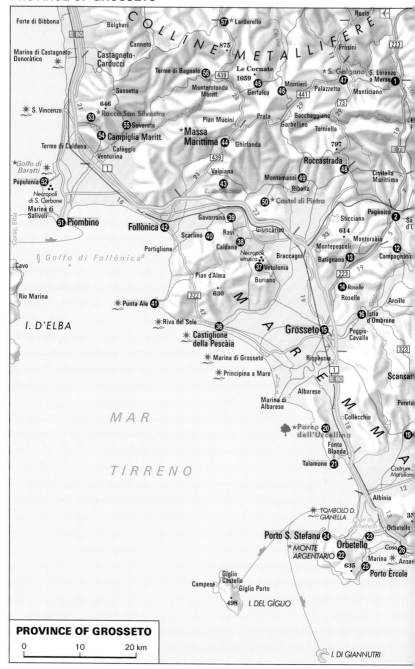

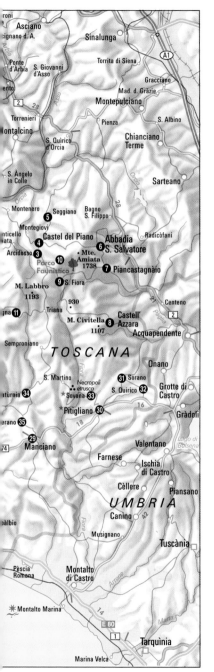

Lorenzo ❶, which was built by the Ardenghesca family around 1200. All remains today are the entrance gate and the late-Romanesque church with a facade that resembles that of the abbey church of Sant'Antimo.

If you continue along the main road to Grosseto, you will reach **Paganico ❷**, about seven kilometers south of the exit to Roccastrada (see p. 164). An impressive 14th-century city wall surrounds the little medieval town center. This is a good point of departure for a tour of the nearby Amiata massif.

*AROUND THE AMIATA

The extinct volcano Amiata (1738 meters), and the mountain peaks Labbro (1193 meters), Buceto (1152 meters), Civitella (1107 meters) and Poggio Zoccolino (1035 meters), form the largely visible border between the provinces of Siena and Grosseto. However, inhabitants of the region's eleven communities swear allegiance only to "their Amiata," and think of themselves as islanders.

The mountains are covered with thick forests of chestnut and beech, and are crisscrossed with brooks and streams. At a height of between about 600 and 800 meters, several springs form a kind of ring around the massif, and there were settlements around them even in prehistoric times. The Etruscans mined red mercury sulfide here, and, until the 1970s, local inhabitants continued to live from mercury mines, together with some agriculture and sheep herding. Since the mines closed, however, all that is left is the timber industry. Thus, the region has placed considerable hopes on tourism, staking out nature parks and clearing hiking trails. As a result of measures to create jobs after the mines closed, therefore, the landscape here is well cared for.

An excursion through the Amiata massif is also a tour through some 3000 years of cultural history. The towns here all de-

Maremma

veloped from medieval fortifications. Since the days of the Lombards, foreign powers have been interested in this border region between the Empire and the Papal States. The pilgrim route *Via Francigena*, which linked the Frankish Empire with Rome, was nearby, and powerful families in the late-Middle Ages and Renaissance hearkened back to the Etruscan mining tradition and stripped the area of natural resources. In modern times, this rather rugged area has escaped widespread notice – thus, preserving its natural beauty.

Some 30 kilometers from Paganico, the SP 26 leads past Montenero and Montegiovi to **Arcidosso ❸**, perched between Monte Amiata and Monte Labbro, on a mountain saddle at an altitude of 679 meters. From a distance, you can see the *Rocca* with its turreted tower (ca. 1000), a testament to the village's medieval origins. During the 9th century, the village

Above: A surprising encounter in the forests around Amiata. Right: The forested hills surrounding Monte Amiata.

belonged to the abbey of San Salvatore. Later it belonged to the Aldobrandeschi, and finally to the city of Siena.

Over the centuries, a little city grew up within the fortress and outside the city walls. For a long time, its economy was centered on the mineral resources of the surrounding mountains. To reach this picturesque old city with its little, winding alleys, take the Corso Toscana through the old city gate with a clock tower, a reconstruction of a 19th-century original. A side street leads off the Corso Toscana to the Porto del Castello, a second city gate, which is adorned with the coats-of-arms of the Medici and Arcidosso families.

North of Arcidosso is the village of **Castel del Piano ❹**, which also once belonged to the Benedictine abbey of San Salvatore, but which was nonetheless administered by the inhabitants themselves. In 1214, the Aldobrandeschi put an end to such autonomy, only to be ousted themselves in 1331 by the ubiquitous Sienese.

Castel del Piano has a medieval city center that is surrounded by a ring of Renaissance buildings and another ring of more modern buildings. The town's five towers and circular city plan are reminiscent of Siena's. Along the Corso Nasini, the houses are built atop the former city wall, and thus form the border of the oldest part of town. In front of this, on the Piazza della Madonna, is the largest church in the Amiata, the Chiesa dell'Opera.

Some seven kilometers north of Castel del Piano, **Seggiano ❺** lies on a gentle rise of land. Streams form a natural border around this former castle, which is numbered one of the oldest in the region. At the entrance to the city, shaded by olive trees, is the Baroque church of Tempio della Madonna della Carità, built by the survivors of a plague epidemic in 1603. The town itself has preserved little of its medieval character, but its little churches do contain a few 14th- and 15th-century masterpieces. Signs direct you to the ruins of the Castello del Potentino (ca.

1040) and the ruins of the monastery of Colombaio, where Saint Bernardino of Siena once stayed.

From Castel del Piano, a road leads east to the peak of the Amiata. On the other side, it leads down again to **Abbadia San Salvatore ❻**, which lies at an altitude of of 812 meters. This town derives its name from the nearby abbey, the Monte Amiata's oldest center of power. Legend has it that Saint Salvatore met the Lombard king Rachis here – reason enough to found Tuscany's first-ever abbey on the spot in A.D. 762. A more probable factual reason was the Lombard interest in this border area between the Frankish Empire and the Papal State. The abbey belonged, in turn, to the Benedictines, the Camaldolians, and the Cistercians. During the 18th century, the monastery was dissolved and turned into residential apartments, but monks returned to inhabit parts of the old buildings in 1939. Next to the abbey is a fortress that developed into a flourishing mining center during the Middle Ages. The

area's wealth of mineral resources meant that the most powerful families in the region – the Aldobrandeschi, Sforza, and Piccolomini – were constantly struggling for control with the Republic of Siena. Until the middle of the 20th century, the town and surrounding communities lived from mercury mining. The local Mining Museum documents the history of this industry in the area.

Despite its having suffered a rather unfortunate course of restorations around 1930, the Romanesque abbey church, consecrated in 1036, is also worth visiting. Noteworthy here are the T-shaped ground plan, the oldest of ist kind in Tuscany; the two-towered facade; the crypt with its 36 tall slender, columns, each decorated with a different capital; a wooden cross that dates from the 12th century; and Francesco Nasini's fresco depicting the Martyrdom of Saint Bartolomeo.

South of Abbadia San Salvatore, amid a chestnut wood with views of the Paglia plain, at an altitude of 772 meters, is the

town of **Piancastagnaio** ❼. This, too, was once an Aldobrandeschi castle that fell into Sienese hands during the 15th century. Witnesses to its past include the 13th-century defensive fortress at the entrance to the Old City; the church of Santa Maria Assunta (1279); the 14th-century Palazzo Communale; the Palazzo del Podestà (13th century) on the former Piazza del Commune; and the Palazzo Bourbon del Monte (1611) on the Piazza Belvedere. Outside the city walls is the convent of San Bartolomeo with frescoes dating from the 13th and 14th centuries.

From Piancastagnaio, the SP 18 leads directly to Santa Fiora, another former mining center on Monte Amiata.

To extend your tour of Amiata, follow the signs to **Castell'Azzara** ❽, the "Fortress of Gambling." Its name originates with the story that two brothers of the Sforza family are said to have thrown

Above: Always eager to spend time with a grandchild. Right: The waters of Santa Fiora flows out of taps 100 kilometers away.

dice, which appear in the castle's coat-of-arms, to determine who should get the medieval castle. Comprised of gray stone houses, the Castell'Azzara is on a steep slope that looks out all the way to Latium. To the west, Monte Civitella blocks the view. The lodes of red mercury sulfide here drew the Umbrians, and later Etruscan settlers.

From Castell'Azzara, it is only about 20 kilometers to **Santa Fiora** ❾. This picturesque village with a pretty old town is popular with vacationers and winter sports enthusiasts. A winding road leads through well-tended woodlands to the town. Along the way, signs indicate individual geothermic drilling holes. Enel, the state-owned electric company, is trying to make use of the underground heat that is present throughout the area.

From the south, a bridge leads into the village, which is divided into three parts. The first building here was the castle, protected by a natural rocky trench and rough cliffs. On the Piazza Garibaldi, you can see what is left of the fortress, a clock tower, and the Renaissance Sforza palace. To the southwest is the old city *Borgo* with the Poor Clares' Convent (1612); the parish church of Saints Flora and Lucia, which contains some terra-cotta works by Della Robbia; and the Jewish ghetto. Outside the old city walls is the quarter of Montecatino, where the Peschiera, an old basin, catches the waters of the Fiora.

The village's monumental cemetery is the last resting place of David Lazzeretti. Called the "Christ of Poor People," he was hunted and shot by the authorities in 1878. His crime was preaching the doctrine of equality and communal property in this impoverished area. In 1872, he founded a Christian brotherhood of peasants, shepherds, and artisans, called the *Giurisdavidici*, and built a church on the peak of Monte Labbro, the ruins of which can still be seen today. His ideas of social renewal have also survived among the inhabitants of this inhospitable region.

From Bagnore you can access Italy's only former cult center, as well as the nature preserve **Parco Faunistico ⑩**, where wolves and elk once again roam wild through the woods.

A lovely, winding road leads to the west, back towards Paganico. After about ten kilometers, you can see the vacation town of Monticello Amiata, perched on top of a mountain at an altitude of 734 meters. This town also grew out of a *castrum*, and a tower rises from its center like a raised index finger, signaling, perhaps, a warning to those with anything more than a pleasant visit in mind.

The SP 7 offers beautiful views as it leads rapidly downhill to Cinigiano, a friendly little town with old city walls, that is at an altitude of just 324 meters. The main sources of income here are agriculture and cattle breeding. The road then leads past Sasso d'Ombrone. From here a bridge leads across the Ombrone River, the source of which is in Umbria, and which is named for the original Umbrian people. Before long, you are out of the mountains, back in Paganico and on the busy expressway between Siena and Grosseto.

WEST OF THE AMIATA

As you go farther west, you reach other villages that peaked during the Middle Ages. Six kilometers before the town of Roccalbegna, at a height of 769 meters, is the castle **Triana**, which is also know as the Piccolomini. This imposing, well-preserved fortress was first mentioned in A.D. 776. Today, it belongs to a religious society and is closed to the public.

Rising behind **Roccalbegna ⑪** in the upper Albegna valley, is a steep cliff that is topped by a fortress. The houses of the town crowd together at the foot of the cliff, and the locals like to joke that, "If the cliff should ever shake, then *addio*, Roccalbegna." Around 1250, this town, too, was under the feudal rule of the Aldobrandeschi. Ruins are all that remain of their once-proud fortress, yet, the town's general medieval character has

been preserved thanks to its narrow little streets. The Romanesque-Gothic church **Santi Pietro e Paolo**, with a triptych by Ambrogio Lorenzetti, is worth visiting, and the Museum of Sacral Art displays other religious treasures.

Campagnatico ⑫ was one of the virtually omnipresent Aldobrandeschis' oldest holdings. But, the late-Middle Ages brought with them destruction, epidemics, decline, and finally oblivion. In the 19th century the Tuscan Grand Duke Leopoldo II brought the little town back to life by encouraging the development of small industries. Some of the town's original medieval character has been preserved in the quarter of Via Casacce. And below the castle ruins, on the Piazza Garibaldi, a former pilgrims' hospice, **Ospedale di Sant'Antonio**, which the Knights Templars administered, can still be seen.

To the right of the SS 223 are the little mountain settlements of Batignano and

Montorsaio. During the Middle Ages, the castle of **Batignano** ⑬ owed its importance to its proximity to silver and lead mines. Before the Republic of Siena took control in the 14th century, vassals of the Aldobrandeschi held sway here. At the edge of town, the convent of Santa Croce is worth visiting. In the summer, it hosts a festival called *Musica nel Chiostro*, or music in the convent (mid-July to mid-August). During the last few years, the Englishman Adam Pollock has staged little-known, rarely performed operas here. In Batignano's town center is the church of **San Martino**. Its oldest sections, taken from a church in Roselle, are from the 8th century.

The archeological excavation site of **Roselle** ⑭ is on a rise of land about seven kilometers from Grosseto. Protected on the west by Lagus Prilius, a lagoon that has since been drained, and by the hill Poggio Moscona to the south, Roselle was founded in the 7th century B.C., and its strategically advantageous position made it one of the Etruscans' twelve most

Above: Grosseto's cathedral is adorned with colored marble.

powerful cities. Its economy was agrarian-based, and although they supplied the Romans with grain, the inhabitants of *Rusellae*, as it was originally known, resisted forming an alliance with the new super-power. When the Romans finally took control in 294 B.C., they quickly added their standard facilities – a forum, amphitheater and thermal baths.

It was in Roselle, in A.D. 862, that the Aldobrandeschis built their first castle. The city became the seat of a bishopric under the Lombards, but had to yield pride of place to Grosseto in 1138, after much of its population had left because the surrounding land was becoming increasingly swampy, bringing disease and other problems in its wake. The last residents abandoned it in the 16th century.

Today, you can see the Etruscans' 3000-meter-long cyclopean city wall, up to seven-meters-high in places, as well as cisterns, water pipes, and parts of the Roman additions, like the amphitheater. The necropolises indicate that people lived here during the Iron Age. Some of the site's artifacts are displayed in the Archeological Museum in Grosseto. During the summer, it is open all day.

GROSSETO

Grosseto ⑮ (population 65,000), the province's lively main city, probably developed from an old Etruscan settlement. The plains, which extend to the sea today, were under water in Roman times. The Etruscans, Romans, and, in the Middle Ages, monks constantly struggled to drain this swampy, malaria-ridden area.

First documented in the year A.D. 803, its castle was originally the property of the Aldobrandeschis. During their dominion, in 1138, it became a bishopric, but in 1336, it was conquered by Siena, and was later incorporated into the Duchy of Tuscany in 1569. Between 1565 and 1593, the Medici had the hexagonal ring wall that encloses the historic center and

the fortress built. It is still well preserved today. Around 1835, Leopoldo II (whose monument stands on the Piazza Dante) had the ring transformed into an area of parks and streets, removing the star-shaped, defensive, navigable moats that had once surrounded the city.

Leopoldo II also joined his predecessors in the fight to drain the Maremma, and thus checking the constant threat of malaria. Using more modern technology, he was more successful, and ushered in a new period of prosperity for the city.

The **Cathedral of San Lorenzo**, with its striped marble facade, dates from the 13th century (the facade was renovated in 1840-1845), as does the simple church of **San Francesco**. The painted wooden cross on the main altar is by Duccio di Buoninsegna (1289). The **Museum of Archeology** displays prehistoric, Etruscan, and Roman artifacts from Roselle, Vetulonia, Pitigliano and the Fiora valley.

THE GREEN HILLS OF THE MAREMMA

In the southeastern part of the province, **Istia d'Ombrone ⑯**, eight kilometers from Grosseto, is a good place to start an excursion through the province's forested hills. As late as the 1920s, fear of malaria drove the well-heeled Grossetans to withdraw from the plains, taking children and possessions, to spend the summer in this former fortress of the Bishops of Roselle. The medieval city wall with the 13th-century *Porta Grossetana*, and the fact that there was a market held here as early as 1032, shows that people were able to appreciate this village's excellent location very early on.

Farther southeast along the SS 323, halfway to the sea, you will come to the village of **Scansano ⑰**, with medieval origins similar to other Aldobrandeschi fortress towns. During the 19th century, this town was official summer headquarters for Grosseto's municipal officials, who

Maremma

fled from the threat of malaria in the hot summer months. Today, Scansano is a modern small city with an agrarian-based economy. It has a medieval town center and a museum.

Continuing towards the coast, you pass **Pereta** ⑱, built on a mountaintop like a fortress. Ranged one against the other, it is the houses themselves that form the city wall, with a high, 12-century tower in the center. A turreted city gate, restored in 1546, leads into the medieval town center. Pereta was the last place of refuge for the aristocratic couple Nello della Pietra and Marghereta Aldobrandeschi, who lived in bigamy and finally had to be separated by armed force.

From here, everything is downhill. The thick woods begin to thin out, and agriculture kicks in again by the time you reach **Magliano** ⑲. Here, once upon a time, was the old city of *Heba*, originally

Above: A shady avenue lined with pines in the Parco dell'Uccellina. Right: Maremma cows with their distinctive horns.

an Etruscan, later a Roman settlement. All that is left of it today are the name and the necropolises, dug out of the tuff stone that forms the surrounding hills. You can learn more about the city's history at *Pro Loco* in Magliano.

The focal point of Magliano is its 1,000-year-old Aldobrandeschi **fortress**, which sits on a hilltop 128 meters above sea level, surrounded by a wood of venerable olive trees that reach all the way up to the fortified city walls. Near the church of Annunziata is the huge "Witches' Tree," said to be the oldest olive tree in Europe. Enter Magliano's Old City through the Porta Nuova, then turn left. On the Piazza del Popolo is the turreted city gate of **San Martino**, near which stands the Romanesque church of the same name, which was completely restored after World War II. On the Piazza Libertà, the Palazzo dei Priori rises up in a blend of the Gothic and Sienese styles. It dates from 1430, and is ornamented with the coats-of-arms of 15th- and 16th-century *Podestà*.

Corso Garibaldi leads to the church of **San Giovanni**, which has a Romanesque floor plan, and is a typical specimen of Renaissance architecture in the Maremma. A short footpath leads through olive groves to the south, to the white ruins of the 11th-century church of San Bruzio. You can still see the apse and its ornate capitals with allegorical figures. A pagan temple supposedly once stood on this site, and was thought to have been linked to the town by a tunnel.

If you are short of time, drive straight to the sea along the SS 323. The road is lined with eucalyptus trees that were supposed to clear the air of malaria germs. Perhaps, however, you will have time to take a short detour to the nearby ***Parco dell'Uccellina** ⑳, a nature preserve between the fishing village of Talamone and the mouth of the Ombrone River. The park was established in 1975 and is one of the few oases in the Maremma where the Mediterranean flora has been preserved in its original state. Roaming around here are wild pigs and porcupines, badgers, ot-

ters, fallow deer, rare birds, and the white Maremma cattle with their sweeping horns, tended by the local shepherds who are known as *butteri*. This region is also a rich lode for archeologists. The oldest finds have been stone tools from the days of Neanderthal Man.

If you have time for this detour, you can enter the preserve, and buy tickets, in Albarese. Bring along sturdy shoes so you can enjoy the nature trails, which are set up around the life cycles of the various indigenous animals. Because of the great crowds between July 1 and September 30, you can only visit the preserve in conjunction with a group tour.

THE SILVER COAST

The "Silver Coast" is a region covered with long sand beaches and pine woods. To explore it, start in the fishing village of **Talamone** ㉑, which sits on a protrusion of rock at the southern end of the Parco dell'Uccellina. It was badly damaged during World War II, and most of the vil-

Above: Evening quiet on the Argentario. Right: Orbetello's old mill.

lage had to be completely rebuilt. This was not, however, its first entry into military history. In 225 B.C., the Romans beat the Gauls at Campo Regio, while in 1860, this is where Garibaldi's 1000 loyal followers stocked up on provisions before they set out to conquer the mainland.

In Antiquity, it was the Argonauts who were said to have founded Talamone – or so, at least, runs the legend. The Etruscans found this to be a good base for their merchant marine, and proceeded to establish a harbor. The ruins of a medieval fortress are the sole testiment to its turbulent and colorful history. What was left of the town's Etruscan temple has been removed and is on display in the archeological museum in Florence.

From Talamone, it is about four kilometers to the Via Aurelia Etrusca (SS 1), which leads to **★Monte Argentario ㉒**, and ultimately on to Rome. This rocky promontory has given its name to the en-tire surrounding coastline. Once an island, two narrow tongues of land, or *tomboli*, now connect it to the mainland. A shallow lagoon has formed between the sand dunes, and a narrow spit of land, like the prow of a ship, thrusts into it from the mainland, forming the narrow spit of land on which **Orbetello ㉓** lies. An artificial causeway (1842) also links the city and the Argentario.

The old Etruscan harbor was first conquered by the Romans, then by Siena in the Middle Ages, and finally by the Spanish, who made it their main naval base. In 1555, Philip II made the city the capital of the *Stato dei Presidi*, a federation that included Porto Azzurro, the Argentario and Talamone. Later, in 1815, the city was incorporated into the Duchy of Tuscany.

Each of these various rulers left their mark. The city's **cyclopean wall**, from the 4th century B.C., is Etruscan; the cathedral (1376) is Sienese Gothic; and the city wall (1557) is Spanish.

Today, Orbetello is a particularly popular destination among growing numbers

of ecologically-minded tourists. The lagoon contains both a World Wildlife Fund nature reserve and an Italian League of Bird Protection observation station. (Don't forget you mosquito repellent!)

Within the pine woods of the *Tombolo della Giannella*, to the north, are other vacation communities. In Santa Liberata, where you can see the remains of a Roman villa, you are deep within in the Argentario, with its dense maquis and the coast's rocky, inaccessible cliffs. To the north is the charming little city of **Porto Santo Stéfano** ㉔, which has been an active harbor since the days of the Etruscans. Today, there are more yachts than fishing boats in its slips, and the lively bay is well suited for more urbane living. The old city with its 17th-century Spanish fortress and vacation villas complete the picturesque setting. A regular ferry to the islands of Gíglio and Giannutri leaves from Porto Nuovo.

On the southern side of the Argentario is the luxurious vacation town of **Porto Ercole** ㉕. Hercules, *Ercole*, is supposed

to have founded this port city, however, it has only been proven that the Romanesque monastery of Tre Fontane was a gift from Charlemagne. After it was conquered by the Spanish in 1557, the town became a naval base. Relics of this period are the Spanish Fort Filippo to the left of the harbor, and the castle opposite.

The 17th-century Fort Stella is in the south of town. On the Cala Galera, where *Feniglia*, the southern spit of land, begins, the painter Michelangelo Merisi, known as Caravaggio, died of malaria.

This tour of the Silver Coast ends at the Lago di Burano. If you are coming from Orbetello, leave the Via Aurelia Etrusca in Ansedonia, which is little more than a collection of vacation homes. From here, you will have an amazing view of the sun setting behind the Argentario.

A bumpy road leads to the excavations at **Cosa** ㉖, on a rock ledge at an altitude of 113 meters. Cosa, dating from 273 B.C., was the first Roman settlement on the Etruscan coast. But by the end of the first century B.C., it was abandoned, and

the Visigoths dealt it the *coup de grâce*. Today, you can see an impressive field of ruins with a small museum (open only in the morning). Below the promontory is Cosa's harbor. Here, in the 15th-century **Torre della Tagliata**, Giacomo Puccini worked on his opera *Tosca*.

At the front edge of the cliff is the *Tagliata etrusca*, an artificial canal that is supposed to guarantee that the seawater can flow freely in and out, preventing the silting up of the harbor. A similar channel is the *Bagno della Regina*, a natural cleft in the rock, 260 meters long and up to six meters wide, which has been artificially enlarged. There is also an artificial drainage canal between Lago di Burano and the sea. All of this was created more than 2000 years ago, and continues to fulfill its function. The World Wildlife Fund has declared the swamp area around **Lago di Burano** to be a protected nature preserve,

Above: Porto San Stéfano. Right: The "Empress" in Niki de Saint-Phalle's sculpture park near Capalbio.

which means entry is forbidden during the summer.

AN ETRUSCAN TOUR

If you want to pay a visit on the ancient Etruscans, you have to be prepared to work for it, because these people preferred to live in high places, at a safe distance from the swamps and their enemies. Spreading from the coastal cities of Vetulonia and Populonia and the early inland settlements of Volterra and Chiusi, they reached all the way into Umbria and Latium. They founded cities and settlements, drained the Maremma with a clever drainage system, and mined ore and minerals from the wooded Colline Metallifere.

Start about ten kilometers inland from Lago di Burano, in **Capalbio ㉗**. You can walk around this well-restored village, which is now a favorite summer residence among Roman television personalities, along its intact medieval city walls. Within the labyrinth of side streets, next

Maremma

to a medieval tower, there is a 12th-century Romanesque church with Sienese-school frescoes. Nearby, the artist Nikki de Saint-Phalle has created what some think of as an irreverent sculpture garden, ★**Giardino dei Tarocchi**. In theory, it is open to the public from mid-May through the end of October, Monday through Saturday, from 2:30 to 6:30 p.m., closed Sundays. (Info. tel: 0564 895 122).

Capalbio is surrounded by thick woods that, during the 19th century, the outlaw Domenico Tiburzi found to be a very effective hiding place. Only wild boar lurk in the shadows today – and hunters, for whom boar hunting is a popular pastime.

From Capalbio, a road leads northwest to **Marsiliana** ㉘ (14 kilometers). This region is predominantly agricultural. At the junction with the SS 74, at the end of an avenue of cypresses, you can see the former **Castrum Marsiliani**, which today belongs to the Orsini princes. Hidden in the undergrowth along the Camarrone are graves from the Villanova-period, as well as Etruscan graves. The Greek and

Phoenician grave offerings that have been excavated here are displayed in the archeology museum in Grosseto.

The Maremmana SS 74, which links the Via Aurelia with Lago di Bolsena, is the fastest way to get to the Etruscan excavations sites in Pitigliano and Sovana. Between fields and forests, the road wends its way up to the 444-meter-high town of **Manciano** ㉙.

Because of its strategically advantageous location, this medieval fortress attracted the Aldobrandeschi, the Orsini, and finally the Sienese. It was the latter who left the 15th-century **castle**, which commands a breathtaking view, within the old city walls. If you have time, you should stroll through the old city and visit the town's Prehistoric Museum, which displays finds from throughout the Fiora valley.

A mere 18 kilometers lie between this town and Pitigliano. In the virtually inaccessible thickets of the Poggio Buco, just before the bridge across the Fiora, there are Etruscan graves and remains of ar-

chaic walls. The forms of the graves indicate that this was one of the Etruscans' early settlements (8th century B.C.).

Before long, the landscape changes, and the thickly forested valleys give way to a barren plateau. *Pitigliano ③⓪ appears without warning after a curve in the road. It sits high above a gorge and looks as if it has grown out of the yellowy-red volcanic tuff stone, an impression that is furthered by the fact that the houses are constructed of the same porous stone as the surface on which they rest.

From the west, Pitigliano can only be reached via a high aqueduct, which was built in 1545. At the entrance to the old city, which is guarded by a stone lion, stands the mighty, turreted silhouette of the 15th-century **Palazzo Orsini**. The Orsini family took over this fortified town from the Aldobrandeschi in 1293. Today, the palace houses the Archeological Museum, home to some 1500 artifacts from

Above: Pitigliano – as if it grew out of the rock. Right: Social hour on the piazza.

prehistoric and Etruscan times. The medieval city center is a warren of tiny streets that are linked by narrow flights of stairs, sometimes ending at a house wall or at the city wall, from which you can look out across the surrounding countryside. The local Baroque church doesn't seem to fit in very well with the village's overall image. In the Middle Ages, Pitigliano was a refuge for Spanish Jews fleeing the Inquisition, as the Jewish cemetery at the village entrance attests.

From Pitigliano, where today most of the inhabitants are elderly people, you can head to the cliff town of **Sorano ③①**. As you approach, your view of the city is blocked by new buildings, but once you pass them, you can see that, like Pitigliano, Sorano is built of and on volcanic tuff. *Columbari*, the characteristic caves in the cliffs, which are today used to store wine, are testimony to the site's Etruscan origins. One noteworthy sight is the broad 16th-century Orsini fortress in the south of the city. You can also see the church of San Nicola, completely renovated in the

17th century; the Palace of the Orsini Counts (1551); and the Sasso Leopoldino with a clock tower (18th century).

Unfortunately, Sorano, like so many other out-of-the-way villages in Tuscany, is slowly dying. Increasing numbers of people are leaving, some of them driven away by the frequent landslides. Its beautiful old city center is decaying because there is no money for renovations, and the future of the village is being left to fate.

In nearby **San Quirico** ㉜, signs indicate the way to the ruins of fort **Vitozza**. Sections of walls and a few subterranean apartments are all that remain of the 12th-century Aldobrandeschi complex, which was occupied into the 18th century.

A gorge between rock walls of porous stone leads to the medieval **★Sovana** ㉝, which was a flourishing Etruscan community during the 7th century B.C. Here, too, time seems to have stood still. Along the cobblestone streets, a handful of buildings of the yellowy-red volcanic tuff attest to the town's glorious past, as do the ruins of the Aldobrandeschi fortress, the

12th-century Romanesque church of Santa Mary, and its coeval cathedral of Santi Peter and Paul, which turns its back, or apse, on the village. The unusual octagonal dome reveals the influence of the Lombards. Sovana was the birthplace of Pope Gregory VII (1073-1085), who forced the Emperor Henry to undertake the Journey to Canossa to petition for forgiveness.

In the area around Sovana, Etruscan graves are hidden by the thick Mediterranean undergrowth. They provide good examples of the period's wide variety of grave architecture. A small trail off the San Martino road leads to the **Grave of the Siren** (3rd-2nd century B.C.). Its name is derived from a relief above the rubble of the grave chamber depicting a somewhat weatherworn mermaid.

Nearby, is the **Tomba Ildebranda** (3rd century B.C.), a luxury grave in the form of a temple with a row of columns, which you can only observe from the outside. Behind the burial mound, you can see a *cavone*, an Etruscan passageway

that was hewn into the rock, and is so narrow that hardly any light penetrates it.

From here, the provincial road leads to another Etruscan center, **★Saturnia ㉞**, which you will smell before you see. The strong odor of sulfur rises from the thermal springs, where first the Etruscans, then the Romans, soaked away their aches and pains. Above the springs is the white town, built of bleached travertine rock. Saturnia is said to be the oldest city on the peninsula, and is dedicated to Saturn, the god of fertility and dissemination. The town's recorded history begins around 800 B.C. Within the old city walls, probably begun even before the Etruscans arrived, is the medieval center with a castle and well-tended piazzas that are surrounded by little stone houses. A walk along the cobblestone Via Clodia leads you through the old Porta Romana and outside the city walls.

Above: Enjoying the pleasures of the warm, sulfurous waters of Saturnia. Right: Herding sheep in the coastal region of the Maremma.

Scattered around the countryside north of the city are funerary urns from the Villanova period and stone Etruscan gravesites. Many of the graves have vanished over the years, and it is said that local residents happily used the blocks of travertine that were lying around the countryside to build their own houses.

The **thermal baths** at the outrageously expensive hotel *Terme di Saturnia* below the city make the sulfurous waters available to wealthy guests and local residents. If you follow the drainage canal, you will come to an abandoned mill where the water forms natural pools and where you can, winter and summer, enjoy the healing waters free of charge. This is particularly fun on romantic moonlit nights.

On the way back to the coast, about seven kilometers from Saturnia, you will reach the picturesque mountain village of **Montemerano ㉟**. This town has a tower that is as crooked as the one in Pisa, just not as famous. Its 13th-century church of San Giorgio contains valuable frescoes and panel paintings, including a lovely

Maremma

polyptych by Sano di Pietro. There is an unusual story behind the *Madonna della Gattaiola*, from the school of Sassetta, that hangs here. For centuries, before it was rescued and returned to its proper function, it was simply used as the door to a grain silo, with a little door cut in it for cats.

The Northern Etruscan Settlements

For further excursions into Etruscan territory, the best point of departure is **Castiglione della Pescaia** ㊱. This pleasant holiday town is set among broad pine forests, with the sea on one side and the gentle slopes of Petruccio, with its medieval fortifications, on the other. The Pisans built this fortress, as well as the impressive city walls, with three gates and eleven towers. Here, where the lagoon of Lagus Prilius flowed into the sea, archeologists have excavated a Roman thermal bath facility.

In the modern part of town, which has developed at the foot of the fortress

mound, there is a harbor for sailors and fishermen, as well as a lovely little sand beach that gets wider to the north, around the vacation complexes Riva del Sole, Roccamare and Le Rocchette. It is the pine woods behind this beach, incidentally, that form the setting for the novel *The Secret of the Pineta* by the successful authors Fruttero and Lucentini.

Continuing north, you will see settlements atop nearly every hill, medieval settlements with fortresses to which people could retreat in the event of Saracen attack.

One such settlement is Buriano, which was a possession of Lamberto Aldobrandeschi around A.D. 900. Just beside it, **Vetulonia** ㊲ sits atop a hill at a height of 344 meters. For years, the Etruscan settlement of *Vetluna* was believed lost. Not until 1850 did experts agree that the city must have been located here, atop the hills of Colonna di Buriano. Further evidence includes coins embossed with the city's emblem, a trident and two dolphins that were discovered in the burial sites.

After Populonia, Vetulonia was the oldest Etruscan settlement, one of the powerful League of Twelve Cities. It peaked during the 7th and 6th centuries B.C., due to the reserves of silver and ore in the nearby Colline Metallifere. Its subsequent decline was a result of the silting up of the lagoon on whose banks it lay, as well as continued attacks from the hostile Saracens.

A little below the town are the funerary complexes with chamber and stone circle graves. The most architecturally interesting are the **Tomba della Petriera**, where a 22-meter-long grave opens into a rectangular, two-story burial chamber, and the **Tomba del Diavolino**, under an earth mound measuring 80 meters in diameter. Excavations have also brought the remains of Roman streets to light. Part of the wealth of artifacts from this site, some dating from the Villanova period, are dis-

played in the Antiquarium at the entrance to Vetulonia, while the rest have been taken to the archeological museum in Florence. The medieval village was built upon, and using, rubble from the ruins of the older city, as can be seen from the remains of the fortification walls.

Somewhat farther north is the village of Giuncarico, a fortified Aldobrandeschi possession that fell under Sienese rule in the 13th century. To the west, you can see the hill of **Caldana** ㊳, which is first mentioned in the year A.D. 940. To reach the old city within the rectangular walls of the 16th-century castle, you go through a medieval city gate. At the end of Via Montanara is the 12th-century church of San Biagio.

Another hill, and another castle, the settlement of **Gavorrano** ㊴ lies amidst thick woods at an altitude of 273 meters. According to tradition, a baptistry supposedly stood here as early as 1188. The elliptical form of the castle walls is notable, as is the marble, 13th-century *Madonna and Child* by Giovanni d'Agostino

Above: An especially notable set of horns.
Right: The picturesque charm of daily life in provincial Tuscany.

in the parish church. The statue was illegally sold at the beginning of the 20th century, but was later returned by a Roman antiques dealer. Until recently, Gavorrano was a center for pyrite mining.

Like an eagle's aerie, **Scarlino** ⓭ is perched atop a hill 229 meters high, and looks down over the surrounding countryside. Its name is derived from the Gothic word *Scheril*, or torch, because this town once served as a kind of lighthouse. Its 12th-century fortifications belonged, in turn, to Roselle, Pisa, and Piombino. Excavations in the courtyard of the castle have shown that this spot has been inhabited since the Bronze Age. The Renaissance palace houses the city's historical archives. To the left of the Gulf of Follonica road are the ruins of the Romanesque collegiate church San Michele.

A little further on, on the same side of the road, a path leads to the overgrown ruins of the monastery of **Monte di Muro**, which was home to the heretical Dolcino monks for one chapter of its long history. It was destroyed by the Turks in the 16th century, and finally abandoned in 1808.

Portiglione used to be the port for shipping the pyrite that was mined in Gavarrano. A nature preserve with a sandy beach, *Cala Violina*, which you can only reach on foot or by bus, begins here. Things are certainly more comfortable in the elegant resort of **Punta Ala** ⓭ (turn left off the SS 322, in Pian d'Alma, nine kilometers). Privately owned until quite recently, the town has a small harbor, lovely sand beaches, pine woods, and luxurious holiday and recreation facilities. The place itself, however, has very little in the way of atmosphere or charm.

COLLINE METALLIFERE

The Etruscans, Romans, Lombards, Sienese and Florentines – they all flocked to the area bordered by the Ombrone to the south, and the Cecina to the north. They were lured by natural resources of

Maremma

copper, silver and iron, and because controlling the Colline Metallifere equaled wealth and power.

During the 15th century, however, people left the territory. The mines closed and there was a constant threat of malaria because of the coastal swamps. People didn't trickle back until the 19th century.

Follonica ⓭ was founded in 1832, when Grand Duke Leopoldo established the region's first iron and steel foundries. These are still the dominant features in what has become the most densely populated community in Colline Metallifere.

This city on the sea is a prime example of how the industrial age, pared with a complete disregard for good city planning, can utterly destroy a picturesque little town and all of the natural beauty that surrounds it. At best, the only sights this locale has to offer are artifacts of industrial archeology, such as abandoned steel foundries, and a couple of public monuments like Carlo Reishammer's church of San Leopoldo (1836), one of Tuscany's first steel buildings.

A mere 15 kilometers further on, however, you find yourself, mercifully, returned to the past at the excavation site of **Lago dell'Accesa** ❸. Almost perfectly round, this glass-clear body of water swallowed up, or so the story goes, an entire village, simply because the town's inhabitants insisted on working, rather than resting, on Saint Anna's Day. Nearby, the remains of an Etruscan settlement, a satellite colony of Vetulonia, have been slowly uncovered since excavations began in 1980. Finds from here can be seen in the museum at Massa Marittima.

*Massa Marittima

Originally a Roman estate (*Massa*) in a coastal region (*Marittima*), this former seat of a bishopric developed, in its heyday, into one of the true gems of medieval Tuscany. **Massa Marittima** ❹ enchants

*Above: The cathedral in Massa Marittima.
Right: An 11th-century relief by an unknown master on the cathedral of San Cerbone.*

with its location alone. Twenty-three kilometers from Follonica, at a height of 380 meters, it looks out over the fertile plain towards the sea. This site was settled as early as prehistoric times, and the Etruscans, Romans, and, later, a number of medieval powers stayed because of the metal resources. In 1310, the world's oldest code of mining laws was passed here.

The town's recorded history began in A.D. 835, when the Bishop of Populonia sought refuge in Castello Monte Regio after pirates had destroyed his own city. Massa its true heyday was in the Middle Ages, and by 1300, 10,000 people lived within its walls. The copper and silver mining industries brought prosperity, and its protected location in the hills allowed this independent city-state to preserve a measure of independence for a considerable period, even after it fell to Siena in 1335. Eventually, as malaria continued to spread, its population dropped to a mere 500. It remained practically uninhabited into the 19th century, which means its historic center has survived almost intact.

The lower, older section of the city is the Romanesque **Città Vecchia** (11th-13th centuries), while to the west is the mainly Gothic **Città Nuova** (after the 13th century), which contains the ruins of the Castello Monte Regio and the Sienese fortress. The fact that the newer part of the city is built above the older is unusual.

Another notable feature is the asymmetric division of the Piazza Garibaldi in the center of the lower city. In the midst of a rather severe ensemble of city palaces is, set as if on a pedestal, the loveliest church in the Maremma, the ★**Cathedral of San Cerbone**. Begun in the 13th century, in the Pisan Romanesque style, it gradually evolved into Lucchese Gothic. Flooded with light, the interior contains such treasures as an ornate baptismal font from 1267 (in the baptistry, to the right) and the altarpiece of the *Madonna della Grazie* by the school of Duccio (1316, in the left transept). The gorgeous early-Christian reliefs on the inner side of the facade are of unknown provenance. The crypt preserves relics of Saint Cerbonius, and stone reliefs on the casket narrate the story of this saint's life. Opposite the cathedral, the Palazzo Pretorio now houses an archeological museum.

From Massa Marittima, the route leads north to the area in which the river Cecina has its source. There, on a small, winding road, at an altitude of 774 meters, is **Gerfalco** ㊺, which was a fortress of the counts of Pannocchieschi in the 13th century, and was destroyed by an earthquake in 1502. Today, a few walls, or sections of walls, are all that remain. It is in the surrounding mountains that the red marble that was used to adorn the cathedral in Siena is quarried.

Towering above the town is the mountain of **Le Cornate**, at 1060 meters, the highest elevation in the Colline Metallifere. Local legend has it that this was the site of the Witches' Sabbath.

Continuing eastwards, you will come to **Montieri** ㊻, at an elevation of 704 meters, among chestnut trees. It is thought that Montieri stands atop the ruins of an Etruscan settlement. Around the year 1000, the town was a bone of contention between Volterra and Siena because both wanted control of its silver mines for the minting their coins. Emperor Frederick II also helped himself to the mines during the second half of the 12th century. Once the mines were exhausted, however, the town began to decline. Today, only its many 13th- and 14th-century buildings attest to its former wealth and glory. The Romanesque parish church of Santi Michele e Paolo, which was renovated in 1540, is worth seeing.

Shortly before the SS 441 intersects with the SS 73 (from Grosseto to Siena via Roccastrada) you can take a detour to the ★**Abbey of San Galgano** ㊼, not far from the road. You might recognize this, one of Tuscany's most impressive ruins, from Tarkowski's film *Nostalghia*. In the Middle Ages this monastery church, of which only the walls, facade, apse and columns remain standing today, was one

of the area's most important Cistercian abbeys. Decline set in, however, during the 16th century, and the Grand Duke of Tuscany dissolved the facility all together in 1783. If you have the time, try to visit this site at sunset, when this broad space, with its overgrown floor and its open ceiling, is illuminated with a special kind of light.

Just above these ruins, perched on top of a small hill, is the burial church of Saint Galgano. This round building is reminiscent of an Etruscan tumulus grave, and in the chapel, which is a later addition, you can see frescoes by Ambrogio Lorenzetti.

Roccastrada ④, on the SS 73, is the largest town in the northwestern part of the Maremma. It sits 475 meters high on a plateau of volcanic rock, from which you have a view across the Grosseto plain and the sea, all the way to Corsica. In the Middle Ages, Roccastrada was a center for

Above: Inside the ruins of the abbey of San Galgano. Right: Etruscan graves in Populonia.

silver and copper mining, and the remains of the old city walls testify to this. From Roccastrada, you can reach Grosseto and the sea by following the SS 73. You will pass a number of old mountain villages, such as Sticciano and **Montepescali**, which is known as the "balcony of the Maremma," and has a commanding view of the entire Grosseto coast. This is where the Greco-Roman hero Herakles (or Hercules) is supposed to have descended to the underworld.

From Roccastrada a small road leads 13 kilometers west to **Montemassi** ④. This medieval *borgo*, with a twice-fortified castle in its center, was once the Aldobrandeschi's most important fortress. The Sienese battle for the city, in 1328, has been immortalized and preserved in a mural by Simone Martini that hangs on a wall of Siena's Palazzo Communale.

On the way back to the Via Aurelia, a little road just past the town of Ribolla leads off to ★**Castel di Pietra** ⑤. It was here that Nino Pannocchieschi impris-

oned his first wife, Pia dei Tolomei, because he wanted to marry Margherita Aldobrandeschi.

Western Colline Metallifere

The Etruscan Maremma extended over the present border of the province and into Livorno, as the name *Riviera degli Etruschi*, or Etruscan coast, indicates.

Populonia was the only Etruscan city that was directly on the sea. Today, you get there by following the Via Aurelia and exiting at Venturina onto the road to **Piombino 🗲**, which lies at the southern end of the maquis-covered peninsula of Massoncello. In A.D. 809, refugees from Populonia founded the town on the spot where the Roman harbor of Falesia had once been located. At that point, the area belonged to the Gheradesca, who turned it over to Pisa in 1013. In 1399, Gherado D'Appiano created the independent principality of Piombino, which also included the islands of Montecristo, Pianosa and Elba. They were far from tranquil times,

because many people wanted to control the harbor and mines of Elba, including Alfonso d'Aragona, Cosimo del Medici, Cesare Borgia and Napoleon Bonaparte. After the principality was turned over to the Duchy of Tuscany in 1815, things became a good deal quieter in this city, which today, as then, has an economy that is based on iron processing. This industry is reflected in the skyline, which is dominated by factory chimneys.

Despite the chimneys, the old city, with its 15th-century Palazzo Communale and the 1377 church of Sant'Antimo, which contains a marble baptismal font by Andrea Guardi, is still pretty. From the terrace of the Piazza Bovia, which juts out into the sea, you can see the islands of Elba and Capraia, and ferries leave for Elba several times daily.

Populonia, 🗲, called *Pupluna* by the Etruscans, is just ten kilometers away, on the road to San Vincenzo. Its history is closely linked with that of the mining of iron ore on the island of Elba and in the Colline Metallifere. The city's heyday

was in the 7th century B.C., although excavations show that copper and bronze were processed here during the Villanova period. In the early Middle Ages, it became the seat of a bishopric, an honor that was transferred to Massa Marittima in A.D. 835. After 1339, it was incorporated into the principality of Piombino. The **fortress** with its restored tower and excellent view, and the remains of the city walls of the upper village **Populonia Alta**, some 180 meters above sea level, both date from this period.

A small **museum** displays Etruscan artifacts from the necropolises of the ★**Gulf of Baratti**. Today, a beautiful sandy swimming bay stands, in the shade of umbrella pines, where a 4th-century industrial center devoted to processing iron ore from Elba once stood. The ancient graves were discovered at the beginning of the 20th century, when people were trying to

Above: The easy pace of life in the village of Campiglia Marittima. Right: The geothermic power plant in Lardarello.

use some of the iron ore slag that was lying around the area.

Near the coastal road are the **Necropolises** of **San Cerbone**, which includes the *Tomba del Bronzetto di Offerente*, a grave shaped like an ancient house (6th-5th centuries B.C.) and the ★**Tomba dei Carri** (7th-6th centuries B.C.), a chamber grave under a 28-meter-wide burial mound with a number of burial sites at the end of a corridor. Many of the graves have been plundered in the course of the years, and everything that was left is displayed in the archeological museum in Florence.

Not far from the vacation town of **San Vincenzo**, tucked away amid the pines, is the exit to Campiglia Marittima. Leading off to the left, near a gravel pit, is a trail that leads to the ghost town of ★**Rocca San Silvestro** ㊵. This Gheradesca family fortress (ca. 1050) was abandoned around 1400 because the mines had been exhausted. Below Rocca is an excavation site where finds demonstrating how the Etruscans processed iron have been discovered. The entire area is now the

Parco Archeologico Minerario (Museum of Mining) and visitors can take tours of the mines.

Campiglia Marittima **54** is a beautiful little medieval city that is dominated by the ruins of a 12th-century castle. On a clear day, you can see from here all the way to Elba. The city doesn't have any particularly notable art works to offer, but its narrow winding streets, old houses, and stone arches make it well worth visiting. Especially attractive are the 15th-century **Palazzo Pretorio** and the church of San Lorenzo (13th century).

Not far away, between vineyards and olive groves, is **Suvereto 55**, which probably gets it name from the cork oak woods (*sughero*) that once covered the hills of this region. Here, in 1313, the corpse of Emperor Henry VII was cremated. His ashes were then taken to Pisa, where they were interred in the cathedral.

Following the Via Moncini, you will pass through the 14th-century Porta alle Sicili and enter the upper city. When the Sienese took over in 1335, they built a fortress around the **Castello Monte Regio**. Just behind the gate is the **Torre del Candeliere**, built by the free citizens of Massa in 1228. Here, in the upper city, is the church of Sant'Agostino (1313) and the former convent of Santa Chiara. In 1380, a son was born to the local Albizeschi family; he later became the Franciscan Saint Bernard.

Twenty kilometers north of Massa Marittima, on the SS 439 near Monterotondo Marittimo, sulfurous water bubbles up in the **Thermal Baths of Bagnolo 56**.

In *Larderello 57**, about 15 kilometers further north on the SS 439, the penetrating smell of sulfur also hangs in the air. At the same time, a number of crevices in the earth bubble and steam, creating a diabolical and hellish impression that has little to do with the usual cliché images of Tuscany.

In 1777, the German chemist Franz Höfer discovered that there was boric

Maremma

acid in the steaming pools of water, which reached temperatures of up to 230°C when heated by volcanic lava that was just under the earth's crust. Less than fifty years later, the Frenchman François Larderel started using this hot steam for industrial purposes. The town that sprung up near this industrial site bears his name to his day.

Since 1905, the steam has also been used to produce electricity. Like thick silver snakes, a tangle of steel pipes winds its way through the countryside, bypassing or connecting with cooling towers and an electric plant. Together with four other geothermic power plants in the Amiata region, so much electricity is produced here in the Valle del Diavolo (Devil's Valley) that the needs of a major city like Florence could easily be covered.

The Palazzina Larderel, built in 1818, houses a **Technical Museum** where you can learn more about the region and the development of the geothermic production of electricity.

PROVINCE OF GROSSETO

ALBERESE (☎ 0564)

Parco Naturale della Maremma, (Parco dell'Uccellina). In the summer only with a guided tour (July 1-Sept 30). At other times you can visit alone on Wed, Sat, Sun and holidays or with a guided tour. For additional information: tel: 407 098, fax: 407 278.

ARCIDOSSO (☎ 0564)

Aiuole, Loc.Le Aiole, tel: 967 300, fax: 966 747. Toscana, Via D. Lazzaretti 47, tel: 967 486, fax: 967 000. Da Lorena, Strada Provinciale 20, tel/fax: 967 162.

Parco Funistico del Monte Amiata, tel: 966 867 and 968 010, fax: 967720; Tue-Sun sunrise to sunset, closed Mon. Best season for hiking is early summer (richest floral beauty) and fall. Well-signed hiking trails and circular walks.

CAPALBIO (☎ 0564)

La Mimosa, Via Torino 34, tel/fax: 890 220. La Palma, Via della Stazione 5, tel/fax: 890 341. La Torricella, SS Aurelia kilometer 125, tel/fax: 890 083.

Da Maria, Via Comunale 3, tel: 896 014; closed Tue. Good, simple Maremma cuisine, tasty vegetable soufflé. La Vallerana, Loc. Vallerana, tel: 896 050; closed Wed. A simple family-run house near Capalbio that serves good traditional Maremma-style dishes.

Giardino dei Tarocchi. tel: 895 122, fax: 895 700. Only open May 15-Oct 23: Mon-Sat 2:30-6:30 pm, closed Sun.

CASTEL DEL PIANO (☎ 0564)

Impero, Via Roma 7, tel: 955 337, fax: 955 025.

Da Venerio, Piazza G. Carducci 18, tel/fax: 955 244. Amiata, Via D. Alighieri 10, tel/fax: 955 407.

CASTIGLIONE DELLA PESCAIA (☎0564)

L'Approdo, Via Ponte Giorgini 29, tel: 933 466, fax: 933 086. Riva del Sole, Loc. Riva del Sole, tel: 933 625, fax: 935 607.

Lucerna, Via IV Novembre 27, tel: 933 620, fax: 933 704. Roma, Via C. Colombo 14, tel: 933 542, fax: 931 175.

Aurora, Via F.lli Bandiera 19, tel: 933 718, fax: 934 358. Il Gambero, Via Ansedonia 29, tel/fax: 937 110.

Baia delle Rocchette, Loc. Rocchette, tel: 941 092, fax: 941 242. Rocchette, Loc. Rocchette, tel: 941 123, fax: 941 112. Santa Pomata, Strada delle Rocchette, tel: 941 037, fax: 941 221.

Corallo, Via Sauro 1, tel: 933 668; closed Tue. Excellent fish dishes in a small guesthouse. Reservations are a must, the earlier the better! La Portaccia, Via San Benedetto Po 13, tel: 935 318; closed Mon. Fresh fish

at moderate prices. Pizzeria Napoletana, Via Roma 5, tel: 935 059; open daily. Pretty location with nice view of the harbor.

FOLLONICA (☎ 0566)

Golfo del Sole, Via Italia 301, tel: 72 111, fax: 260 422. Lampada di Aladino, Via Firenze 10, tel: 53 535, fax: 53 558. Piccolo Mondo, Via Carducci 2, tel: 40 361, fax: 44 547.

Leonardo Cappelli, Piazza XXV Aprile 32, tel: 57 360; closed Sun dinner and Mon, except July and Aug. Elegant surroundings, first-class cuisine at fairly high prices, excellent wines.

Museo del Ferro e della Ghisa (Iron Museum), Area Ex-Ilva. Info about opening hours: tel: 59 201.

GROSSETO (☎ 0564)

APT, Via Fucini43, tel: 454 510/527, fax: 26 571. Tourism Office, Via Scrivia 10, tel: 484 111, fax: 281 063.

Bastiani Grand Hotel, Piazza Gioberti 64, tel: 20 047, fax: 29 321. Lorena, Via Trieste 3, tel/fax: 25 501.

Maremma, Via Fulceri de Calboli 11, tel: 22 293, fax: 22 051. Nuova Grosseto, Piazza Marconi 26, tel/fax: 414 105. San Lorenzo, Via Piave 22, tel: 27 918, fax: 25 338.

Quattro Strade, V. Aurelia Sud 1, tel/fax: 25 581. La Pace, Via della Pace 10, tel: 456 280. Mulinacci, Via Mazzini 78, tel: 28 419.

Canapone, Piazza Dante, tel: 24546; closed Sun. Traditional home-style cooking. La Buca San Lorenzo, Viale Manetti 1, tel: 25 142; closed Sun. Good fish dishes, imaginative combinations. Fairly expensive. Il Terzo Cerchio, Istia d'Ombrone, Piazza Castello 2, tel: 409 235; closed Mon. The daily menu is highly recommended. Prices are quite reasonable. Osteria del Ponte Rotto, Istia d'Ombrone, Via Scansanese 636, tel 409 373; closed Wed. Traditional Maremma cuisine, good fish. Il Pescatore da Pizzica, Via Orcagna 61, tel: 491 035; closed Sun. Pleasant family-run trattoria in an old farmhouse.

Roselle Archeological Excavation Site, tel: 402 403; 9:00 am-6:30 pm. Museo Archeologico e d'Arte della Maremma, Piazza Baccarini, Tue-Sun 9:00 am-1:00 pm and 4:00-6:00 pm (March 1 - April 30), 10:00 am-1:00 pm and 5:00-8:00 pm (May 2 - Oct 31), 9:00 am-1:00 pm (Nov 1 - Feb 28), closed Mon.

LARDERELLO (☎ 0588)

Geothermic Museum, Mon-Fri 9:00 am-12:30 pm and 1:30-6:00 pm, Sat and Sun 10:00 am-12:30 pm and 1:30-7:00 pm. Closed Jan 1, Easter and Christmas. For guided tours tel: 67 724.

MAGLIANO IN TOSCANA (☎ 0564)

Aurora, Chiasso Lavagnini 12/14, tel: 592 030;

closed Wed. Typical old city restaurant with traditional cuisine. **Sandra**, Via Garibaldi 20, tel: 592 196; closed Mon. Good food at decent prices in pleasant surroundings.

MANCIANO (☎ 0564)

Terme di Saturnia, Saturnia, Via della Follonata, tel: 601 061, fax: 601 266.

Il Boscaccio, Via P. Pascucci 9, tel: 620 283, fax: 620 380. **Villa Acquaviva**, Loc. Acquaviva, tel/fax: 602 890. **Rossi**, Via A. Gramsci 3, tel/fax: 629 248.

MASSA MARITTIMA (☎ 0566)

Il Sole, Corso della Libertà 43, tel: 901 971, fax: 901 959.

Duca del Mare, Piazza Dante Alighieri 1/2, tel: 902 284, fax: 901 905. **Il Girifalco**, Via Massetana Nord 25, tel/fax: 902 177.

Museo Archeologico (Archeological Museum) in Palazzo del Podestà. Medieval paintings and archeological finds. Tue-Sun 10:00 am-12:30 pm and 3:30-7:00 pm (April-Oct), 10:00 am-12:30 pm and 3:00-5:00 pm (Nov-March), closed Mon. **Museo della Miniera** (Mining Museum), Via Corridoni. Temporarily closed. Information tel: 902 289. **Museo di Arte e Storia della Miniera** (Museum of the Art and History of Mining), Piazza Matteotti. Temporarily closed.

MONTE ARGENTARIO (☎ 0564)

Baia d'Argento, Porto S. Stéfano, Loc. Pozzarello, tel/fax: 812 643. **Il Pellicano**, Porto Ercole, Loc. Lo Sbarcatello, tel: 833 801, fax: 833 418. **Villa Portuso**, Porto Ercole, Loc. Poggio Portuso, tel: 834 181, fax: 835 351.

Marina, P. Ercole, Lungomare A. Doria 30, tel: 833 123, fax: 836 057. **Belvedere**, Porto S. Stefano, Via Fortino 51, tel: 812 634.

MONTEMERANO (☎ 0564)

Caino, Via Canonica 3, tel: 602 817; closed Wed and Thu lunchtime. Good, home-style food.

ORBETELLO (☎ 0564)

Telamonio, Talamone, Piazza Garibaldi 4, tel: 887 008, fax: 887 380.

I Presidi, Via Mura di Levante 34, tel: 867 601/2, fax: 860 432. **Sole**, Via Colombo 2, tel: 860 410, fax: 860 475. **Piccolo Parigi**, Corso Italia 169, tel: 867 233, fax: 867 211.

Il Nocchino, Via del Mille 64, tel: 860 329; closed Wed during the winter. Good vegetable and fish dishes at moderate prices.

PITIGLIANO (☎ 0564)

Corano, Loc. Corano, SS Maremmana, tel/fax: 616 112. **Guastini**, Piazza Petruccioli 4, tel: 616 065, fax: 616 652.

PORTO SANTO STEFANO (☎ 0564)

Orlando, Via Breschi 3, tel: 812 788; closed Thu.

House specialty is fish soup, fair prices. **Siro**, Corso Umberto 1, tel: 812 538; closed Mon. Beautifully located with a view of the sea, fish dishes.

PUNTA ALA (☎ 0564)

Cala del Porto, Via del Pozzo, tel: 922 455, fax: 920 716. **Gallia Palace Hotel**, Via delle Sughere, tel: 922 022, fax: 920 229. **Golf Hotel**, Via del Gualdo 2, tel: 923 290, fax: 923 302.

ROCCASTRADA (☎ 0564)

Sant'Umberto, Loc. I Piloni, tel: 575 466, fax: 575 419.

SANTA FIORA (☎ 0564)

Eden, Via Roma 1 tel: 977 033. **Fiora**, Via Roma 8, tel: 977 043, fax: 978 154.

SATURNIA (☎ 0564)

Il Capriccio, Via del Poggio 113, tel: 607 711; Mon, Tue, Thu and Fri evenings only, Sat and Sun also lunch, closed Wed. Traditional cuisine, also exotic dishes such as snails and frogs legs.

Thermal Springs, downhill from the hotel.

SOVANA (☎ 0564)

Taverna Etrusca, Via Pretorio 16, tel: 616 183.

Scilla, Via Rodolfo Siviero 1/3, tel: 616 531; closed Tue. Traditional cuisine with homemade pasta dishes.

PROVINCE OF LIVORNO

CAMPIGLIA MARITTIMA (☎ 0565)

Rossi, Via Indipendenza 190, tel: 851 256. **I Cinque Lecci**, Via della Stazione 30, tel: 851 021.

Parco Archeologico Minerario San Silvestro, Via di S. Vincenzo 34B, tel: 838 680; Tue - Sun 9:00 am to 8:00 pm (June, July and Sept), daily 9:00 am to 8:00 pm (Aug), Sat, Sun and holidays 9:00 am-sunset (Oct - May).

LIVORNO (☎ 0586)

APT, Piazza Cavour 6, tel: 898 111, fax: 896 173. **Rex**, Loc. Antignano, Via del Littorale 164, tel: 580 400, fax: 509 586.

Gennarino, Viale Italia 301, tel: 803 109, fax: 803 450.

La Chiave, Scali delle Cantine 52, tel: 888 609; closed Wed. Good fish dishes, relatively high prices. Also see *INFO* page 190.

PIOMBINO (☎ 0565)

Ariston, Via Ferrer 7, tel/fax: 224 390. **Collodi**, Via Collodi 7, tel: 224 272, fax: 224 382. **Esperia**, Lungomare Marconi 27, tel/fax: 42 284.

POPULONIA (☎ 0565)

Parco Archeologico di Baratti, tel: 29 002; Tue-Sun 9:00 am-sunset (March-May), Wed-Mon 9:00 am-8:00 pm (June, July and Sept), daily 9:00 am-8:00 pm

Maremma

TUSCAN ARCHIPELAGO

ELBA
GÍGLIO
GIANNUTRI

Elba

The islands of Elba, Capraia, Gorgona, Pianosa, Montecristo and, further south, Gíglio and Giannutri, form the Tuscan Archipelago, which was once connected to the mainland. These "islands of pirates and saints," which are rich in history and legends, were inhabited as early as 50,000 B.C. Today, they guarantee visitors idyllic opportunities for undisturbed swimming.

Some of the islands are uninhabited, while others, like Pianosa and Gorgona, which once housed prisons, are closed to tourists. Montecristo is a bird sanctuary and a permit is required for visits.

**ELBA

The largest of the islands, Isola d' Elba, covers an area of 223 square kilometers and is just ten kilometers from the mainland. To the west, the countryside is almost Alpine in character, with a kind of stark, intense beauty. Contrasting with this is the agricultural character of central Elba, with its low hills, and the terraced countryside in the east, which was built up over the years with residue from the iron mines. Its mild climate and beautiful

Preceding Pages: In Gíglio Castello on Isola del Gíglio. Left: Making oyster-baskets on the island of Elba.

swimming coves make Elba a popular vacation destination.

Elba's (from Latin *ilva*, iron) rich resources of iron ore have always made it a desirable object. Early on, the Etruscans shipped the metalliferous rock to the mainland, where there were more trees to fire their kilns. Later, unhappy with the Etruscans' monopoly in the iron trade, the Romans made Elba one of the first objectives in their conquest of Etruria.

The island was also a bone of contention in conflicts between the northern Barbarians and southern pirates. During the 11th century, under the Pisans, things calmed down. Yet, in 1392, when Elba was incorporated into the Principality of Piombino, its troubles began again. In the history books, Elba is noted as the site of Napoleon Bonaparte's exile in 1814, and his departure point for Waterloo ten months later. Finally, in 1815, Elba was given to the Grand Duchy of Tuscany. The island's blast furnaces were destroyed in World War II, and since then, tourism has been its main industry.

Coming from Piombino or Livorno (Leghorn) you land at the island's capital of **Portoferráio ❶**. Construction of this city on a rocky promontory in the north of the island began in 1548, under Cosimo di Medici. It became a masterpiece of military architecture with a circular wall

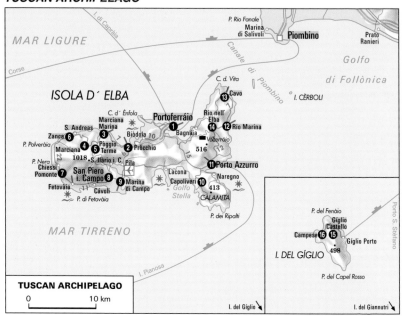

TUSCAN ARCHIPELAGO

0   10 km

that starts at the old port; an octagonal watchtower; **Forta Stella**, shaped like a star; and **Forta Falcone**, set above the rest, and from which there is a fine view.

The **Porta a Mare**, or Medicea, is the gate to the old city. Along Via Garibaldi, past the city hall, where you can find a granite Roman sacrificial altar in the courtyard, you come to the **Villa dei Mullini** – once Napoleon's city residence, today a museum. The exiled emperor also spent part of his 300 days on Elba in the **Villa San Martino**, located just off the road to Procchio. The Neo-Classical facade was later added by Prince Demidoff, who also assembled the **Napoleon Collection**.

If you feel like a refreshing swim after visiting the museum, there are the city beaches **Le Viste** (sand and rocks) and **Le Ghiaie** (gravel), a picturesque bay with a gravel beach at the camp site **Camping Enfola**, and one of Elba's most beautiful sand beaches at the **Gulf of Biodola**.

Right: Fishing boats in Portofino's harbor.

If you follow the winding road, you come to **Prócchio ❷**, a busy vacation resort with a white sand beach. From here, you can take a short trip to the Etruscan mountain settlement of **Monte Castello**. Charred remains of houses were discovered hidden under Roman cobblestones, a sign that the village was not abandoned in a wholly peaceful manner.

Seven kilometers further, you come to **Marciana Marina ❸**. Its 12th-century Saracen tower, the **Torre Pisano**, can be seen from afar, and its quaint old city quarter and lively seaside promenade are popular vacation spots. Marciana Marina was once the harbor for the small town of **Marciana ❹**, defensively located 400 meters higher. Marcian was the seat of the Appiani, from where they ruled their Principality of Piombino between 1399 and 1634. The Casa degli Appiani (15th century) and the mint, where the princes coined their gold and silver pieces, both date from this period. Located amid terraced vineyards and dense forests, and due to its narrow streets with many stairs,

 Info p. 177

Elba

it can best be explored on foot. A small archeological museum displays finds from the area, and near the 15th-century fortress by the city gates, a well-marked path leads to the island's oldest pilgrimage chapel, **Madonna del Monte**, with its miracle-working picture of the Madonna (15th century). A **cable car** runs from Marciana to the summit of **Monte Capanne**, which at 1018 meters is the highest point on the island.

Not far from Marciana is the terraced spa town of **Poggio Terme** ❺, known for its spring of curative mineral waters, the Fonte Napoleone. Churchill, di Chirico and Delacroix are among the many who have vacationed here. The town makes a good departure point for hikes up Monte Capanne or visits to the hermitage of **San Cerbone**, where the Bishop of Populonia retreated when he was fleeing from the Lombards in A.D. 572. The path that leads there starts at the town's cemetery.

From here, a road leads inland, through chestnut and pine forests, to **Monte Perone** (630 meters), whose flat peak af-fords a good view of the entire island. West of Marciana, the coastal road winds along the steep slopes of Monte Giove. The vacation resorts of **Zanca** ❻ and **Sant'Andrea** have tiny sand beaches, and there is excellent diving off the coast.

Roman and Greek artifacts from ancient shipwrecks have been salvaged all along the west coast, a reminder of how treacherous the sea here can be. It is difficult to reach the coast from the road, but there is a path that leads to the lighthouse Faro di Punta near **Patresi Mare**. Just before Chiessi, you reach **Punta Nera**, the island's westernmost point. **Pomonte** ❼ is a modest seaside resort with a rocky coast and gravel beach. It is a good starting point for hikers who want to explore the island's mountainous interior.

After the long stretch of rocky coast, the white sand beaches of the resorts of Fetovaia, Seccheto and Cávoli are very appealing. Two kilometers past Cávoli is the road to **San Piero in Campo** ❽. Its two-aisled Romanesque church of San Nicolò (12th century) has 14th- and 15th-

century frescoes. Nearby, the charming mountain village of **Sant'Ilario in Campo** is worth visiting.

Marina di Campo ❾ has everything a tourist's heart desires: a seaside promenade, a sand beach, shops, fishing boat and yacht harbors, even a surfing and sailing school. The main attraction in the neighboring town of Lacona is Spiaggia Grande, a wide, sandy beach.

Continue past Golfo Stella, with its small beaches and coves, and you will come to the **Calamita Peninsula**, the part of the island richest in natural mineral resources. The magnetite ore in Monte Calamita is said to affect the compasses of passing ships. Surface iron ore mining gradually transformed the hills here into a terraced landscape of vineyards and olive groves. A winding road leads to the town of **Capoliveri ❿**, a picturesque hilltop town that is popular with visitors and surrounded by vineyards. Its crooked side

Above: Discussing the latest happenings in Gíglio Castello.

streets converge at the town square. *Caput Liberum*, the mountain of liberty, was a place of refuge for Roman citizens in trouble with the law. By the sea, 140 meters below, is the 16th-century pilgrimage church of **Madonna delle Grazie**. At the far end of the peninsula, around which you can bicycle on a trail that is open only to local traffic, there are small swimming beaches and the *Costa dei Gabbiani*, a nature preserve.

Opposite Capoliveri on the east coast is the Spanish **Forte Focardo** (1678) with its flat sand beaches. Across the bay is the vacation port of **Porto Azzurro ⓫**. The nearby pilgrimage church, which houses a replica of the black **Madonna di Monserrat**, was built by the Spanish.

The northern part of eastern Elba is known for its rare minerals, and experts and laypeople alike will find plenty of interest in the collections in the town of **Rio Marina ⓬**. The history of this town has been linked to iron ore mining for 2500 years. Early on, it was a loading port, and the octagonal watchtower, which was built in 1534, served as the town's first line of defense. Built of stone that, because of its high iron content, actually rusts, most of the residential houses were constructed around 1800 when the administration of the ore mines was moved to Rio nell'Elba. With the closing of the mines in 1982, the fate of the town was sealed.

On the northern tip of the island, the neighboring town of **Cavo ⓭**, which was popular even with the Romans as a summer residence, is where the mine directors lived. From here, the road passes south through lush greenery as well as barren country to **Rio nell'Elba ⓮**.

Every building in this town is built like a small fortress because the inhabitants had to defend themselves against pirate attacks or enemy siege. Today, the small houses where the miners once lived are summer cottages. From here, an unpaved road leads to the **Bay of Nisportino**, with its small, sandy beach, and the tourist center of Nisporto.

On the way back to Portoferraio, a road to the ruins of **Volterraio** branches off just after Bagnaia. Located at an elevation of 400 meters, this 13th-century island landmark was built by the Pisans, supposedly upon the ruins of an Etruscan settlement. For a long time, this fortress with a commanding view of the bay was the safest point on all of Elba. (For the ascent, which takes about 30 minutes, you should only use the marked trail, from the southwest. Do not try to climb down from the viewpoint further up the road because there is a real danger of falling!). Shortly before returning to Portoferráio, near the **San Giovanni Thermal Baths**, you will pass the Roman **Villa delle Grotte**.

★GÍGLIO AND GIANNUTRI

Gíglio, measuring just 21 square kilometers, is the archipelago's second-largest island. Ferries run the 14 kilometers from Porto Santo Stefano several times daily. The inaccessible coast, which has few beaches, is popular with divers. Tourism and farming fuel the economy.

This rocky island is overgrown with maquis and has three main towns. Gíglio Porto is the port on the east coast. **Gíglio Castello** ⓯ is a charming little inland town with narrow winding streets, a 13th-century fortress, and an ivory sculpture of Christ by Giambologna in its parish church. And **Campese** ⓰, on the west coast, sports the picturesque Torre del Campese, which was used as a defense against the attacks of barbarian pirates.

Giannutri (2.6 square kilometers), the southernmost of Tuscany's islands, is inhabited only in summer. The island has the ruins of a 1st-century B.C. Roman villa, and around A.D. 1000, Cistercian monks arrived. At the end of the 19th century, Captain Gualtiero Adami voluntarily lived here for 40 years, as a kind of modern-day Robinson Crusoe.

ELBA (☎ 0565)

CAMPO NELL'ELBA
🛏️ 😊😊 **Montecristo**, Via Nomellini 11, tel: 976 861, fax: 976 597. **Hotel dei Coralli**, Viale degli Etruschi 81, tel: 976 336, fax: 977 748.

CAPOLIVERI
🛏️ 😊😊 **Antares**, Loc. Lido, tel: 940 131, fax: 940 084. 😊 **La Voce del Mare**, Loc. Naregno, tel/fax: 968 455. **Miramare**, Loc. Pareti, tel/fax: 968 673.
❌ **Il Chiasso**, Via Sauro 9, tel: 968 709; closed Tue in the winter. Fish dishes, fairly expensive.

MARCIANA
🛏️ 😊😊😊 **Desirée**, Loc. Spartaia, tel: 907 311, fax: 907 884. 😊😊 **Corallo**, Loc. Pomonte, tel: 906 042, fax: 907 270. **Delfino**, Loc. Procchio, tel: 907 455.

MARCIANA MARINA
🛏️ 😊😊😊 **Gabbiano Azzurro II**, Viale Amedeo 94, tel: 997 035, fax: 997 034. 😊😊 **La Conchiglia**, Via XX Sett. 43, tel: 99 016, fax: 99 488. **Marinella**, Viale Margherita 38, tel: 99 018, fax: 996 875.

PORTO AZZURRO
🛏️ 😊😊 **Belmare**, Banch. IV Nov. 21, tel: 95 012, fax: 958 245. **Cala di Mola**, Loc. Mola, tel: 95 225.

PORTOFERRÁIO
ℹ️ **APT**, Calata Italia 26, tel: 914 671.
🛏️ 😊😊 **Airone Hotel**, Loc. San Giovanni, tel: 929 111, fax: 917 484. **Hermitage**, Loc. Biodola, tel: 936 911, fax: 969 984. 😊 **Grotte del Paradiso**, Loc. Le Grotte, tel: 933 057, fax: 933 452. **Punta Pina**, Loc. Bagnaia, tel: 961 077, fax: 961 191.
❌ **Emanuel**, Loc. Enfola, tel: 939 003; closed Wed in the winter. Good fish restaurant.
🏛️ **Napoleon Museum**, Villa dei Mulini, Mon-Sat 9:00 am-7:00 pm (4:00 pm Nov-March), Thu-Sat till midnight (July & Aug), Sun 9:00 am-1:00 pm.

RIO MARINA
🛏️ 😊😊😊 **Ortano Mare**, Loc. Ortano, tel: 939 160, fax: 939 154. 😊😊 **Cristallo**, Loc. Cavo, tel: 949 898, fax: 949 960. **Maristella**, Loc. Cavo, tel/fax: 949 859. **Rio**, Via Palestro 31, tel: 924 225.

SAN MARTINO
🏛️ **Napoleon Museum**, Res. Estiva, Loc. S. Martino, Mon-Sat 9:00 am-7:00 pm (4:00 pm Nov-March), Thu-Sat till midnight (July & Aug), Sun 9 am-1 pm.

GÍGLIO (☎ 0564)

PORTO
🛏️ 😊😊 **Arenella**, Via Arenella 5, tel: 809 340. **Castello Monticello**, Via Provinciale, tel: 809 252.

CAMPESE
🛏️ 😊😊 **Campese**, Via della Torre 18, tel: 804 003.

ALONG THE ETRUSCAN COAST TO LUCCA

ETRUSCAN RIVIERA

LIVORNO

PISA / PROVINCE OF PISA

LUCCA

ETRUSCAN RIVIERA

Steep, or gentle and sandy; lined with pine forests; the "Etruscan shoreline," or *Riviera degli Etruschi*; the stretch of coast that reaches from Piombino to Livorno, has something to offer everyone. There are tempting opportunities for swimmers; in the hilly hinterland, architecture and history buffs can explore the small fortified towns that grew up around monasteries and *castelli* in the Middle Ages; and there is plenty to occupy lovers of nature.

Take the SS 1 northward, and turn right eight kilometers after the resort of San Vincenzo, to **Castagneto Carducci ❶**. This town was named for author and Nobel Prize winner Giosuè Carducci, who spent his youth here and in neighboring Bólgheri. By the year 1000, the aristocratic Lombard family Gherardesca had taken possession of the *castello* outside the city gates. They still own the castle ruins in **Donoratico**, and the fortress in ***Bólgheri ❷**, which is linked to the SS 1 by a famous five-kilometer-long avenue that is lined with cypress trees.

Near La California, a road leads up into the hills and to the picturesque town of

Preceding Pages: Evening in Marina di Pisa. Left: A view of Pisa's cathedral and baptistry from the Leaning Tower.

Guardistallo ❸. In 1846, an earthquatke destroyed ts 11th-century fortress, but the medieval town center, with its narrow, winding streets has remained intact. From here, you can look down to the sea and the plains around **Cecina ❹**, near the mouth of the river of the same name, the source of which is in the hills around Volterra. In 1818, only one man lived here, but the town is now a popular vacation destination for Italian families who fill the long, inviting gravel beach of the swimming resort **Marina di Cecina** every August. An archeological museum with Etruscan finds from the Cecina valley is located in the neighboring town of **Rosignano Marittimo ❺**, in the Palazzo Bombardieri.

LIVORNO (LEGHORN)

The foundation stone of present-day **Livorno ❻** was laid on March 28, 1577, at the behest of Cosimo I di Medici. His reason for reestablishing the old town of *Liberna* at the defensive tower **Mastio di Matilda** (1103) was to replace the former Roman naval base of Portus Pisanus, which was Pisa's harbor during the Middle Ages, but which had since become unusable. The architect Buontalenti drew a new city plan that had both the **Fortezza Nuova** and the cathedral within pentago-

ETRUSCAN
RIVIERA

0   10 km

nal city walls. In 1534, the 11th-century Fortezza Vecchia was expanded by Antonio di Sangallo. Livorno soon flourished, and during the 18th century it became the second-largest city in Tuscany, a position it still holds today.

From an art-historical perspective, the modern, busy city has little to offer, since many of the old city's buildings were destroyed during World War II. Still worth visiting, though, are the Medici monuments, the Quartiere Venezia and the old sailors' and fishermen's quarter, which is crisscrossed with canals. Everything else in Livorno revolves around the harbor, Tuscany's largest commercial and passenger port. Ferries leave here for Elba, Corsica, Sardinia and Sicily.

At the beginning of the 20th century, the painters Amadeo Modigliani and Giovanni Fattori, whose works now hang in the **Museo Civico Giovanni Fattori** in the Villa Fabricotti on Via della Liberta, helped bring the city a degree of fame. The museum also houses a collection of archeological finds.

Halfway between Livorno and Pisa begins the nature preserve of **Migliarino**, where wild boar and fallow deer can be seen between the oaks and pines. On its southern edge rises the magnificent Romanesque basilica of **San Piero a Grado**, which was built in the 11th century on the remains of a previous Lombard construction (6th century). In the interior of the church, which has a three-aisled nave with three apses in the east and one in the west, there are frescoes depicting scenes from the life of Saint Peter and portraits of the popes.

★★PISA

In ancient times, the Arno River flowed into a lagoon off the sea, which silted up during the Middle Ages. On the south bank of this lagoon, on the site of present-day Livorno, Emperor Augustus founded the naval base of Portus Pisanus. On the opposite bank, **Pisa **❼**, a settlement that existed as early as the days of the Etruscans, developed. After the fall of the Western Roman Empire in A.D. 476, all of Tuscany suffered under the attacks of plundering invaders – cities and rural areas alike became destitute and depopulated. Only the seaport of Pisa, now 12 kilometers inland, and the Lombard town of Lucca escaped this fate. Pisa was even able to expand its marine supremacy. Its fleet successfully defended itself against the Saracens, and in 1063, it defeated the Arabs at Palermo, after which, Pisa was undisputed ruler of the Mediterranean. It developed trade connections and increased its wealth unchecked. This led to a significant upswing of art and culture between the 11th and 13th centuries, and the Pisan Romanesque style was soon reflected by architecture throughout the Mediterranean.

On land, Pisa's enemies were the cities of Lucca and Florence, both of which wanted free access to the sea. At sea, the city's main competitors were Amalfi and Genoa, with the latter finally dealing Pisa a devastating defeat in 1284. The powerful maritime republic of Pisa never recovered from this blow. Not until the 16th century did Pisa experience a revival, after Medici patronage led to the building of houses, bridges, and a connecting canal to the sea, in addition to the expansion of the city's university.

If you enter the old city through the west gate of the medieval city walls, you will find the vast and awe-inspiring piazza **Campo dei Miracoli ❶** spreading out to your left. Nearby, the cathedral, baptistry, famous leaning bell tower, or campanile, and monumental city cemetery, are richly decorated with white Carrara marble, with blind arches on the ground floors, and elevated passages with arches and pillars.

Above: Cypress trees line the five-kilometer-long road to Bólgheri.

Along the Etruscan Coast to Lucca

Construction of the cathedral began in 1064, financed by the spoils of the battle in Palermo. To give himself room to play with, the architect Buscheto, whose background was Byzantine, chose a building site on the edge of town. Popular wisdom had it that one motivation for this choice was to make the neighboring Lucchese jealous. Unfortunately, it rapidly became clear, even in the course of construction, that the swampy alluvial land was not an ideal surface on which to build. Solid proof of this fact is the city's hallmark, the Leaning Tower.

The **Cathedral ❷** consists of a five-aisled nave, expanded by Rainaldus in the 12th century; a three-aisled transept; and a presbytery that is rounded off by an apse. The cruciform church was crowned with an oval dome, which was unique at that time. You enter through bronze doors dating from around 1180, with reliefs depicting scenes from the lives of the Virgin and Christ. The two-tone pointed arches that line the nave echo the architecture of Islamic mosques; the mosaic of the apse,

part of which was executed by the painter Cimabue (1302), also betrays Byzantine influence. The pulpit, by Giovanni Pisano (1302-1311), is decorated with dramatic reliefs depicting scenes from the New Testament; this masterpiece, however, was broken in 1559, and the restoration that was carried out in 1929 was not quite true to the original. In the right transept is the tomb of Henry VII, Holy Roman Emperor and patron of the city, who died in Buonconvento in 1313. Further treasures are displayed in the Museo dell'Opera del Duomo, the cathedral's museum.

In planning the artistic decoration of the ****Baptistry** ❸ (1153), the architect Diotisalvi remained true to the plan of the cathedral's facade, with blind arches and a columned gallery. The Gothic stylistic elements were added by Giovanni and Nicola Pisano a century later. Not until 1358 was the baptistry, with its vaulted roof, finished and topped with the figure

Above: A relief sculpture on the door of the Baptistry in Pisa.

of Christ that you see today. The baptismal font is by Guido Bigarelli (1246). The real showpiece, a hexagonal pulpit by Nicola Pisano, is the first example of Gothic sculpture in Italy. Its reliefs depict scenes from the New Testament.

In 1173, construction began on the famous **Leaning Tower**, the 55-meter-high ****Campanile** ❹, with its 180 columns, according to designs by either Diotisalvi or Bonanno. But, because the alluvial sand kept giving way during construction, it wasn't completed until a century later. Attempts to compensate for the tilt by actually bending the tower in the other direction proved unsuccessful. Recent attempts to stop, and even reverse the leaning of the tower appear to have been successful and it is expected to re-open to visitors in 2001.

Begun in 1277, the cemetery of **Campo Santo Monumentale** ❺, completes the ensemble of the "Square of Miracles." A colonnade surrounds the elongated courtyard of this rectangular, walled site that is filled with soil supposedly brought

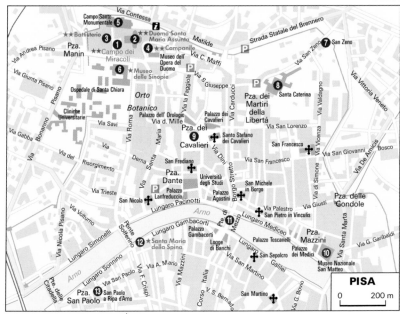

Along the Etruscan Coast to Lucca

from the Holy Land. Gravestones are set into the ground, while on the wall you can make out remains of the frescoes that were almost completely destroyed during World War II. Sketches of these frescoes, which are displayed in the **★Museo delle Sinopie** ❻ on the opposite side of the Campo, show just how much was lost.

Because of the overwhelming impression made by the Campo dei Miracoli, it is easy to lose sight of the fact that the city has other things to offer. Furthermore, there doesn't seem to be much interest in trying to acquaint visitors with other parts of the city. Signs to other points of interest are few and far between. If you want to get to know Pisa, therefore, arm yourself with a good city map and the curiosity of an explorer.

There is, for instance, the Benedictine church of **San Zeno** ❼ (10th/11th centuries), located at the east gate of the old city. Even the Pisans didn't really discover it until 1972, when the stucco was removed. Restoration exposed a facade of yellow tuff stone that is adorned with Ro-

man capitals. Its vestibule, which resembles a portico, is rather unusual.

On the nearby Piazza Martiri di Libertà is the 13th-century Dominican church of **Santa Caterina** ❽, with a Romanesque marble facade with blind arches and a rose window. The sculpture on the main altar is by Nino Pisano. From the opposite side of this square, Via San Lorenzo leads to the **Piazza dei Cavalieri** ❾, the center of maritime Pisa. In the 16th century, the order of the Knights of Saint Stephen commissioned Giorgio Vasari to redesign the square. Accordingly, the palace of the Anziani family became the Palazzo dei Cavalieri with a painted facade (today, it houses the renowned Scuola Normale Superiore), while two medieval towers were turned into the Palazzo dell' Orologio. In the Hunger Tower, Count Ugolino della Gherardesca, held responsible for the city's defeat by the Genoese in 1284, was sentenced to starve to death. Vasari also built a church on this square.

Follow the shopping street Via Oberdan, with its splendid arcades, and you will reach the banks of the Arno. Housed in a former Benedictine convent at Lungarno Medoceo, **Museo Nazionale San Matteo** ⑩ displays Tuscan, specifically Pisan, sculptures and paintings, featuring painted wooden crosses (12th/13th centuries) and original architectural models of the baptistry.

You can cross the Arno on the single-arched **Ponte di Mezzo** ⑪, site of the historic festival *Gioco del Ponte* every June. On the riverbank is the church of ***Santa Maria della Spina** ⑫, which is basically an oversized stone reliquary for a small thorn thought to be from Jesus' crown. This small church with ornate Gothic gables, the only surviving 14th-century religious building, had to be moved in 1871 because of the rising waters of the Arno.

Further downriver in a westerly direction, is **San Paolo a Ripa d'Arno** ⑬, a monastery church of the Vallombrosan order, with a two-tone marble facade and the same architectural elements as the cathedral. This jewel of 12th-century Pisan Romanesque architecture includes the octagonal chapel of Sant'Agata with its pyramidal dome.

PROVINCE OF PISA

The area surrounding Pisa also profited from the fortunes of the maritime republic. Around the year 1000, this territory began to fill up with people. Settlements were founded and fortresses and churches built. Development was furthered by the steady stream of travelers along the trade route of the Frankish Road.

The hilly region of Monte Pisano, foothills of the Apuan Alps, extends between Pisa and Lucca. The resort town of **San Guiliano Terme** ❽, a former Roman spa, is the area's largest community. Well into the 19th century, it was popular with the aristocracy, who built their summer villas

Right: The beautiful view of Lucca from the Torre Guinigi.

here. A typical example is the 16th-century Villa Roncioni, surrounded by a romantic park, in the Pugnano quarter.

East of Pisa, in the Valle Graziosa, is **Calci** ❾, a town with a turbulent history. The site has been occupied by Etruscans, Romans, Lombards, Pisans and Florentines, in turn. It is also said to be the place where, in 1375, Saint Catherine persuaded the British plunderer John Hawkwood to place his troops in the service of the church. Noteworthy sights here are the Pisan Romanesque parish church (11th/12th centuries), a gem of sacral architecture, and the nearby **Certosa di Calci**. This monastery was founded in 1399, but didn't receive its present Baroque appearance until the 17th century. Its cloisters and fresco-decorated halls can only be visited with an official guide. Also, a museum of nature and local history recently opened.

On the steep slopes of Monte Verucca (587 meters), behind the Carthusian monastery, are the ruins of the abbey of San Michele and a fortress that was razed in 1342. It is said that an underground passageway connects the fortress with a watchtower in Caprona, and even with distant Pisa, but there is still no proof.

From Calci, a winding road passes Trecolli and leads to the medieval fortress of **Vicopisano** ⑩, a possession of the Bishop of Lucca since the 10th century. The 13th-century towers that rise above the houses were restored by Brunelleschi after Florence conquered the town in 1407. The Romanesque parish church houses valuable wooden sculptures.

You can also glimpse the living past in the small villages nestled in the mountains south of the Arno, where the people make a living from their vineyards and olive groves. **Pontedera** ⑪, however, is known for its role in more recent history. This is where Vespas, the motor scooters that have been virtually synonymous with the Italian way of life since the 1950s, are produced.

Approximately 16 kilometers south of Pontedera is **Casciana Terme** ⑫, where Roman citizens, and later the Margravine Mathilde, went to be treated for gout and rheumatism. Passing Lari and the former Pisan castle Ponsacco, from which you can detour to the nearby Medici Villa Camugliano (1533), you will return to the expressway connecting Pisa to Florence.

**LUCCA

Just 20 kilometers separate Pisa and Lucca. But the two cities aren't so much separated by Monte Pisano, as much as by a long history of rivalry that led to frequent warlike conflicts. Halfway between them is the Nozzano Castle, which was built in 1126, by Matilda of Canossa, to ward off Pisan attacks. In the neighboring town of Ripafratta, Pisa built a defensive castle for exactly the same purpose.

A Roman military base with streets laid out in a chessboard pattern, with a forum and amphitheater, standing on the swampy soil of the Serchio valley – that was **Lucca** ⑬ in 180 B.C. (*luk* is Etruscan for marsh). In A.D. 568, the Lombards chose this town to be their capital in Tuscia. They left behind a number of Romanesque churches and the pilgrimage road *Francigena*, a route that was beneficial to the Lucchese's cloth trade. During the 11th century, Lucca's citizens declared their city politically autonomous and expanded their sphere of influence to include Versilia and the Garfagnana. With a few brief interruptions, Lucca remained an independent republic until 1799, when the French marched in. The city was appointed to the duchy of Parma in 1815, and after 1847, belonged to the Grand Duchy of Tuscany.

The impressive fortification wall with its 11 bastions, measuring more than four kilometers in length, up to 30 meters in width, and standing 12 meters high, completely encircles the city. In the days of the Romans, the town already boasted a city wall, albeit of far more modest proportions, of which you can still see a few remains. In the late Middle Ages, a sec-

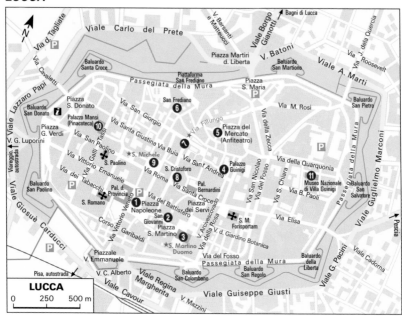

ond circular wall was built to encompass the suburbs of Santa Maria Forisportam in the east, and San Frediano in the north.

Today, the center of Lucca is the tree-shaded **Piazza Napoleone** ❶ and its magnificent **Palazzo Ducale** (Ducal Palace), begun in 1578 and continually renovated ever since. Via Duomo, on which the church of **San Giovanni** ❷ is located, also starts at the piazza. Until the 8th century, this church was the seat of the bishopric. The present-day construction dates from the 13th century, but the rectangular baptistry, with its lancet arch cupola, was added a hundred years later. The facade was added around 1600. Recent excavations in the church's interior have unearthed Roman remains. Nearby is one of Italy's oldest churches, the ★**Cathedral of San Martino** ❸ (6th century). It was fundamentally changed early in the 12th century, and a campanile was added in 1233. On the ground floor of the Roman-

Right: The Piazza dell'Anfiteatro echoes the oval of the former Roman amphitheater.

esque facade, with three stories of blind arches, three columned arcades lead into the vestibule. The stone labyrinth on the right pillar is a symbol of *Francigena*, the pilgrimage road. By peering through two hatches in the portals, travelers, who had to leave town before sunrise, could take one last look at the face of Jesus on the wooden crucifix that is known as the *Volto Santo*. This sculpture, which is borne through the city in a ceremonial procession every September, is one of the most famous works of Christianity. Popes and kings have come to Lucca just to see it, and according to a legend that is recounted by the frescoes on the inner side of the facade, it is the work of one of Jesus' apostles and miraculously turned up in Lucca in the 11th century.

Yet another world-famous work of artis housed inside the church: the marble tomb of Ilaria del Carretto by the Sienese sculptor Jacopo della Quercia. It was commissioned in 1406, by the ruler Paolo Guinigi, in memory of his wife, who died prematurely. In the aisle on the right, a

painting by Tintoretto depicts the disciples of Jesus at the Last Supper (1590).

Just behind the cathedral, Via Arcivescovato leads to the **Palazzo Guinigi ❹**. In Lucca, it is said that the most powerful man is he who can see the farthest, and indeed, from the observation platform atop the 230 steps of the **Guinigi Tower**, you can actually see the entire city and surrounding area, and thus have the feeling that things are under control.

Via Guinigi runs into Via Mordini, which follows the course of the old Roman wall. This is where the Roman amphitheater, incorporated into residential dwellings during the Middle Ages, once stood. This explains the elliptical shape of **Piazza del Mercato ❺** (Anfiteatro). Behind the piazza is the church of **San Frediano ❻**, with a 12th-century **mosaic** on its facade. The campanile and the high interior with an open roof truss are typical of the Lucchese Romanesque style. In the first side chapel on the right, there is a 12th-century baptismal font, and to the back, on the left, in the Trenta Chapel,

there is a marble altar by Jacopo della Quercia (1422).

From here, ★**Via Fillunga ❼**, which is lined with pretty shops, leads back to the center of town. Set into the plain facade of the church of **San Cristoforo ❽** is an iron cross that is comprised of two measuring-sticks. This was used, in case of doubt, to determine whether or not a cloth dealer had sold a customer short. If he had, his stand was smashed to pieces, or *bancarotta* – hence the word bankrupt. Via Roma ends at what was once the site of the Roman forum, the Piazza San Michele. Today it is the site of the church of ★**San Michele in Foro ❾** (12th century), a stone expression of the pride of citizens who erected it in defiance of the bishop's power. The facade, with its blind arches and pillars, is reminiscent of the cathedral in Pisa. Its decorative highlight is the ornate facade with its four-story pillared gallery.

From here, it isn't far to the birthplace of the opera composer Giacomo Puccini (*Tosca*, *La Bohème*) on Via Poggio. Also

nearby, on Via Galli Tassi, is the city palace of the Mansis (17th century), home of the **State Gallery of Paintings** ⑩. However, it is the **National Museum** ⑪ in the **Villa Guinigi** (1418), on Via della Quarquonia, that lovers of art from earlier periods enjoy the most. It display Etruscan and Roman sculptures, Lombard jewelry, and of course, examples of the Lucchese weavers' art.

Grandiose villas of rich city merchants are a typical feature of the countryside around Lucca. The parks are lavishly decorated with statues, flower beds in geometric patterns, waterworks, and topiary labyrinths. Some fine examples are located northeast of the SP 435 in the direction of Pescia. In particular, the **Villa Mansi**, near Segromigno Monte, and the **Villa Reale** in Marlia, which had one of the most famous estate gardens during the 17th century. Near Camigliano, the park at **Villa Torrigiani** (16th century) is also a masterpiece of landscape gardening.

Above: On the Piazza San Michele.

RIVIERA DEGLI ETRUSCHI

CASTAGNETO CARDUCCI (☎ 0565)
🛏 ⊖⊖ **La Torre di Donoratico**, Loc. La Torre 42, tel/fax: 775 268. **Zi' Martino**, Loc. S. Giusto, tel: 766 000, fax: 763 444. **Hotel il nuovo Bambolo**, Via del Bambolo 31, tel: 775 206, fax: 775 346.

🅰 **Belmare**, Via del Forte 1, tel/fax: 744 092, during the peak season tel/fax: 744 264. **International Etruria**, Via della Pineta, tel: 744 254, fax: 744 494.

❌ **Da Zi' Martino**, Loc. S. Giusto 264, tel: 763 666; closed Mon. Trattoria at the exit to Bolgheri. **Da Ugo**, Via Pari 3A, tel: 763 746; closed Mon in the winter. Serves game specialties and offers an excellent selection of wines.

ROSIGNANO MARITTIMO (☎ 0586)
🛏 ⊖⊖⊖ **Villa Parisi**, Via Romolo Monti 10, tel: 751 698, fax: 751 167. ⊖⊖ **Atlantico**, Via D. Martelli 8/12, tel: 752 440, fax: 752 494. **Miramare**, Via Marconi 8, tel: 752 435, fax: 751 151.

🅰 **Campo dei Fiori**, Loc. Campo del Fiori, tel: 770 096, fax: 770 323. **Tripesce**, Via Cavalleggeri 88, tel: 788 167, fax: 789 159.

SAN VINCENZO (☎ 0565)
🛏 ⊖⊖⊖ **Park Hotel I Lecci**, Via d. Principessa 116, tel: 704 111, fax: 703 224. ⊖⊖ **Il Delfino**, Via Colombo 15, tel: 701 179, fax: 701 383. **La Vela**, Via V. Emanuele II 72, tel: 701 529, fax: 701 384.

🅰 **Park Albatros**, Loc. Pineta di Torre Nuova, tel: 701 018, fax: 703 589.

❌ **Gambero Rosso**, Piazza della Vittoria 13, tel: 701 021; closed Mon and Tue (only closed for lunch in the summer). One of Italy's best restaurants. **Il Bucaniere**, Via Marconi 8, tel: 703 387; open daily. In former public baths. Same owners as Gambero Rosso, but lower quality and prices.

LIVORNO (☎ 0586)

🇮 **APT**, Piazza Cavour 6, tel: 898 111, fax: 896 173. **Ufficio Informazioni** (April-Oct) Porto Mediceo, tel: 895 320.

🛏 ⊖⊖⊖ **Rex**, Loc. Antignano, Via del Littorale 164, tel: 580 400, fax: 509 586. ⊖⊖ **Gennarino**, Viale Italia 301, tel: 803 109, fax: 803 450. **Universal**, Loc. Antignano, Viale Antignano 4, tel/fax: 500 398.

❌ **La Chiave**, Scali delle Cantine 52, tel: 888 609; closed Wed. Good fish dishes, but fairly high prices. **Il Sottomarino**, Via Terrazzini 48, tel: 887 025; closed Thu and Sun evening. Simple traditional cuisine, local fish dishes. **Trattoria Antico Moro**, Via E. Bartelloni 59, tel: 884 659; closed Wed. Classical Italian menu and atmosphere.

🏛 **Museo Civico G. Fattori**, Villa Mimbelli, Via San La-copo, Loc. Aquaviva; Tue-Sun 10:00 am-7:00 pm, closed Mon.

PROVINCE OF PISA

CALCI (☎ 050)

🏛 **Certosa di Calci**, tel: 938 430; Tue-Sat 9:00 am-6:00 pm, Sun and holidays 9:00 am-noon, closed Mon (May 1-Sept 30); Mon-Sat 9:00 am-4:00 pm, closed Sun and holidays (Oct 1-April 30). Tours hourly on the hour.

PONTEDERA (☎ 0578)

🏛 **Piaggio Works**, tel: 272 111. Tours available for groups of 8 or more.

PISA (☎ 050)

ℹ️ **APT**, Piazza Duomo, tel: 560 464, fax: 40903, and at train station, tel: 42 291.

🛏 😊😊😊 **Hotel dei Cavalieri**, Piazza della Stazione 2, tel: 43 290, fax: 502 242. 😊😊 **Casetta delle Selve**, Pugnano (near Rigoli), tel/fax: 850 359. Idyllic location, family atmosphere. **Francesco**, Via S. Maria 129, tel: 554 109, fax: 556 145. **Grand Hotel Duomo**, Via S. Maria 94, tel: 561 894, fax: 560 418. Verdi, Piazza della Repubblica 5, tel/fax: 598 944. **Villa di Corliano**, Rigoli, 12 km along SS 12 to Lucca, tel: 818 193, fax: 818 897.

❌ **Da Bruno**, Via L. Bianchi 12, tel: 560 818; closed Tue. Traditional food. **La Mescita**, Via Cavalca 2, tel: 544 294; closed Mon. Imaginative cuisine, fair prices. **Sergio**, in Hotel Villa di Corliano, Rigoli, tel: 818 193; closed Wed. Outstanding cuisine. **Vecchia Livorno**, Via Scali delle Cantine 34, tel: 884 048; closed Tue. Risto-rante-Pizzeria (except Sat evening), good fish dishes.

🏛 **Campo Santo** and **Baptistry**, daily 8:00 am-8:00 pm (summer), admission until 4:40 pm in the winter. **Ca-thedral**, Mon-Sat 10:00 am-7:40 pm, Sun 1:00-7:40 pm (from March), until 4:40 pm in the winter. **Museo Nazio-nale di S. Matteo**, Tue-Sat 9:00 am-7:00 pm, Sun and holidays 9:00 am-1:00 pm, closed Mon. **Museo del-l'Opera del Duomo**, daily 9:00 am-8:00 pm (summer), 9:00 am-5:20 pm (spring and fall), 9:00 am-4:20 pm (winter). **Museo delle Sinopie**, daily 8:00 am-7:40 pm (summer), 9:00 am-5:40 pm (spring and fall), 9:00 am-12:40 pm and 3:00-4:40 pm (winter). **San Piero a Gra-do**. Visits via pre-registration with Don Mariotel, tel: 960 065. Romanesque basilica at what was once the mouth of the Arno, accessible via plane-tree-lined avenue that leads towards the sea.

🎉 **Luminara e Regata Storica per San Ranieri**. On the evening of June 16, the town is illuminated by count-less wax candles; the next afternoon there is a historical rowing regatta on the Arno in honor of the city's patron saint. **Gioco del Ponte**. Sporting competition in medi-eval costumes, between the districts of the city that lie north and south of the Arno. Held annually at the end of June at the bridge Ponte di Mezzo.

📷 **Parco Naturale Regionale di Migliarino Tenuta di San Rossore**, entrance at Viale delle Cascine; Sun and holidays 9:00 am-sunset. Nature reserve between mouths of Arno and Serchio Rivers. Red deer, roe deer and wild boar inhabit thick pine and oak forests.

LUCCA AND SURROUNDINGS

BALBANO (☎ 0583)

🛏 😊😊 **Villa Casanova**, tel: 548 429, fax: 368 955.

LUCCA (☎ 0583)

ℹ️ **APT**, Piazzale Verdi, tel: 419 689, fax: 312 581.

🛏 😊😊 **La Luna**, Corte Compagni 12, tel: 493 634, fax: 490 021. **Universo**, Piazza del Gíglio 1, tel: 493 678, fax: 954 854. 😊 **La Torre**, Piazza del Carmine 11, tel: 957 044. Pleasant tower house in central location.

❌ **Antica Locanda dell'Angelo**, Via Pescheria 21, tel: 47 711; closed Sun evening and Mon. Hearty dishes have been served here since 1414. **Canuleia**, Via Canuleia 14, tel: 467 470; closed Sun. Refined, tra-ditional cuisine. **La Mora**, Loc. Ponte a Moriano, tel: 406 402; closed Wed. Best Garfagnana cuisine, fair prices. **Caffè Di Simo**, Via Fillungo 58; closed Mon. Historical coffee house. **Taddeucci**, Piazza S. Michele 34. This is where you can eat the best Buccellato, a ring-shaped bread/cake, one of Lucca's specialties.

🏛 **MUSEUMS: Museo di Villa Guinigi**, Via della Quarquonia; Tue-Sat 9:00 am-7:00 pm, Sun and holi-days 9:00 am-2:00 pm, closed Mon. **Pinacoteca Na-zionale di Palazzo Mansi**, Via G. Tassi 43, Tue-Sat 9:00 am-7:00 pm, Sun 9:00 am-2:00 pm, closed Mon. **Casa Natale di Puccini** (Puccini's Birth House), Via di Poggio, tel: 584 028, Tue-Fri 10:00 am-1:00 pm, Sat and Sun 1000 am-1:00 pm and 3:00-6:00 pm (Jan 2-Feb 28), Tue-Sun 10:00 am-1:00 pm and 3:00-6:00 pm (March 1-May 31, Oct 1-Dec 31), 10:00 am-6:00 pm (June 1-Sept 30), closed Mon.

📷 **SIGHTS: Torre Guinigi**, Via Sant'Andrea 41, 9:00 am-7:30 pm. Lovely panoramic view of the city. *Luc-chese Villas:* **Villa Mansi**, daily 10:00 am-12:30 pm and 3:00-7:00 pm (summer); 10:00 am-12:30 pm and 3:00-5:00 pm (winter). **Villa Reale**, guided tours at 10:00 and 11:00 am, noon, 3:00, 4:00, 5:00 and 6:00 pm (March-Sept). **Villa Torrigiani**, daily 10:00 am-12:30 pm and 3:00-7:00 pm (summer), only groups with reservations in Nov, closed Dec and Jan.

🎉 **Luminara di Santa Croce,** Sept 13. Procession for the "Volto Santo" through the illuminated city.

PELLERIA (☎ 0583)

❌ **Da Giulio**, Via delle Conce 45, tel: 55 948; closed Sun and Mon. Lucchese cuisine at low prices.

Along the Etruscan Coast to Lucca

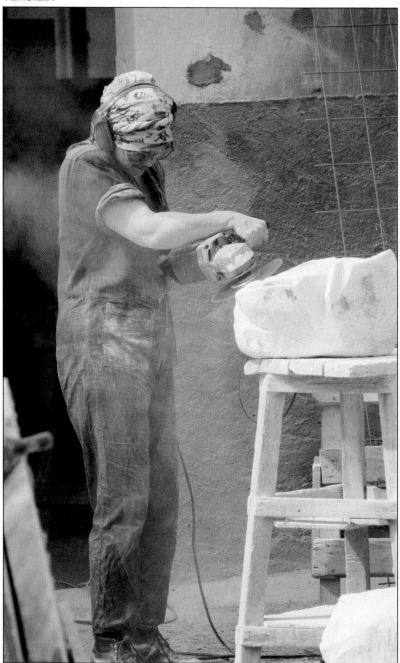

VERSILIA AND LUNIGIANA

VERSILIA / VIAREGGIO
WHITE GOLD / CAMAIORE
PIETRASANTA
SERAVEZZA
MASSA / CARRARA
LUNIGIANA

★VERSILIA

Versilia – white beach, white light, white marble. If you are taking the expressway from Lucca to this stretch of coast, which is more than 18 kilometers long and up to ten kilometers wide, your first view will be of the nature preserve on Lake Massaciuccoli, stretching away to your left. This, Tuscany's largest marshland, is home to more than 250 species of nesting birds, some of them extremely rare. The swampland once extended further north, but it has been drained, and a sea of red roofs among the pines now borders the coast.

After the final draining of the coastal strip, the area was reforested to protect the dried-up swamps from the brackish salt water. To the right of the expressway are wooded hills scattered with little villages.

Behind them are the looming forms of the Apuan Alps, where marble is still legally quarried today, despite the fact that part of the region was declared the Parco Naturale delle Alpi Apuane in 1985. This apparent contradiction continues to be a heated source of discussion, not to say controversy.

Left: Artists come from around the world to work marble in Pietrasanta.

This mountainous country, with its narrow valleys, peaks that reach heights of up to 2000 meters, broad gullies, chestnut forests, green meadows and rugged cliffs, has everything hikers, mountain climbers and spelunkers could wish for.

A hundred years ago, this coastline boasted only a few scattered fishing villages. The marshes and malaria effectively squelched interest in the area until the region, under the direction of the Venetian Bernardino Zendrini, was drained in the 18th century. But, it wasn't until swimming became fashionable around 1890 that the real boom began. The wealthy arrived first, followed by intellectuals and artists eager for the chance to unwind in Versilia's mild climate and enjoy the broad sand beaches that slope gently into the sea. Today, this stretch of coast still relies on tourism, and its main industries focus on leisure activities.

★VIAREGGIO

A trip through Versilia begins in the city of ★**Viareggio** ❶. Naturally, this coastal city existed well before the 19th century, even if the architecture of its elegant city villas and public baths tend to contradict that impression. As early as 1172, the Genoese and Lucchese erected, on the site that today is occupied by the

VERSILIA

0   10 km

ish poets Lord Byron and Percy B. Shelly, who drowned here.

The center of Viareggio is the coastal promenade. For anyone strolling from the Burlamacco Canal at the harbor basin to the casino Principe de Piemonte (1938), the Art Deco buildings from the 1920s, decorated by artists such as Galileo Chini and Lorenzo Viani, make a marvelous backdrop. Only the Chalet Martini, with its exotic oriental gable, a wooden Liberty construction that stands next to the imposing Caffè Margherita, survived the devastating fire at the beginning of the 20th century. Another ornamental Art Deco highlight is the memorial to fallen soldiers (1927) on the Piazza Garibaldi.

Towards town, parallel to the promenade, you will notice two large pine forests, the *Pineta di Ponente* and the *Pineta di Levante*. They are particularly inviting on hot summer days, when they offer you a chance to rest in the shade.

For over 120 years, Viareggio has been the capital of the Italian carnival. Every Sunday during the carnival season (usually mid-February) you can watch as parades with magnificent floats move down the promenade.

South of the city is the **Torre del Lago** quarter, which has developed around the 15th-century watchtower that was built by Paolo Guinigi on the shore of Lake Massaciuccoli. The city's fame is due, in part, to the composer Giacomo Puccini, who lived and worked here. His house, the Puccini Villa directly on the lake, was built on the ruins of the Guinigi Tower. Today it is a museum, and every August it hosts a *Pucciniano* festival.

Directly north of Viareggio is the town of **Lido di Camaiore** ❷. Although first documented as early as 1293, the site was not actually settled until early in the 19th century. Before that, the swamps made any kind of established life here impossible. The poet Gabriele d'Annunzio came here a century later, ushering in an era of illustrious guests.

watchtower Torre Matilde (1544), a fortress that allowed them to keep an eye on Pisa, their mutual enemy. The early fortress was named Via Regia, King's Street, because it stood on a road controlled by Emperor Frederick Barbarossa. In 1599, the church of San Pietro was added. (The church was re-christened Santi Annunziata after a later expansion.) Apart from these, all that remains from this period are the dilapidated houses along Via Catena.

After the swamps were successfully drained in the mid-18th century, the area rapidly developed into a popular summer residence for the Lucchese.

Viareggio has Marie Louise, the duchess of Bourbon, to thank for its chessboard layout, tree-lined boulevards, and the port of Darsena Europa (1820), where shipyards now build large luxury yachts.

It was this period that saw the opening of the first public pools and luxury hotels, which attracted visitors from home and abroad. Among the guests were the Brit-

Right: A popular beach in Versilia.

Versilia and Lunigiana

For many years, marble from the quarries of Seravezza was shipped to destinations around the world from ★**Forte dei Marmi ❸**. The small fort for which the town was named was commissioned by Grand Duke Leopoldo, in 1788, to defend the port and its residents from any nasty surprises from the sea. Since 1900, the town's fabulous location and white beach have attracted visitors from all over the world, including Aldous Huxley, Thomas Mann and the Italian actress Eleonora Duse. Forte dei Marmi has remained an elegant vacation spot where tradition dictates that you show yourself once a day on the breakwater that stretches more than 300 meters into the sea.

THE WHITE GOLD

What looks like patches of snow shimmering in the sun on the mountains is actually marble. While in other areas you find wine roads with signs for tourists, here, running parallel to the coast from Pietrasanta to the neighboring district of Massa-Carrara, there is a "marble road" through the **Apuan Alps**. Past traveling cranes, marble workshops and souvenir stands, the road leads to quarries, where, for over 2000 years, massive blocks have been cut out of the mountain, to be tooled and carved by stonemasons and artists.

Calcium carbonate is the main component of this valuable white stone. Its history begins some 200 million years ago, when the Apuan Alps were still under water. The bodies of dead sea creatures drifted down to collect on the ocean floor, where they slowly turned to limestone. Then, 30 million years ago, Africa and Europe began to slowly drift towards each other, pressing the soft limestone together into crystalline marble, and thrusting it upward to form mountains. Thus were the Apuan Alps, with their veins of white treasure, born.

The process that nature began was continued, many years later, by man, when people began using chisels to force shape upon the hard substance. The colonial power of Rome was the first to discover

the "white gold," which it used to adorn its temples, villas and baths. When this impressive stone again reached the height of fashion during the Renaissance, architects, builders and sculptors traveled from afar to test the shimmering rock for their purposes. Leading the way was Michelangelo Buonarroti, who wanted Apuan marble and nothing else for his David and his Pietà. He personally climbed down into the quarries of Monte Altissimo to select his own *statuario*, which had to be as white as snow, fine as porcelain, and solid as rock.

The list of fellow-artists from later centuries who came to Versilia for its white rock is long, reaching from such past giants as Donatello, Bernini, and Canova to such 20th-century luminaries as Henry Moore, Giò Pomodoro, Hans Arp and Fernando Botero. Some of their contemporaries have settled in the area because

nowhere else on earth can you find such a collection of talented craftsmen who are able to realize an artist's ideas in marble. Actually, these stonemasons are artists themselves. Many of them learned their craft at the art school in Pietrasanta or in their fathers' workshops. Today, however, people complain that there is a lack of young blood. The trade demands a apprenticeship, and it is often hard to tell whether someone really has the talent for this kind of work until after several years of training.

Standing in front of a magnificent church facade, or marble sculpture in a museum, it is easy to forget that these masterpieces are also made of sweat and tears. In the precipitous mountains of Versilia, however, you can get some idea of just how difficult it was to pound the marble out of the mountain by hand – without the aid of any machinery – and transport it to the coast. The Romans had their slaves do the work. They bored holes in the cliffs, inserted wooden stakes and poured water over them until they ex-

Above: Marble quarries are eating away at the Apuan Alps. Right: Even with modern technology, this is a dangerous place to work.

Versilia and Lunigiana

panded enough to pry the blocks from the mountain. After this, the blocks, each of which weighed tons, were lowered down the mountain on ropes, centimeter by centimeter, a process that cost countless stonecutters their lives. In later years, the quarrymen worked with explosives. They carried out repeated explosions until they managed to blast out a block of the size they desired, an inexact process lead to tons of valuable rock being wasted. You can still see the debris lying around.

It has only been since the 19th century that blocks have been cut from the mountain with the aid of water and steel cables, which nowadays are studded with industrial diamonds. The huge blocks are then transported down to the sea on trucks, along steep, often unsafe roads. Recent statistics show that this is still dangerous work – the quarries claim an average of 13 lives every year.

Even today, when the economies of the surrounding regions are fueled by tourism, the mining of marble has remained Versilia's most important industry. Every year, approximately one million tons of marble is mined, to be shipped, either as building material or in processed form, all over the world. Don't miss the chance to see the stonemasons at work. Watching them use jackhammers, chisels and years of experience to hew works of art, kitsch and replicas from the rough blocks of marble is a fascinating experience.

CAMAIORE

Around **Camaiore ❹**, the capital of the district of Versilia, there are few indications that the bustling marble industry is located nearby.

From this quiet little town it isn't far to the countryside and the little villages, like Casoli or Trescolli, that are ideal departure points for long, peaceful hikes.

In 1255, Camaiore's **Borgo Nuovo** was designed on the drawing board, as it were, at the same time as Pietrasanta. Lucca needed it as an outpost to control the Via Aurelia, long stretches of which coincided here with the Frankish Road that linked the Frankish Kingdom and southern Italy. The **Piazza San Bernardino** and the 13th-century collegiate church of Santa Maria Assunta, which contains remarkable art treasures, are in the center of town. Next to the 10th-century church of **San Michele** on the Piazza Diaz is a museum of sacral art. Among the museum's treasures is a magnificent Flemish tapestry from 1516.

At the cemetery, the abbey church of **San Pietro**, which was restored in 1100, presents a fine example of the simple 11th/12th-century Lucchese architecture. The emphasis is on correct proportions, while decorative elements, like those that appear in Pisan architecture of the same period, were omitted altogether.

Three kilometers further along the road to Lucca, a road branches off to the **Pieve San Stefano**, which, dating from the 9th century, is one of Versilia's oldest parish churches. After another five kilometers, turn right to get to **Massarosa ❺**, where there are a few ruins from Roman times, including the ruins of a thermal spa complex and a villa from the 2nd century B.C.

PIETRASANTA

Take the SS 439 to Pietrasanta, at the foot of the "white mountains." If you have the time, you can take a little detour into the hilly countryside. At the cemetery shortly before Pietrasanta is the exit to **Valdicastello Carducci**, home of the famous poet Giosuè Carducci (1835-1907). The townspeople have converted his birthplace into a **museum**.

***Pietrasanta ❻**, was named after its founder Guiscardo Pietrasanta, *Podestà* (mayor) of Lucca. It developed between 1242 and 1250, below the Lombard fortress of Rocca di Sala, and was expanded between 1316 and 1328 by the Lucchese Grande Castruccio Castracani Antelmi-

Right: A man of marble patiently waits to be completed.

nelli. In 1513, this fortified town became the property of the Medici, and as such, was later incorporated into the Grand Duchy of Tuscany. However, it wasn't until 1824, after Leopoldo II had the neighboring swamps drained, that the city began to flourish. Because of its abundance of marble, Pietrasanta soon became a Mecca for sculptors. There are numerous **artists' studios** and **marble workshops**, and the entire city seems to be made of the white rock – even the curbs and benches!

The **Porta a Pisa** at the small fortress, **Arrighina** (1324), is the last intact gate to the old city. From here it is just a few steps to **Cathedral Square**, where the city's most significant monuments are located. The cathedral of **San Martino**, built in 1330 atop a earlier construction from 1255, has a white marble facade with a fabulous Gothic rosette by Riccomanni. The red campanile (16th century) provides a nice contrast. The most notable elements in the interior of this three-aisled church, which was altered in the 17th century, are the marble pulpit by Stagio Stagi (1504) and the beautiful staircase by Andrea Baratto (17th century). The other church on Cathedral Square, **Sant'Agostino**, is supposed to have been erected at the behest of the obsessive builder Castruccio Castracani. Its facade, with blind arches and rows of marble Gothic columns, give the impression that more was supposed to have been added to it. In the cloisters of the adjacent monastery (1500), home to the **Museo del Bozetti** and its collection of sculpture models, there is a depiction of the life of Saint Augustine. Next to the church and monastery is the beginning of the street that leads up to the remains of the fortress, Rocca di Sala.

SERAVEZZA

The small marble-mining center of **Seravezza ❼** is located five kilometers

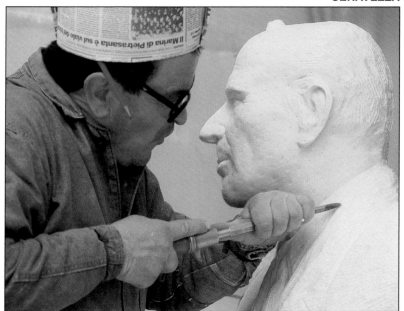

further north, at the confluence of the Serra and Vezza Rivers. It was from the spectacular quarries of nearby Monte Altissimo (1589 meters), where you can still watch how the "white gold" is cut out of the mountain, that Michelangelo selected the raw materials for his sculptures.

The Romanesque parish church of **La Cappelle**, near Azzana, on the way to the marble quarries, profited from Michelangelo's journeys. The artist himself is said to have designed the marble rosette that is above the portal, which is known, therefore, as "The Eye of Michelangelo."

Seravezza itself, nestled in a narrow green valley, has a few significant monuments. Among them is the **Cathedral of San Lorenzo**, which was built on the remains of an ancient temple in 1422, and was enlarged 200 years later. Its splendid decor is an ode to marble. Another noteworthy building is the **Palazzo Mediceo** on the bank of the Vezza, which the Medici prince Cosimo I had built, according to plans by Ammannati, in 1560. The stone trout on the courtyard fountain re-

fers to the legend that Cristina de Medici once caught an enormous trout here.

Seravezza is an ideal departure point for excursions to the nearby mountains, either on foot or by car. It isn't far from **Stazzema**, which is one of the most beautiful towns in this part of the Apuan Alps. From here, you pass marble quarries as you follow the old Via d'Arni deeper into the Garfagnana, which forms the eastern boundary of the Apuan Alps, beyond the Cipollaio tunnel.

MASSA AND CARRARA

Stessa spiaggia, stesso mare – the same beach, the same sea. Although the province of Massa also has a stretch of coast with long, sandy beaches and pine forests, tourism takes a back seat to the marble industry in the overall hierarchy of the region's economy. Try, then, to be understanding, rather than annoyed, that there are no signs marking the way to the ruins of **Luni** (2nd century B.C.), a Roman town that was deserted in the 13th century

Versilia and Lunigiana

and was only recently rediscovered, just two kilometers from the sea. To get there, follow the SS 1 and, at about the latitude of Marina di Carrara, follow the signs to the restaurant Chioccia d'Oro. Luna's well-preserved **amphitheater** is worth searching for. More than 2000 years ago, it was from Luni that the prized marble, which back then was known as Luni marble, was shipped to sites throughout the ancient world. Additional Roman finds are displayed in the adjacent archeological museum.

The ruins of **Castello di Aghinolfi** rise out of a thick forest near Montignoso, off a small minor road that links Seravezza and Massa. Occasionally, this octagonal tower is provided as an example of the Lombard style of fortress-building, and sometimes it ascribed to the Byzantines. From here it is only four kilometers to **Massa ❽**. This small provincial capital that developed below the medieval fortress of Malaspina was first mentioned in a document from A.D. 882. Although the city had a certain importance even in the Middle Ages, due to its location on the important north-south axis, the rise and fall of Massa was closely linked to the fortunes of the Malaspina family from Fosdinova, who were princes of the city between 1442 and 1790. As solid proof of his power, Alberico Cybo Malaspina had a Renaissance palace built next to the fortress, and linked the two buildings by an archway. In 1557, another **palazzo**, belonging to the family **Cybo Malaspina**, was built on the **Piazza degli Aranci** in the center of town: the facade of this palazzo, however, was not completed until 1701. The **cathedral** in Massa, at the end of Via Dante, has a modern marble face (1936), but the structure dates from the 15th century. Inside, you will find, among other things, a fresco by Pinturicchio, above the Baroque altar; a triptych by F.

Right: Tendola, a small village in Lunigiana, Tuscany's northernmost district.

Lippi; a 16th-century terra-cotta crèche; and a 13th-century wooden crucifix. Also here are the tombs of all of the princes and bishops from throughout the city's history.

That the features of Tuscany's most famous marble town, **Carrara ❾**, are also dominated by the fine white stone should come as no surprise. Since 1473, when a Malaspina obtained the feudal rights to the city, its political fortunes have been closely linked to those of Massa. One hundred years later, a member of the Cybo Malaspina family had the city wall built. He also commissioned the palaces on Piazza Alberica and the princely Renaissance palace (which has served as the **Accademia di Belle Arti** since 1805), next to the medieval watchtower. The Romanesque-Gothic **Cathedral of San Andrea** (11th-14th centuries), with its Pisan facade also received a new marble facing in this period. If you are interested in knowing more about the history of marble, you should visit the **museum** on Via XX Settembre, near the stadium.

Narrow, winding roads lead from Carrara to the mining area, most of them along watercourses that are white with marble dust. About six kilometers away are the **Fantiscritti quarries**, where you can still see the train tracks along which, until 1962, stone was transported to the port of Marina di Carrara.

The small dusty mountain village of **Colonnato** (532 meters), nestled in the mountains, was originally a Roman slave colony. It later became a settlement for the quarrymen.

Heading north on the SP 446, a gray asphalt strip along the Canale di Gragnana, continue on to Fosdinovo and on into Lunigiana. On the way, there is a side road to the right that leads to the vacation spot of **Campo Cecina ❿** (1357 meters). To escape the summer heat, the residents of Versilia come here. Most of them, instead of lying on overcrowded beaches, prefer to hike along the marked trails in

the quiet mountains, where they can rest in the *Belvedere* and *Carrara* huts.

Fosdinovo ⓫ sits at an altitude of 500 meters on a steep mountain spur. It was from here that the counts of Malaspina controled the area's important transportation routes during the Middle Ages. Their 13th-century castle at the end of town was converted into a grand **palace** during the Renaissance. Also notable is the parish church of **San Remigio**, which contains the tomb of Galeotto Malaspina and the Bianchi **Oratory** (1666).

*LUNIGIANA

From here it is only a hop, skip and a jump to Lunigiana, which snakes its way into Emilia Romagna. Although this small river valley at the junction of Tuscany, Liguria and Emilia Romagna was once a pivotal spot in Italian history, it is now practically forgotten. Many inhabitants had to leave their old, gray houses to search for work elsewhere. Little known, even among the Tuscans, the

Magra river valley enjoyed its heyday in the Middle Ages, when pilgrims, singly or in droves, passed through on their way to Rome. There was a castle atop almost every hill, and a total of 160 of them were built to keep an eye on the roads and valleys. Many of them are examples of the building frenzy of the extended family of the counts of Malaspina, who wanted to leave their mark on Lunigiana. Some of these castles are still intact, while the romantically dilapidated state of others, including the charming remains of the Comano Castle, call to mind the glorious days of troubadours, noblewomen, evil knights and scheming sextons. It is here that legends and reality, tragedy and minnesong, blend together.

Similarly, the area's churches, gathering places of the townspeople and examples of the Romanesque Lombard style, also reflect the turbulent developments and the cultural streams that have passed through this valley. One impressive example is the church of **Santa Maria Assunta** (10th century) near Crespiano, with an old, long-deserted town crouching behind it. Unfortunately, the church has been changed for the worse due to constant "improvements" in recent years. One of the oldest examples of Romanesque church architecture in Lunigiana is the **Chiesaccia**. Together with a pilgrim hospice, the church was located near a one-time ford of the Magra, directly across from the village of **Lusuolo** (north of Aulla), with its characteristic terraces, which stretches alongside a road on a mountain crest, on the opposite bank of the river.

After gaining independence early, the valley lost it again around 1300 and rapidly fell into insignificance, from which it has yet to rise. This has helped to preserve Lunigiana's austere and charming beauty, and transformed it into a popular destination for hiking excursions. You can become familiar with the impressive and constantly changing landscape step by step, by following in the pilgrims' footsteps, so to speak. Once place to do this is along the marked **walking trail** that leads from Podenza to Pontremoli and back to Aulla.

The main arterial road for motorists with a little extra time, on the other hand, is the SS 62, the Cisa Pass road, from which numerous smaller roads branch off into the green valleys. It passes through **Aulla** ⑫, where pilgrims who were making their way to Rome stopped to rest and eat before marching on to Lucca or undertaking the strenuous crossing of the Apennines. It also goes through the town of **Pontremoli** ⑬, known as the "keyhole to the Apennines" because no traveler, whether emperor or soldier, bishop or pilgrim, could pass through unseen.

Before heading north and finally leaving Tuscany, you have the opportunity to stop at an old castle and see one the most puzzling art collections in all of Italy – the ***Stelae Museum**, which contains prehistoric stone sculptures that are ancient and yet somehow modern.

VERSILIA

CAMAIORE (☎ 0584)

🏨 ⑤⑤ Cerú, Loc. Gombitelli, V. Gombitelli, tel/fax: 971 901. Le Monache, Piazza XXIX Maggio 36, tel: 989 258, fax: 984 011. Restaurant serves good food with game and mushroom specialties. Conca Verde, Loc. Misciano, tel: 989 686, fax: 60 091.

❌ Il Vignaccio, Loc. S. Lucia, Via S. Lucia 26. tel: 914 200; evenings only except Sat and Sun, closed Wed (winter). Attractive location, small menu with typical regional dishes. Bernardone, Via Nocchi 110, tel: 951 118; closed Tue (winter) and Wed. Traditional Lucchese cuisine.

LIDO DI CAMAIORE (☎ 0584)

🏨 ⑤⑤⑤ Villa Ariston, Viale Colombo 355, tel: 610 633, fax: 610 631. Colombo, Viale Colombo 161, tel: 619 651, fax: 618 363.

⑤⑤ Brunella, Viale Pistelli 102, tel: 617 258, fax: 618 220. Gigliola, Via del Secco 23, tel: 617 151, fax: 617 172.

❌ Ariston Mare, Viale Colombo 660, tel: 904 747; closed Mon. Good food, located in public baths.

🍸 Cavalluccio, Viale Europa 1, Sat and Sun. Agorà Caffè, Viale Colombo 666, Thu-Sun.

FORTE DEI MARMI (☎ 0584)

🏨 ⑤⑤⑤ Augustus, Viale Morin 169, tel: 787 200, fax: 787 102. Byron, Viale Morin 46, tel: 787 052, fax: 787 152.

⑤⑤ Marsiliana, Via N. Sauro 19/21, tel: 787 151, fax: 787 436. Bandinelli, Via Torino 3, tel: 787 455, fax: 787 083.

❌ Lorenzo, Via Carducci 61, tel: 84 030; closed Mon. Outstanding fish dishes, fairly expensive. Le Bistrot, Viale Franceschi 14, tel: 89 879; closed Tue. An elegant "in" restaurant. Recommended fish specialties.

MASSAROSA

🏛 Museo Antiquarium, Sat 10:00 am-1:00 pm and 3:00-6:00 pm, Sun 9:00 am-noon and 3:00-6:00 pm.

PIETRASANTA (☎ 0584)

🏨 ⑤⑤ Pietrasanta, Via Garibaldi 35, tel: 793 726/27, fax: 793 728. Charmin hotel in a 17th-century nobleman's palace that has been lovingly restored. Grappolo d'Oro, Loc. Strettoia, tel: 799 422/23, fax: 799 153. Palagi, Piazza Carducci 23, tel: 70 249 and 70 498, fax: 71 198. ⑤ Da Piero, Via Traversagna 3, tel: 790 031, fax: 794 196.

❌ Da Coppo, V. Aurelia 121, tel: 70 350; closed Mon. Traditional Tuscan/Lucchese cuisine. Da Sci, Vicolo Porta a Lucca, tel: 790 983; closed Sun. Especially good vegetable soup and dried cod, very decent prices.

Marble Workshops: **C.S.N.C.** and **Cervietti Franco**, Via S. Agostino 53. Numerous copies of classical sculptures. **Studio Sem e scultori associati**, Via S. Agostino 51. Legendary workshop in which, among others, Henry Moore and Arp have worked. **Museo dei Bozzetti**, Via S. Agostino 1; evenings in July and Aug, otherwise afternoons. Copies of classical sculptures.

TORRE DEL LAGO (☎ 0584)

Bosco Verde, Viale Kennedy 5, tel: 359 343, fax: 341 981; April-Sept. **Burlamacco**, Viale Marconi 142, tel: 359 544, fax: 359 387.

Museo Villa Puccini, tel: 341 445; Tue-Sun 10:00 am-12:30 pm, afternoon opening hours vary, closed Mon.

VALDICASTELLO

Casa Natale di Giosuè Carducci, Tue-Sun 5:00-8:00 pm (June 15-Sept 15) closed Mon; Sat 9:00 am-noon, Sun 3:00-6:00 pm (Sept 16-June 14).

VIAREGGIO (☎ 0584)

APT Versilia, Viale Carducci 10, tel: 962 233, fax: 47 336.

Esplanade, Piazza Puccini 18, tel: 53 815, fax: 53 638. **Excelsior**, Viale Carducci 88, tel: 50 726, fax: 50 729. **Palace Hotel**, Via F. Gioia 2, tel: 46 134, fax: 47 351. **Regina**, Viale Carducci 64, tel: 407 440, fax: 407 444. **Bristol**, Viale Manin 14, tel/fax: 46 441. **Liberty**, Lungomare Manin 18, tel: 46 247, fax: 46 249. **Miramare**, Viale Carducci 27, tel: 48 441, fax: 963 637. **La Pineta**, Via dei Lecci, tel/fax: 383 397. **Paradiso**, Viale del Tigli, tel: 392 005, fax: 387 206. **Viareggio**, Via Comparini, tel: 391 012, fax: 395 462.

Gusmano, Via Regia, 58/64, tel: 31 233; closed Tue. Specialty: spelt with fish. Refined fish dishes, but also rustical cuisine, fair prices. **Il Patriarca**, Viale Carducci 79, tel: 53 126; closed Wed. One of Versilia's most famous restaurants, appropriately high prices. **Tito del Molo**, Lungomolo del Greco 3, tel: 962 016; open daily. Classical Tuscan cuisine. **La Darsena**, Via Virgilio 150, tel: 392 785; closed Sun. Old fish trattoria in the harbor district, good prices. **Osteria N.1**, Via Pisano 140, tel: 388 967; closed Mon. Simple fish menu, good food.

Carnival: Excitement and political satire characterize the Italian carnival season here, which ranks next to Venice in importance.

PROVINCE OF MASSA-CARRARA

CARRARA (☎ 0585)

Michelangelo, Corso F.lli Rosselli 3, tel: 777 161/162/163, fax: 74 545.

MARINA DI CARRARA (☎ 0585)

Maestrale, Via Fabbricotti 2, tel: 785 371, fax: 634 651. **Mediterraneo**, Via Genova 2/H, tel:

785 222, fax: 780 530. **La Pineta**, Viale Colombo 119, tel/fax: 633 390.

L'Enoteca, Viale Verazzano 11E, tel: 634 420; closed Sun. Little snacks with the finest wines in the "osteria," or refined fish starters and homemade pasta in the restaurant – everything is delicious.

MASSA (☎ 0585)

Galleria, Viale della Democrazia 2, tel: 42 137, fax: 489 106. **Annunziata**, Via Villafranca 4, tel/fax: 41 023 and 810 025.

Il Passeggero, Via Alberica 1, tel: 489 651; closed Sun. Typical regional dishes, good starters with an excellent Lardo di Colonnata and homemade desserts.

APT Massa-Carrara, Viale Vespucci 24, tel: 240 046, fax: 869 015.

Excelsior, Via C. Battisti 1, tel: 8601, fax: 869 795. **Eco del Mare**, Via Verona 1, tel: 245 200, fax: 245 262. **Bellamarina**, Via Zolezzi 17, tel: 869 731.

MARINA DI MASSA (☎ 0585)

APT Massa-Carrara, Viale Vespucci 24, tel: 240 046, fax: 869 015.

Excelsior, Via C. Battisti 1, tel: 8601, fax: 869 795. **Eco de Mare**, Via Verona 1, tel: 245 200, fax: 245 262. **Bellamarina**, Via Zolezzi 17, tel: 869 731.

LUNIGIANA

AULLA (☎ 0187)

Pro Loco, Via Gramsci 1, tel: 409 960 and 421 439.

FOSDINOVO (☎ 0187)

Don Rodrigo, Via Cucco 5, Loc. Foseta, SS 446, tel: 68 861, fax: 68 978.

FIVIZZANO

Medieval Procession of knights, noblewomen, flag throwers and pages, followed by archery competition. Second Sun in July.

PONTREMOLI (☎ 0187)

Piazza del Comune, tel: 833 278 and 460 111.

Golf Hotel, Via Pineta, tel: 831 573, fax: 831 591. **Napoleon**, Piazza Italia 2B, tel: 830 544, fax: 830 544.

La Puledra, Fraz. Coloretta, tel: 447 066.

Da Bussé, Piazza Duomo 31, tel: 831 371; closed Fri. Classical Lunigiana cuisine. **Trattoria del Giardino da Bacciottini**, Via Ricci Armani 4, tel: 830 120; closed Sun evening and Mon (winter). Sausage and ham from own slaughter, homemade pasta.

Museo Civico Ubaldo Formentini (Stelae Museum), Via Curtatone; Tue-Sun 9:00 am-noon & 3:00-6:00 pm (April-Sept), 9:00 am-noon & 2:00-5:00 pm (Oct-March), closed Mon. Bronze & Iron Age stelae.

Versilia and Lunigiana

GARFAGNANA

GARFAGNANA
SERCHIO VALLEY
UPPER GARFAGNANA

*★GARFAGNANA

Garfagnana – large magnificent forest. This is what the early natives called the fertile Serchio valley that begins north of Lucca, and is bordered by the Apuan Alps in the west and the Apennines in the north. Along the wild mountain streams that run down the narrow side valleys, ruins of small fortresses, Romanesque chapels and lonely monasteries document an eventful past.

The history of the valley goes back to the times of the Visigoths, Lombards and Franks, who fought with the residing feudal rulers over its ownership. In 1248, Frederick II decided to cede the area to the city republic of Lucca, which then lost it to the d'Este family from Ferrara in 1451. After this, a long period of peace ensued. In 1847, the valley once again became part of Tuscany.

THE SERCHIO VALLEY

If you are driving from Lucca through the lower, here still idyllic, Serchio valley, you can choose one of two routes. Either take the main SS 12, which takes you directly to Borgo a Mozzano, where the

Preceding Pages: Going to work near Bagni di Lucca. Left: An old watchtower in Lunigiana.

Garfagnana begins, or a small road that leads along the right side of the river, past hamlets and Romanesque churches. The symbol of the small industrial town of **Borgo a Mozzano ❶** is the 14th-century Magdalena Bridge, also called the Devil's Bridge, which arches steeply across the Serchio like the curve of a cat's back. Near Fornoli, the SS 445 branches off into the wild upper Garfagnana, while the SS 12 takes you to the Lima valley and the spa resort of **Bagni di Lucca ❷**, which was sought out by everyone from Roman consuls to, during the late Middle Ages, the Tuscan Margravine Matilda, and Frederick II. Yet it wasn't until the Duke of Bourbon, Charles Louis (1824-47), discovered the curative powers of the town's thermal baths for himself that the little it became a fashionable resort. It was during this initial development that its grand Neo-Classical monuments were built. Four Romanesque churches stand on a side street that leads out of town. Among them is one by Controne, which has been rebuilt several times after the main portal has been buried in landslides. Hikers should take the road up to the mountain village of **Montefegatesi** (842 meters), from which a mule trail leads to one of Tuscany's most impressive natural spectacles, the **Canyon Orrido di Botri**, a narrow gorge in which golden eagles

Map p. 209, Info p. 211

Garfagnana

that are in danger of dying out, have built their nests.

Back on the SS 12, if you look up to your right, you will see, high above you, **Crasciana**, "the grandiose." Its symbol is, in addition to its fabulous palazzi, the 10th-century campanile of San Frediano. Ten kilometers further along the SS 12, an exit to the right leads to the castle ruins of **Lucchio**, one of Lucca's former outposts, located opposite the Florentine fortress of Popiglio. Initially, construction workers lived in the stone-gray houses that cling to the mountain, later it was the castle's guards.

The town of **Ghivizzano** has, in addition to a castle and a Romanesque church, a *sassola*, or covered street. From here, a side road leads from the SS 445 through thick chestnut woods to the pretty mountain village of **Coreglia Antelminelli ❸**, which is famous for its traditional plaster

Above: The Devil's Bridge across the Serchio, in Borgio a Mozzano. Right: Many Tuscans are friendly, but detached.

nativity figures. Some of these are displayed in a small **museum** in the Palazzo Rossi. The parish church of **San Michele** (13th century) has an annunciation group worked in the finest marble and a beautifully crafted gold crucifix from the 15th century.

Back in the Serchio valley, the road on the opposite bank of the river leads to **Fabbriche di Vallico**. Here, you can still see the old, 10th-century water wheels that made the people's work easier and helped them to prosperity.

The center of lower Garfagnana is the silk town of **Barga ❹**, which was under the jurisdiction of the bishops of Lucca and in 1186, was fortified by Frederick Barbarossa. One hundred years later, the town fell under Lucchese rule, only to be turned over to Florence in 1341. In the center of the old town with its steep, narrow side streets is the **Cathedral of San Cristoforo** (12th century), a monumental edifice whose Romanesque-Lombard facade once formed the nave of a 9th-century church. Panes of Egyptian alabaster

　　　　Info p. 211

Garfagnana

filter the light that shines on a 1000-year-old figure of Saint Christopher, a 13th-century marble pulpit that is supported by lions, and terra-cotta reliefs from the workshop of Della Robbia. From the cathedral's forecourt there is a breathtaking view of the mountainous scenery that spreads out below. Palazzi dating from the time of the Florentine occupation are tucked away in the winding side streets of the old city.

You have to cross the river once again to reach the **Hermitage of Calomini**. It hangs on the steep face of a cliff like a balcony, and the Madonna is said to have appeared here around the year 1000. This place of pilgrimage was at first simply a chapel in the rocks, and later, in the 18th century, it was enlarged to a monastery. The road up to it begins at the pretty little town of **Gallicano**, where one of the oldest Luccan baptisteries (7th century) once stood. At the end of the serpentine valley road, near **Fornovolasco**, the stalactite cavern ★**Grotta del Vento** ❺ might lure you in to visit its underground passage-

ways. From Gallicano, it isn't very far to **Molazzana** and **Cascio**, where you can still see the old defensive walls that the inhabitants put up after they rebelled against the d'Este rulers in 1613.

The small textile town of **Castelnuovo di Garfagnana** ❻ owes its wealth to this very same d'Este family from Ferrara. It was to this family that, in 1429, because they had had enough of the Lucchese government, the residents of this medieval fortress voluntarily pledged their allegiance. And this, the main town in the Garfagnana, remained the administrative seat of the d'Este in Tuscany until the French occupation in 1796. From the town's storybook castle (12th century) and the old city that developed within its walls, Via Testi leads to the simple cathedral of Saint Peter (16th century). This, like the entire old city, was heavily damaged in World War II, and had to be rebuilt from the ground up. Every Thursday morning there is a bustling market in Castelnuovo – a good time to get to know this lively little town a little bit better.

UPPER GARFAGNANA

The second part of the trip through the Garfagnana is a bit more adventurous, because the countryside is rougher, the mountains are higher and the roads more winding. From the river valley and the SS 445, a number of smaller valleys branch off, each one concealing hidden beauties that are waiting to be discovered on foot, on horseback, by bicycle or by car.

One example is the **Via d'Arni**, which leads from Castelnuovo to the Apuan marble quarries and continues to a reservoir and **Isolasanta**, an almost deserted town where a pilgrim hospice stood in the Middle Ages. Hiking trails of varying degrees of difficulty now cross through the undisturbed mountain country.

The town of **Poggio** ❼ is just eight kilometers north of Castelnuovo. Its main architectural treasure is the 13th-century church of San Biagio and its flat-topped

Above: Built directly into the cliff – the Hermitage of Calomini.

campanile. On a small road that was once used by the d'Este for their own early postal service, you can reach the mountain communities of **Vagli di Sotto** and **Vagli di Sopra** in the **Nature Preserve of Apuan**. These villages, two of the oldest communities in the Garfagnana, are located on the banks of an artificial reservoir, **Lago di Vagli**, where you can take a refreshing swim. The spire of a church of the town *Fabrica di Careggine*, which was flooded in 1953, can be seen sticking out of the middle of the lake. Shortly before Vagli di Sopra, set up above the road, there is a tiny hermitage that is built into the cliffs. It was founded by the 8th-century Scottish missionary Bishop Viano, who later became a hermit in these secluded mountains.

On the other side of the Serchio valley, between Camporgiano and Piazza al Serchio, both headwaters of the Serchio meet. Here, too, is the *Nature Preserve dell'Orecchiella* ❽ (52 square kilometers). After successful reforestation, it is again home to a wide variety of animals.

There are two different ways to return to Castelnuovo. The most direct route is along a high road past Corfino and **Villa Collemandina**. In 1920, an earthquake destroyed the latter, Romanesque church and all – local residents painstakingly rebuilt the church, stone by stone. The other route passes through Orzaglia and on to **Verrucole**, where you can see the remains of a mighty castle on "Wart Hill." The rest of the way to Castelnuovo is flanked by a series of Romanesque churches – San Jacopo with its Baroque bell tower in **San Romano**; the 12th-century baptistry of **Sambuca** wedged between two cliffs; and a third church in **Pian di Cerreto**, of which only the Romanesque apse remains from the original construction.

Finally, for one final excursion from Castelnuovo, take the SS 324 to the 1529-meter-high mountain pass **Foce delle Radici ❾**, where you can look out over the whole of the Garfagnana. Along the way you pass the fortress of **Castiglione Garfagnana ❿**, which was strengthened with bulwarks and, in 1371, was used by the Lucchese to defend their island in the sea of d'Este possessions.

This scenic town is picturesquely located on a rock ledge and overlooks the entire Serchio valley. It is a popular summer spot, and its well-preserved old city and 13th-century church of San Michele, with a beautiful Gothic-Romanesque facade of colored marble, are worth seeing.

The next stop is **San Pellegrino in Alpe ⓫**. At 1523 meters, it is the highest inhabited town in the Apennines. What started out as a 14th-century pilgrim hospice later became a postal station and eventually expanded to include a farming museum. Travelers have met here since time immemorial and it is the starting point for a number of marked hiking trails into the surrounding mountains. Brave motorists can return to Castelnuovo along the winding route of the first real road to have ever been built in the Garfagnana.

GARFAGNANA

BAGNI DI LUCCA (☎ 0583)
😊😊 **Pensione Serena**, Via Paretaio 1, Bagni Caldi, tel: 87 455. **Silvania**, Via Immagine, Loc. Lugliano, tel: 805 363, fax: 86 570.
😊 **La Frantoia**, Via Tovani 25, tel: 87 983.

BORGO A MOZZANO (☎ 0583)
😊😊 **Milano**, Via del Brennero 9, Loc. Socciglia, tel: 889 191, fax: 889180.
😊 **Il Pescatore**, Via 1 Maggio 2, Ponte Pari, tel: 88 071.

CASTELNUOVO GARFAGNANA (☎ 0583)
😊 **Da Carlino**, Via Garibaldi 13, tel: 644 270, fax: 62 616. **The Marquee**, Via Provinciale 14B, Piano della Pieve, tel/fax: 62 198.
Da Carlino, Via Garibaldi 15, tel: 644 270; closed Mon (winter). Specialties: spelt soup and trout from the Serchio River. Classical Tuscan cuisine.
Parco Regionale delle Alpi Apuane. The starting-point for the area's mountain tours and hiking is located in Castelnuovo Garfagnana. Info: tel/fax: 644 242.

CASTIGLIONE GARFAGNANA (☎ 0583)
😊 **Il Casone**, on the SS 324, Passo delle Radici, Casone Profecchia, tel: 649 090, fax: 649 048. **Lunardi**, Loc. Passo delle Radici m 1529, tel: 649 071, fax: 649 079. **Villa Verde**, on the SS 5, Località Cerageto, tel/fax: 68 127.
Il Casone di Profecchia, Via Statale 324, Loc. Il Casone di Profecchia, tel: 649 028/090; open daily. Former 18th-century soldiers quarters, the best Garfagnana cuisine.

COREGLIA ANTELMINELLI (☎ 0583)
😊 **Il Cacciatore**, Via Roma 3/5, tel: 78 022. **Il Grillo**, Loc. Al Lago, tel/fax: 78 031. **La Posta**, Via Antelminelli 2/4, tel: 78 027.

FORNOVOLASCO (☎ 0583)
Grotta del Vento, daily, 1-, 2- or 3- hour tours from 10:00 am-noon and 4:00-6:00 pm (April 1-Sept 30). In the winter the cave is open on weekdays for 1-hour tours only. Tour info under tel: 722 024.

GALLICANO (☎ 0583)
😊😊 **Mediavalle**, Via Roma 73A, tel: 730 074, fax: 730 288.

CAMPORGIANO (☎ 0583)
Parco Naturale dell'Orecchiella, unusual species of animals and plants can be seen here. Entrance is free and organized tours with a guide are available. Tours are organized by Garfagnana Vacanze, tel: 65 169, fax: 648 435.

Garfagnana

CHIANTI WINE
From Quantity to Quality

During the 1960s, the characteristic *fiaschi*, bulbous, straw-covered bottles filled with Chianti wine, flooded the shelves of supermarkets throughout the European Community. Back then, anyone who overindulged in Chianti in the evening ran the risk of experiencing a big fiasco the next morning – and the Chianti vintners also found that their fiaschi were something of a fiasco. In 1970, they produced a massive 240 million bottles, but they could hardly cover the costs of production. The country was in the throes of radical social changes that were altering the traditional farming structures and methods of cultivation. Some of the problems from this era persist today, but connoisseurs of good wine can still make new discoveries in Tuscany.

Tuscany's vast areas of cultivated land are comprised of a range of different soils and locations, and the vintners who try their luck here are of equally diverse skills and have differing senses of responsibility with regard to the quality of their products. Over the past decades, the traditional vineyards with their alternating rows of grapevines and olive trees have practically disappeared. The landscape is increasingly dominated by monotonous vineyards, a result of industrial production. These acres produce a veritable sea of wine each year. The quality and character of the product varies greatly – from pale supermarket swill to fruity and well-balanced, top-quality products.

Strictly speaking, the historic region of Chianti is a small triangular area that is bordered by Florence, Arezzo and Siena (*Chianti classico, Chianti colli fiorentini*). Today, however, the cultivable areas for Chianti extend south beyond Monte-

pulciano (*Chianti Colli Senesi*), west to Pistoia (*Chianti Montalbano*) and into the area between Pisa and Volterra (*Chianti Colline Pisani*), and *Chianti Rufina* comes from east of Florence. But not every Chianti is a Chianti – the "real," typical Chianti wines come from the historic Chianti area and the Rufina region.

"You are in the world of *Gallo Nero*," roadside signs inform you as you drive south of Florence. The black rooster, a trademark of the Chianti League during the Middle Ages, is today the trademark of the consortium that markets *Chianti classico*. The beverage that bears this historic name is, however, a relatively recent invention. It wasn't until a century ago that Baron Ricasoli, in his castle Brolio, hit upon the idea of blending red and white grapes: 75-90% Sangiovese, 5-10% Canaiolo and 25% white Trebbiano and Malvasia – proportions that the DOCG (*di origine controllata e garantita*) regulations stipulate today.

Because of its white wine content, Chianti genuinely matures early, and can be served as early as March 1, of the same year. However, a vintner's real expertise, or lack of it, is demonstrated in his *riserva* products, which are aged in a cask for at least three years. A good Chianti can be recognized by its brilliant ruby red color, its fruitiness and its mild fragrance. It is the proportion of white grapes that gives it a pleasant lightness despite its full body. Even in temperate Tuscany, you can't be sure that every year will present you with a favorable wine-growing climate. The year 1990 was especially memorable, while '83, '85, '88, '91 and '97 were also good.

The DOCG marking has only partly solved the problem of regulating the quality of Chianti. The yield per hectare has been officially reduced, as has the percentage of white grapes used in the mixture. The use of wines from other regions has been restricted, but is not forbidden everywhere – using other grapes, such as

Preceding Pages: Excited spectators at the "Giostro del Saracino." Harvesting olives. Left: Aging the juice of the noble grape.

Chianti Wine

Cabernet, is permitted. The tangle of red tape and controlling bodies can surely accomplish a great deal, but there is one thing it still can't guarantee: a truly outstanding product from every vintner.

Excellent Chiantis made according to the classic blend are produced by the same vintners who make first-rate wines from old varieties of Sangiovese grapes without the addition of any other variety. At any the *Enoteca* in every well-known wine-producing town, you can get more information about local products. You can also taste them for yourself.

The fate of Ricasoli, the "inventor" of *Chianti classico*, and his vineyard illustrates the situation of Chianti vineyards today. Sold to a beverage group in 1974, the vineyard was run into the ground, to be reclaimed by the Ricasoli family, in a state of almost total ruin, some years ago. The family is now trying to regain their

Above: Most Tuscans purchase their wine before it is bottled. Right: It is grapes like these that yield the Vino Nobile di Montepulciano.

former reputation. Another committed producer, Giovanella Stianti of Castello di Volpaia, is demonstrating one way to achieve success. She cultivates her vineyards ecologically, without the use of artificial fertilizers and pesticides, and by systematically cultivating old grape varieties while preserving the tradition of mixed cultivation with olive trees. In addition to her traditional *Chianti classico*, her *Coltassala* from Sangiovese grapes, and her *Balifico* have also become famous.

The same can be said for family businesses such as the small Fattoria Vigna Vecchia in Radda, run by Franco Beccari. Both his *Chianti classico riserva*, and his *Raddese* are superb. Other vineyards that produce high-quality Chianti wines include Castellare and Castello di Fonterutoli, both of which are near Castellina; Podere Il Palazzino near Gaiole; Vecchie Terre di Montefili near Greve; and, last but not least, Fattoria Isole e Olena in Barberino Val d'Elsa.

It is also worth visiting some of the lesser known Rufina wineries in the Sieve valley, whose wines are robust and solid. Between Florence and Pistoia is the small wine-producing region of Carmignano, where an excellent red wine is pressed using four classic Chianti grapes and an admixture of *Cabernet Sauvignon*.

The *Vino Nobile di Montepulciano* from the south of Tuscany is, on the other hand, is produced like a Chianti, but it doesn't compare well with the best Chiantis.

Not far from here, in the Montalcino area, the unique *Brunello* is produced. During the 19th century, the Biondi-Santi vinters began producing a wine from Sangiovese-Grosso grapes, aged in oak casks. A *Brunello* takes at least four years to age, and since the wine has recently become fashionable, countless suppliers have flooded the market, often with wines that don't quite conform to the strict principles of Biondi-Santi that made *Brunello*

famous and guarantee its distinctive character. Accordingly, you should be a bit more critical when considering this first-class wine. A few of the more reliable vintners include Poggio Antico, Poderi Costanti in Colle al Matrichese, and the Fattoria of Nello Baricci in Colombaio di Montosoli.

In Chianti and the other regions of Tuscany, vintners are experimenting with new varieties of grapes and types of wine. Yet these rather expensive products, often oriented toward a French taste, seem to lack the typical Tuscan element that characterizes a good Chianti. Nevertheless, committed and experimental young oenologists have created some surprisingly good wines in the past few years, often from areas previously thought of as mediocre. Examples of these are the excellent *Sassicaia* from Bolgheri and the award-winning red wine from the Fattoria Sorbaiano in Montecatini Val di Cecina in the Montescudaio region, west of Volterra. There is also a popular *Vino frizzante*, sold under the bland name of

Matre, that is produced by the Capalbio cooperative of Malvasia and Trebbiano.

The region's ordinary white table wines often taste good at the local wine festivals, but they neither travel, nor keep very well. The Fattoria Buonamico and the Carmignani families in Montecarlo, near Lucca, produce good white wines. There is also an excellent white from Pomino, east of Fiesole.

The better-known white wines that are made from the Vernaccia grape in the district around San Gimignano are generally of rather mediocre quality. One of the few exceptions is the *Vernaccia* that is made by Fattoria Ponte a Rondolino. A good *Bianco* is also produced around Cortona and in the far south near Pitigliano.

Finally, don't miss the chance to take home a bottle of *Vin Santo*, an excellent dessert wine that tastes similar to sherry.

One thing to keep in mind is how difficult it is to find truly good products like those from Avignonesi in Montepulciano, Castello di Volpaia, or Isole e Olena in Barberino Val d'Elsa.

Chianti Wine

219

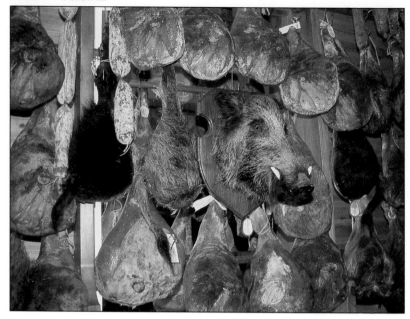

TUSCAN CUISINE

The same is true of Tuscany as of Italy in general: every region, every area has its own cuisine, based on whatever the local forests, fields, or waterways happen to offer. This is a guarantee that everything you are served arrives at your table fresh and without any additives.

In general, it can be said that traditional Tuscan cuisine is free of unnecessary refinement. It is simple cooking, a little on the rough side, hearty, and strongly spiced so it goes well with the unsalted bread that is served in abundance with every meal. The number of typical Tuscan recipes is rather limited. Olive oil is always a major ingredient; wild herbs, such as fennel or sage, are generally popular; and the region is known for its hearty soups and stews. On the coast, there is plenty of fish available; predominant in

Above: Wild boar delicacies. Right: A typical snack. Far Right: Harvesting tomatoes can be a laborious task.

the country's wooded interior are game dishes and different kinds of mushrooms. Vegetables are eaten everywhere, and every region has its own particular local specialty.

The following is an attempt to introduce a few of these specialties and shed some light on how they are prepared.

Let's begin in northern Tuscany, in the green valleys of the Garfagnana, where basic grains such as barley and spelt are still cultivated and used to produce hearty soups. One of the region's typically hearty soups – a thick stew enriched with beans, bacon, and various vegetables, that is especially popular in the mountain regions on cold winter nights – is made with cornmeal (*Infarinata*).

Along the coast, fish is served in every imaginable manner. Particularly well-known are the *triglie alla livornese* from the coast of Livorno, which has the most fish of any part of Italy. For this dish, otherwise known as "Red mullet, Livorno style," the fish are simmered slowly in a sauce of tomatoes, garlic and herbs, then

the whole thing is brought to your table and served in the pan. Also well-known, and equally popular, is the spicy, creamy fish soup known as *cacciucco*.

Every visitor to Florence quickly becomes familiar with the word *bistecca*. This wonderfully tender, tasty piece of sirloin comes from the white Chianina cows, from the Chiana valley, which are bred solely for this rather tragic purpose. "Tragic" because the young animals of this fast-growing breed are slaughtered at the age of between six and seven months, and are confined exclusively to their stalls for the entire span of their brief lives. But their meat, cooked on the grill and drizzled with fine olive oil, is simply poetic.

Typical of the area around Florence, but popular throughout Tuscany, are the white beans called *fagioli*, which are served in soups or as a side dish, drizzled with olive oil and perhaps garnished with a couple of slices of onion. A simple but tasty dish is *pappa al pomodoro* – old bread is softened in water and then mixed into a thick tomato soup.

Maremma is a region that is particularly blessed with fertile earth, which, since the draining of its swamps about a century ago, has produced fruit and vegetables in abundance. The leanness of past years, however, can be seen from such holdovers as *acquacotta*, which translates as "cooked water," and proves, on closer examination, to be a soup of onions, eggs, vegetables, olive oil, and toasted bread. A little *pecorino* (ewe's cheese), which is so excellent in this region that it is allowed to have its own protected label (DOC), is then grated over the soup

In the forests of the hinterland there is an abundance of wild game, mushrooms, and chestnuts. Truffles are found in parts of the Maremma, and wild boar, above all, is served in every trattoria in a wide variety of dishes – roasted, as ham or salami, or as *salsiccia* (sausage). And on the coast here, there is also plenty of fresh fish, which in the evening, after your swim, you can buy directly from the men on the fishing-boats that have just come in for the night.

ARTS AND CRAFTS

See Florence differently, for once! Not, in the usual manner, to follow the stations of the great artists, the painters, sculptors, or architects, but rather to seek out the *artigiani*, the artisans. Since the Middle Ages, they have ensured that Florence is known far and wide for its crafts and applied arts; together with the merchants, they helped ensure the city's reputation and wealth.

As early as the end of the 12th century, the city's artisans were forming guilds to help regulate production and trade. The guilds quickly came to wield significant political power, something that was demonstrated, for example, by the Weavers' Revolt of 1378, which helped a member of the still-unknown Medici family take political office for the first time. At the same time, the guilds acted as commissioners and patrons of public projects, thereby playing an important role for the city's cultural and artistic development.

Wandering through Florence, you encounter traces of this past everywhere. Take the church Orsanmichele, a former granary that the guilds transformed into their temple and meeting-place. Countless streets and piazzas bear the names of old guilds or professions; the *Palazzo dell'Arte della Lana*, the guild house of the wool merchants, still stands on Via Calimala; and many houses still bear the coats-of-arms of various professions over their doors.

The oldest guild in Florence is, in fact, that of the Calimala; its name is derived from the name of the street that runs between the old marketplace, now Piazza Reppublica, and the Mercato Nuovo, where the members of the guild, mainly cloth traders had their shops. Later, these wool traders were the most powerful guild; at the end of the 13th century, they had more than 300 factories available to them and employed about a quarter of the city's population. The guild of Por Santa Maria, which at first included only dealers in notions and goldsmiths, didn't become powerful until the silk makers joined its ranks; the latter's most valuable product was brocade cloth, which was in great demand. The patterns on these fabrics were designed by such artists as Lippi, Botticelli and Ghirlandaio. Among the so-called "higher" guilds were those of the moneychangers, judges and notaries, doctors and pharmacists. The "middle" guilds included shoemakers, tanners, butchers, blacksmiths, stonemasons and carpenters. Many of the other professions were all lumped together in the "lower" category.

On your excursion into this Florentine past, you will notice that the borders between artisans and artists often blur. Art and artisan guilds, *arte e arti*: even the Italian language doesn't make much of a distinction. Our separation of art as an intellectual, spiritual expression as opposed to the mechanical workmanship of artisans is a relatively modern development. In the days of Leonardo da Vinci, art was not produced in studios, rather in workshops. Painting and sculpture were considered to be "applied," rather than "fine," arts. Artists like Michelangelo, Giotto, or Ghirlandaio were simply the best in their guilds. The sculptor Andrea Verrocchio created monumental sculptures, but also banners for tournaments; the painter Botticelli earned extra money by decorating dowry chests; and, like nearly all sculptors of his day, Donatello had trained not as a sculptor, but as a goldsmith.

In Florence today, you can watch the descendants of the great masters, recipients of artisan wisdom that has been passed through the generations, as they work wood, stone or metal according to the traditional methods. They are masters of the old techniques, know all of the ins and outs of their trade, and can make old

Right: Alabaster fruit and eggs – Volterra has something to suit every taste.

things look new or new things old. For many years, Florence's artisans were content with merely copying the venerated objects of the past. Today, however, it is once again difficult to differentiate between artist and artisan. These women and men, often true masters of their trade, now employ both traditional techniques and modern shapes and forms, creating pieces that are true works of art(isanship).

Don't put off paying a visit to a traditional workshop. Even though there are still masterful artisans, less expensive industrial production is, inevitably, taking over, and the traditional techniques are slowly dying out. And fewer and fewer young artisans are coming along to take up the torch. For the time being, however, production continues, both in Florence and throughout Tuscany.

There is a particular flurry of activity in the streets around Santa Croce and Santo Spirito, neighborhoods that it was once advisable to frequent only in broad daylight. Those employed in the legions of small workshops here build new furniture or restore old pieces; carve and gild picture frames; repair musical instruments; weave or sew fabric; or throw ceramics. The air is filled with the smells of clay and glue, paint and wax.

In the side streets to the left and right of the Arno, too, you can find artisans who make objects to order or ably repair broken porcelain and ceramic heirlooms with patience and skill. Some have even achieved world renown, such as the woodcarver Bartolozzi on Via Maggio, who, with the help of a few photographs, was able to recreate the choir pews of the Benedictine monastery of Monte Cassino, after it was destroyed in World War II.

And before you know it, your tour has become a shopping expedition. One typical souvenir from Florence is stone inlay work. With the old technique of *pietre dure*, a paste of powdered gum resin, marble and shell is used to create marvelous patterns in stone. There are also true artists among the ranks of potters, who use their wheels to create marvelous traditional or modern ceramics.

On the Ponte Vecchio, you can see the monument that the old goldsmiths' guild erected to their great master Benvenuto Cellini – perhaps in part to remind themselves of the great creative heights to which members of their profession can rise. Where today gold is melted, shaped and soldered was, until the 16th century, a center for the city's butchers. Because of the stench of their rubbish, which they threw directly into the Arno, they were forced to clear the site and move further out of town. Near the water, too, are the leather tanneries, where, now as then, leather is tanned, cut, gilded, chased, and transformed into elegant boxes or book-covers.

If you would like to see how *carta marmorizzata*, the marbled paper that is so typical of Florence, has been produced for centuries, you can go to Giannini, on the Piazza Pitti, and watch as the bizarre

Above: Florentine artisanship continues to enjoy an excellent reputation. Right: Old copper pots.

and beautiful patterns form atop a tank of water. In the neighboring quarter of San Frediano you can find the *Antico Setificio Fiorentino*, where marvelous silk fabrics continue to be produced, by hand, on traditional looms.

But it isn't only within the city where fine artisanship to be found – it is spread throughout the region. You don't have to go all the way to Venice, for instance, to find fine hand-blown – or mouth-blown – glass. Since the Middle Ages, the secrets of this art have been handed down from father to son (or daughter) in Colle Val d'Elsa. There is reportedly a "Benvenuto Cellini of crystal" at work here, carving patterns in the glass as if telling a story (Boreno Cigni on Viccolo delle Fontanelle).

In Cortona, too, the artisan traditions date back to the Middle Ages. The old city is scattered with carpenters, furniture restorers and blacksmiths, who still in demand all over the world by virtue of their abilities. And those who like beautiful ceramics flock to this old Etruscan city for the typical sunflower pattern that is featured on its pottery.

In Carrara, of course, everything centers on marble. In marble working, the fine line between art and craft becomes particularly difficult to draw.

In Coreglia Antelminelli, on the other side of the Apuan Alps, smaller accessories are modeled from plaster. A museum documents the history of this trade.

If you are looking for basket weaving or raffia work from Tuscany – a Florentine hat or bag – you may strike it lucky in Fiesole, in the Caldine quarter, on Via di Coverciano. But there are hardly any *trecciaiole*, women who braid the fine straw, left in Tuscany. Even the hand-plaited *fiaschi* from Greve in Chianti, the round-bellied wine bottles in straw casings, are few and far between. But here, in the heart of Chianti, one old Etruscan tradition has been preserved – blacksmithing, or metalworking. This is also home to Ferruccio Ferrucci, born in 1909, Chianti's last basket-weaver, on the road between Greve and Figline.

The town of Impruneta is virtually synonymous with fired earthenware. Even the Renaissance master Brunelleschi favored tiles of this material, and used them in the construction of his masterpiece, the dome atop the Duomo in Florence. Today, the principal product of the town's kilns seems to be decorative flowerpots.

Lucca, on the other hand, has been able to guarantee the high quality of its silk and gold products for almost a thousand years. Like their hated rivals, the Florentines, Lucca's citizens based their prosperity on their abilities as artisans and merchants. But if you want a pipe carved from a real tree root, you will have to go into the Maremma, to Massa Marittima, where you can also find handmade lutes.

Pescia has a large flower market and handmade copper wares. If you have time and can speak Italian, Maestro Giovanni Donnini, near the Porta Fiorentina, loves to discuss the finer points of his trade.

Before it is too late and the traditional artisan methods are lost forever, the town of San Gimignano, where the main crafts are cabinet-making and embroidery, has opened a trade museum. Handmade lace and crossbows are the signature products of Sansepolcro, the home of Piero della Francesca. In Sesto Fiorentino, on the other hand, besides the fine porcelain of Richard-Ginori, handmade ceramics are crafted on the potters' wheels, in a range of shapes and patterns that are both traditional and modern.

What is the difference between a Florentine, Neapolitan and Sardinian knife? In Scarperia, the knife capital north of Florence, you will surely be able to find an expert who is able to give you the answer. And in Volterra, you can see that Tuscany's artisan traditions still bear an Etruscan stamp. After visiting the museum displaying antique alabaster urns, you can visit the shop of a modern craftsman and see how he, today, works the "stone of light" that comes from the belly of the earth.

Arts and Crafts

TUSCANY'S CULTURAL LANDSCAPE

The village of Monticchiello, south of Siena, had problems. In fact, emigration to the cities is an ill that has been suffered by many of the region's towns. During the 1960s, the people steadily left, houses stood empty, and the land lay fallow. The number of village residents dropped by more than half. Those who remained behind were afraid that they, too, would have to give up their living space, and would be forced have to turn it over to city slickers or other strangers.

Since 1967, however, Monticchiello has taken great steps to help itself with its *Teatro Povero*, or poor theater. The residents chose spoken drama as a means by which to defend themselves against this development, to give themselves a new sense of community. They write the plays themselves and also act in the performances, which are held every year at the end of July and the beginning of August. No one really remembers why exactly they decided to do theater all those years ago. Perhaps it was because there is a long tradition of folk theater in Tuscany, including marionette plays, spring festivals, and rhymed verse performed in song. The village's first production was a costume theater devoted to the historic theme of the eternal struggles between Siena and Florence. But then the Montichiellese hit upon a form of their own – representing their own problems as a way of seeking to establish a new sense of identity. The famous Milanese stage director Giorgio Strehler has found the appropriate name for this form of theater: *autodramma*.

Drama has brought the inhabitants of Monticchiello together again, and they have been able to prove that while the horizons of the province may be rural, their creativity is limitless.

Right: An open-air performance of the Teatro Povero, in Monticchiello.

Monticchiello's *Teatro Povera* is only one of many open-air summer cultural events held throughout Tuscany between June and September, when the regular theaters are closed for the summer. The natural beauty of this countryside is already a work of art in itself, a work, moreover, that has been refined through the years into a marvelous play of contrasting lines, colors and proportions by the hands of the farmers. During this time of year, the landscape becomes the backdrop for a wealth of musical and theatrical productions, a veritable explosion of every sort of cultural activity, both state and private.

During the Middle Ages and the Renaissance, it was painters, sculptors and architects, like Leonardo da Vinci, Piero della Francesca, Filippo Brunelleschi and Michelangelo Buonarotti who created the incomparable works that continue to attract millions of visitors to Tuscany's museums, churches and monasteries.

Today, on the other hand, the central focus of Tuscany's cultural landscape has shifted to the performing arts and *cultura popolare*, folk culture.

Throughout the province, cloisters are restored, undergrowth is cleared from old ruins, churches are cleaned out, or the village square is simply declared a cultural venue, in order to make room for every conceivable sort of spectacle. The summer festivals have various forms and contents, and are of equally varying degrees of quality. There are improvisational theaters and traditional plays, avant-garde and ultra-conservative productions, plenty of mediocrity, but also some productions of real quality that have a great deal to offer audiences. In some places, the performances remain simply a colorful mixture of theater, music and dance, a little bit of everything, something for everyone. Some of the organizations, however, have managed in a remarkably short period of time to make their events veritable Meccas for artists and spectators alike.

Tuscany's summer calendar begins in Florence, in May, with the *Maggio Musicale Fiorentino*, Musical May. This oldest of all Italian music festivals has been attracting fans of classical modernism to Florence with its first-rate performances for more than 60 years. In the past, you could hear all of the great orchestras here, the very best conductors (Bruno Walter), singers (Maria Callas), and works – there were opera productions that set standards for decades (Verdi's *Macbeth*), staged in historic settings by legends of the stage (Gustav Gründgens).

In recent years, however, the *Maggio Musicale* has lost a bit of its erstwhile glamor. This is partly due to every city of any size is trying, now, to get a festival of its own up and running. But part of the blame also lies with power-hungry politicians, who are all too fond of filling the festival's administration with their own (political) allies.

Not quite as spectacular, but another reason for lovers of classical music to visit Tuscany in July, is Fiesole's *Estate Fiesolana*, Cultural Summer. In the Roman amphitheater and the cloister of the Abbey of Badia Fiesolana, audiences can watch films, music, and dance or theater performances.

For the entertainment of beach guests, from mid-July to the end of August, Versilia offers the festival *La Versiliana* with a number of theater and dance performances as well as concerts. At nearly the same time, and not far away, is the *Festival Pucciniano* in Torre del Lago, where every year the great composer Giacomo Puccini is commemorated in the town where he composed some of his most important operas. These are performed in magnificent stagings on a large open-air stage built over the lake.

These large festivals, of international renown and with very high budgets, are the hallmarks of Tuscany's cultural summer. But specialists and genuine fans often prefer to attend the legion of smaller summer festivals that truly bring the province's theater and musical landscape to life.

Festivals

At the beginning of July, for example, theatergoers in the province of Florence have an important date with the *Volterra-teatro*, in the Etruscan city of Volterra, where classical, modern and even children's theater is presented in the city's loveliest squares.

You can hear contemporary tones in June and July at the *Festival delle Collini* in the Medici's summer palace in Poggio a Caiano. Fans of street performers and musicians, commonly known as buskers, should make sure they are in the picturesque little town of Pelago, near Pontassieve, at the beginning of July.

In Florence itself, there are two private organizations to insure – not only in the summer – that there is always a musical tidbit or two on the program. Responsible for classical music in general, and chamber music in particular, is the *Associazone Amici della Musica*, an exclusive union of music lovers that has been around since 1919. Similarly serious music is on the program of the *Centro Flog*, which is dedicated to researching and documenting folk traditions and music from around the globe. Its showcase is the *Festival Musica dei Popoli*, held from late June to early July, which presents the music of peoples the world over.

And while we are on the subject of ethnic music, this list of summer festivals would not be complete without inclusion of the largest blues festival in Italy, the three-day *Bluesin*, which is held in Pistoia at the beginning of July. Classical-music lovers, however, may prefer the Pistoiese Culture Summer in July, in the gardens of the town's old villas.

In the neighboring province of Lucca, in the silk center of Barga, there is a festival celebrating modern serious music from France and Italy. The spa town of Bagna di Lucca, on the other hand, takes the minds of its guests off their aches and

Right: Folk culture as depicted in the Teatro Povero, in Monticchiello.

pains with chamber music, theater performances and ballet between July and September.

A highlight of summer's cultural calendar in the province of Pisa is the *Pisa Estate*, a festival that offers excellent theater and music events. At about the same time, lovers of modern dance theater should attend the festival in Castiglioncello, in the province of Livorno.

Musica nel Chiostro, a series of concerts in the cloister of Santa Croce, in Batignano, in the province of Grosseto, is one of many praiseworthy private events that have come into being thanks to the magic Tuscany's landscape and culture have worked on a foreign artist. In this case, it is the Englishman Adam Pollock, who, every summer at this small festival, presents musical works that are rarely, if ever, performed elsewhere.

Not far from Batignano, near Capalbio, there is another remarkable cultural project – a bizarre sculpture park, filled with pieces by the French artist Niki de Saint-Phalle, is in the yard of the artist's own summer home. The park, which resembles a colorful fairytale garden, is popular with children as well as adults, and admission is free in the months of June and July. Anyone who likes traditional folk theater should stay in the neighborhood, here in the Maremma, at the end of July, to attend the festival in the Etruscan city of Sorano.

For more than 50 years, the *Accademia Musicale Chigiana* has presented a select series of chamber concerts, orchestral concerts and operas in the city of Siena, in July or August. At the same time, Siena also hosts a kind of jazz summer school that includes a number of evening concerts. This festival is known as *Siena Jazz*.

In fact, the entire province of Siena, which is also home to the theater village of Monticchiello, has cultural tidbits of one form or another to offer all summer long. In Castelnuovo Berardenga, for ex-

ample, classical music is presented, while in Abbadia San Salvatore, on Monte Amiata, presents theater and musicals for a discriminating public.

Bruscello, the traditional form of local peasant theater, is presented in Montepulciano's main square, where it has to share facilities with an extraordinary cultural undertaking, the *Cantiere Internazionale d'Arte*. Together, students and artists create avant-garde works in theater and music workshops, and ultimately perform them before audiences. The founder and leading light of the festival is the well-known German composer Hans Werner Henze.

In the province of Arezzo, there are no fewer than three unusual musical events: the *Concorso Polifonico Internazionale "Guido d'Arezzo,"* a competition in which choirs of every imaginable style vie with one another; an organ festival in the monastery of San Francesco in La Verna, where you can hear organists from throughout Europe; and a festival in nearby Sansepolcro, where unpublished

chamber music from several countries is performed before an interested public. All of which is still an incomplete listing of the region's multi-faceted cultural calendar.

Before leaving this topic, another welcome variation of Tuscan culture should be mentioned. For several years now, museums that are devoted to documenting peasant life have been opened throughout the region. These are often financed privately and initiated by foreign guests who comb the area for grains of lost or vanishing tradition. In the wake of many *cultura popolare*, folk culture, initiatives, like the *Teatro Povero* in Monticchiello, interest in the region's long neglected past has grown and is continuing to grow.

Particularly noteworthy among these museums are the Farmer's Museum in Gaville near Figline; the Museum of Folk Culture, in Palazzuolo sul Senio; the ethnographic center, in the Bisenzio valley; and, last but not least, the Ideale Museum of Leonardo da Vinci, in Vinci, the master's home town.

Festivals

FEASTS AND CIRCUSES

If you drive through the Tuscan countryside during the summer, you will see bright posters plastered across tree trunks or the walls of houses announcing a bewildering variety of impending *sagra* – *Sagra del Tartufo*, *Sagra di Tortellini*, *Sagra del Cinghiale*. The name of this church festival announces a whole schedule in itself, for a *sagra* has, basically, one purpose: it offers the rural population, and any visitors from the city who happen to be around that weekend, the chance to sit at long wooden tables and eat local specialties, thereby forgetting the long winter. To aid this processing of forgetting, these proceedings are fueled with plenty of local wine. And because a sagra is a great opportunity to meet neighbors and friends under the open sky and spend a few convivial hours together, there is also usually a band provide dance music.

Sagras, like the festival of a patron saint that is hosted by a given congregation, or the party festivals of the old Italian Communist Party, the ever-popular *Festa dell'Unità*, have long been a focal point of village life and one of the year's highlights. But if you are looking for the ancient tradition underlying this widespread custom, you will be disappointed.

Sagras are the offspring of popular culture, born in the postwar era when, seeking a new identity of their own, young people in the country began to express themselves more creatively within their landscape and community, social surroundings and countryside. It wasn't that there had previously been a dearth of popular culture in Tuscany – the region looks back on a long history of folklore traditions, some of them deriving from a mixture of heathen customs and religious rites, often seasonal, that are still celebrated enthusiastically throughout the

Right: In the fall, Tuscans gather at chestnut festivals.

area – but many of these traditions were abandoned for a time, and weren't pulled out of mothballs until the 1960s. Today, few other regions in Italy have such a vivid awareness of their own authentic folklore and festivals as does Tuscany.

The annual festival calendar begins on January 6 with a children's festival that centers on the *Befana*, a friendly witch who gives children, according to how they have behaved in the course of the preceding year, a reward in the form of a small gift or punishment in the form of a lump of coal placed in front of their bedroom door. The next important folklore event is carnival season, which in days gone by was often the only chance a young peasant girl had to go out dancing and look around for a husband. The high point of Tuscany's carnival celebrations are the parades in Viareggio that are filled with colorful, allegorical floats and imaginative choreography. At the same time, many village squares host *bruscello*, a grotesque-erotic form of peasant theater centering on the subject of fertility.

During the Holy Week, the proceedings are far more decorous, with penitential processions and passion plays. In the town of Grassina, near Florence, in the night of Good Friday, the residents reenact the life and suffering of Jesus.

On Easter Sunday, Florentines meet in front of the Duomo to participate in a religious Easter ceremony, the *Scoppio del Carro*, and watch how, with the help of a clay pigeon, the "holy fire" is ignited on an oxcart. This tradition reaches back to the days of the Crusaders.

Tuscan through and through is the *Canto del Maggio*, an old song festival that ushers in the spring, particularly in the coastal regions. On the night of April 30, a group of young people, known as the *maggiolanti*, go singing and dancing from house to house, which is supposed to ensure a good harvest. In the Lunigiana and the Garfagnana, a local version of this tradition, the *Maggio Drammatico*, is

a mixture of tradition and folk theater that links the dualities of winter and spring, and good and evil, to historic events, and presents them in earthy verses.

Lucca, too, has its own religious-folkloric ceremonies. On September 13, the *Volto Santo*, the early medieval figure of Christ from the cathedral, the origins of which are obscured in a web of legend, is borne through the city in a festive torchlight procession.

Christmas in Tuscany has a tradition all its own, although today this has followed the lead of the rest of the Western world and degenerated into the normal consumer orgy of gift-giving under a Christmas tree adorned with lights. It used to be, however, that a *ceppo*, a triangular rootstock, held the central role on Christmas Eve. It was decorated with fruits and laurel leaves, sprayed with wine, and finally burned slowly in an open fireplace in a mixture of religious ritual and praise to the wine god Bacchus. In city apartments without fireplaces, the *ceppo* was imitated by a pyramidal set of shelves, in

which presents and sweets were set. Another part of the Christmas tradition here is the viewing of the various Nativity scenes that are displayed throughout the region. Old and new, they are often comprised of living figures, such as the one in Equi Terme in Lunigiana, where the entire village population enacts the Christmas story on Christmas Eve. In a grotto in Porto Santo Stéfano, there is even one that is under water.

In the ranks of Tuscan festivals and holidays, the historic games of various towns hold a very special position. These are generally magnificent costume pageants, albeit often with imaginative rather than historic costumes, that are supposed to reawaken the population's sense of its history and its past. Usually, they are accompanied by splendid parades or linked to a banquet or feast. One major impetus for such forms of popular entertainment is the tourist traffic that they encourage, but the games are taken very seriously by their protagonists as well as by the local spectators. In recent years, such pageant-

games have seen a veritable renaissance throughout Tuscany.

A typically Tuscan element of these games is that they are virtually all competitions, a fact that supposedly originates from a characteristic of the Tuscan soul. Of the *maledetti toscani*, the accursed Tuscans, as the writer Curzio Malaparte referred to his fellow-countrymen, it is said that they amuse themselves best in pairs. As soon as a third party enters the picture, people immediately begin to take sides and start amusing themselves at the cost of their opponents. What appears to tourists and visitors to be an entertaining costume party often becomes deadly earnest for the people who are actually involved. Not infrequently, someone comes out of the games with an ear torn off or a broken arm. This somewhat dubious form of entertainment may have its origins in

Above: You have to start early if you want to be a good flag-waver. Right: After the Palio, the Sienese continue celebrating at the huge banquets that are set up in the city's streets.

the fact that the Tuscans, in the course of their eventful past, were nearly always engaged in conflicts of one sort or the other, and through the centuries this has become part of their flesh and blood, part of their cultural identity.

Take, for example, the *Calcio in Costume* in Florence (June 24), which is a wild free-for-all between two teams over a ball. It is a kind of soccer game played in historic costumes, although feet are mainly employed to deliberately inflict damage upon the members of the opposing team. It seems rather brutal now, but may have made sense in 1530, when the Florentine men challenged the Imperial troops who were occupying the city to a "game." Back then, for the Florentines, the prize of victory was the privilege of being allowed to collect food supplies. Today, however, there is really no justification for the kind of brutality that is sometimes seen on the playing field.

Another tradition that dates back to the 16th century is the *Giostra del Saracino*, held on the last Sunday in June and first

Sunday in September, on Arezzo's Piazza Grande. This is another competitive game in which riders from different quarters of the city joust with lances against a huge puppet, who hits back with a heavy whip if you don't hit him exactly in the middle.

In the medieval *Gioco del Ponte* in Pisa (last Sunday in June), strong men struggle to push, pull or shove each other off a bridge into the Arno. The former maritime republic presents another spectacle, the *Regatta Storico di San Ranieri*, a rowing regatta on the Arno that is held on June 17, to honor the city's patron saint.

Also dedicated to a saint, this time Bernard, the *Balestro del Girifalco* (May 20 and the second Sunday in August) in Massa Marittima, is a competition between crossbow archers shooting at falcons. Dating back to the Middle Ages, it was resumed in 1959. It is for Saint Jacob that, on July 25, Pistoia holds its *Giostra dell'Orso*, an equestrian tournament with roots in the 13th century. After a picturesque parade, twelve riders tilt with their lances at two stylized bear figures. This tournament is the climax of the "Pistoiese July," a festival that combines cultural, athletic and folklore events.

For the last 600 years, the *Palio della Balestra* has been held in Sansepolcro. The second Sunday in September sees crossbow archers compete against rivals from the Umbrian town of Gubbio, in the name of Saint Aegidius. In May, the costumed archers from Sansepulcro parade over to Gubbio, where the opposing team formally challenges them to the contest. The participants' costumes are replicas of the clothes depicted in old frescoes, and the weapons they use actually date from the 14th century.

Unchallenged monarch of Tuscany's games is the *Palio* in Siena (July 2 and August 16), a horse race on the Piazza del Campo. Uninitiated visitors could easily leave with the impression that the fanatical Sienese could take the death of horses and riders in stride as long as the riders representing their city neighborhood succeeded in capturing the contested banner, the *palio*, and thus the victory.

233

HIKING IN TUSCANY

Hiking is the most romantic and perhaps the most intensive way to travel. A hiker is part of the landscape, and actively takes it in with all five senses. Traveling on foot, you approach towns, people, or sights gradually, at a human pace. Meetings and chance encounters take place that would be impossible for someone traveling by car, cut off from his surroundings. A hiker's route generally bypasses overcrowded spots and leads through solitary landscapes that have retained their original, natural qualities, and allow real insight into the land's true character.

Tuscany is perfect hiking country. And this mode of travel is actually the best way to discover this region. The land is, in many places, like a giant garden. Its winding paths, which often lead up hill and down dale, constantly yield up new vistas or open out on unexpected panoramas.

Tuscany is comfortable hiking country as well. The trails are not overly difficult or demanding, and they are suited to walkers of all ages and levels of physical condition. The climate is mild – apart, of course, from the hot summers and cold winters – and you can plan your trips hour by hour or map out a route that will take you several days. You can embark on a walk around one of the smaller villages, which often lie on hilltops; you can walk from one town to the next; or you can avoid civilization altogether and plunge into the region's unspoiled nature. Overnight accommodation of all kinds is available at every turn – in farmhouses or village inns, in hotels in the larger cities, or campgrounds throughout the countryside. In mountainous regions, there are even mountain huts and hostels.

If you would like to plan out your hiking route carefully before you set out, the tourist offices in every town can furnish

Above: Tuscany is ideal country for a riding vacation. Right: After all those hills, a little refreshment is in order.

you with a wealth of material. In addition, there are plenty of books available with various routes, tips and background information. A few such titles are listed in the "Guidelines" section of this book.

Tuscany, of course, isn't just for hikers. Another intimate way to explore and experience this region's magnificent landscape, with its gentle colors, intense smells and unbelievable tranquility, is on horseback. "Tranquility" is a better term to describe the absence of civilization than "silence," for it is hard to believe the cacophonous din of bird song, especially in spring, that rises from the dense maquis undergrowth that provides birds with an ideal natural habitat. This is punctuated with the cries of the pheasants that flourish here, and are popular targets for the hordes of passionate sport hunters who flock to the countryside in season.

Another popular target of the hunters are wild boar, although these certainly don't seem much bothered by the hunters – they have procreated at an alarming rate all over Tuscany, and have become a real nuisance. At night, they force their way into farmers' gardens and vineyards and help themselves to fruit and vegetables. The payoff for this is that, especially in the wooded parts of the region, you can find all kind of delicious wild boar specialties.

If you opt to take a car along the narrow, notably winding and often very steep mountain roads, you will encounter, especially after working hours or on weekends, what at times seems a constant stream of cyclists in bright jerseys, either grimacing and battling with their slender racing bikes up a steep incline or zooming down again without much evident care for approaching traffic. If you are not as ambitious as these cyclists, but would still like to explore Tuscany *en plein air,* yet at a slightly faster pace than a pedestrian, you may still find a bicycle to be the perfect way to go. There are all kinds of tours, at all levels of difficulty – although be warned that nowhere in Tuscany is the land altogether flat, which is exactly why it is so lovely.

Hiking

235

FOREIGNERS IN TUSCANY

"The land where the lemons blossom..." Since Goethe's famous *Italian Journey*, or even earlier, the Apennine Peninsula has been a paradise for all of those who seek to rediscover the romantic Italy of yesteryear. The works of Shelley and Byron had a similar effect. Writing down their observations and experiences, these poets unwittingly unleashed an avalanche. First individually, then in groups, today *en masse*, tourists from around the globe converge on Italy, and seem particularly drawn to Tuscany. After all, this region is Mediterranean without being too foreign. Its cuisine is southern without threatening the digestion. And its people, its inhabitants are southern, temperamental, spirited, and yet "somehow civilized."

The first great wave of vacationers broke over Tuscany in the 1960s. It was this that leveled the way for the onslaught of mass tourism. Today, tour groups in Florence are herded along the well-trodden routes – Duomo, Piazza Signoria, Ponte Vecchio – after which they are taken off, in the afternoon, to photograph the skyline of San Gimignano and the Leaning Tower of Pisa.

Then there were the academics, and other scholars, who have for centuries come south for purposes of study, their gaze trained firmly on the past. For a long time, these travelers to the temples of art overlooked the fact that it could also be fun to mingle with the people of the region. Today, young people come to Florence, Pisa and Siena not only to learn about the sun-drenched Renaissance culture, but also the art of *saper vivere*.

In the 1970s, increasing numbers of travelers arrived for whom the second-most important vacation book, after the *Blue Guide* or *Baedeker*, was their check-

Right: The dream of many who visit Tuscany – transforming an old villa in a beautiful setting into a vacation home.

book. These people bought themselves a piece of vacationland, thereby joining the club of English aristocrats and intellectuals who were buying up villas in the hills around Florence as early as the beginning of the 20th century. But, instead of integrating themselves, many preferred to remain among themselves in an imported, British atmosphere. If an Italian did set foot in one of their salons, he was likely to be a member of an old Florentine family – for the local aristocracy, at least, knew a bit of English and had a proper feeling for the importance of a proper afternoon tea.

The modern vacation settler, however, is more likely to hail from Zurich, Oslo or Munich, and is probably a university professor, filmmaker, or therapist. A well-paying job enables him to retreat for a few months every summer into his simple Tuscan country house, so he can "find himself" anew. These summer guests embark, well-armed, on their search for the meaning of life. They are usually fluent in the local language, seek out contact with the locals, and generally love all things Italian – the wine, the food, the clothes, the lifestyle. And when autumn begins and the rains start, they return, rested and content, to their comfortable city apartments north of the Alps, where some of them even write a new chapter of the Tuscan myth.

For a while, a few modern romantics even tried to flee the pressures of an achievement-oriented society by retiring here altogether. They could be spotted at local markets in colorful, hand-knitted garments, trying to sell cheese made of ewe's milk or painted pottery of their own design. Later, they created imaginative self-help seminars for like-minded people. Eventually, their illusions of the joys of a primitive life popped one-by-one like soap bubbles. They learned to fear cold winters in damp houses, and the Italian tax authorities. They learned, too, that today it is practically impossible to survive without a steady monthly income, prefer-

ably from one's own country – even in paradise.

The Italianophilic summer guests who own property here will doubtless remain faithful to "their" Tuscany. They have a great time here, and they are tolerated by the locals. After all, they spend their money in the local shops and at the bar, and don't miss a single *sagra*, or local summer festival. They ask for help and advice in pruning their olive trees and grapevines – for, of course, a price – and happily help gather in the grape harvest – for free!

The Tuscans themselves look with equanimity, sometimes with a bit of amusement, but generally with distance upon these comings and goings. Certainly they are happy that guests bring money into the local economy. The rural population is glad to see decrepit houses being bought and restored. They have the greatest respect for anyone who doesn't shrink away from hard work in the stony soil. And since the population here has watched, for centuries, wave after wave

of foreigners coming through, be they pilgrims, merchants or soldiers, they are not particularly impressed, much less intimidated, by this peaceful invasion.

As for foreigners who live and work in Tuscany, such as myself – that is a subject unto itself. Many of them came here hoping to discover the Italy of Antiquity, and ended up colliding head-on with the actual Italy of today.

"You live with Italy as you would with a lover – today quarreling mightily, tomorrow in adoration," Schopenhauer pithily noted during one of his stays in Florence. Anyone who wants to stay here for a long time has to be aware that he will need all his strength and energy to reach a compromise with the country. There is no room here for imported illusions, habits, expectations and other baggage. Nor is there any place for half measures. If you prefer things a little calmer, you would do better to stay in a place like Germany, where life, also according to Schopenhauer, is "like life with a housewife, without great anger, but without great love."

Foreigners

FRESCOES
The Television of the Renaissance

We, as children of the television generation, think that the concept of conveying information through pictures is a terribly modern innovation. But it is really not all that new. In Tuscany, 600 years ago, pictures were already being used as a medium to communicate the experiences of the then-contemporary world. And for a modern visitor, these pictures can be the key to opening the door to the history of the cities and their culture. They remain fascinating because, even today, they still have so much to say.

In 1338, the painter Ambrogio Lorenzetti was commissioned to decorate the walls of the Sala della Pace, in Siena's Palazzo Pubblico, with frescoes. This room was the meeting-chamber of the Council of Nine, a body that passed the laws that

Above: The results of the Ideal Government – Ambrogio Lorenzetti's fresco in the Palazzo Pubblico, in Siena.

regulated the city's life down to the smallest detail. These laws were written down in the Tuscan dialect, and lay in the town hall to be read by any citizen who wished to do so. In 1339, both Lorenzetti's frescoes and a new body of laws were completed, and the painter's frescoes can be seen as a kind of illustration of these legal texts.

At that time, visitors entered the room through the old entrance in the corner of the central wall. The two frescoes that he saw above him if he turned his head depicted the victory of Justice on the right, and, on the left, her defeat. The right-hand image shows a majestic woman on a throne; on the left, she is lying bound on the floor, and her scales are broken. The visitor can decide between these two alternatives, and the consequences of his decision are immediately illustrated – peace or war. These topics are treated in detail in the rest of Lorenzetti's frescoes.

The bad, unjust government naturally leads to a state of tyranny, in which the city decays, the streets are unsafe, and the

workshops are plundered. Murder, thievery and rape are shown next to allegorical figures of arrogance, greed, betrayal, cruelty, and war. Fear rules the countryside. Roads, bridges and farmhouses fall into disrepair, and armed men march across the fields.

Under the good government, however, the ideal of the Council of Nine in Siena, the city and the surrounding countryside flourish. The city overflows with goods, the people are dressed elegantly, and everywhere you see people who are working, learning and building (the frescoes offer an excellent illustration of the building techniques that were in use at that time). Even the countryside is depicted in graphic detail – you can easily recognize the Arbia valley. Fields and vineyards are well-tended, and the roads are crowded with traveling merchants. A winged image of security overlooks the scene.

The allegorical figures at the sides of this fresco represent the virtues of peace, strength, intelligence, courage, temperance and justice.

"Talking pictures" is the term one art historian coined for Lorenzetti's frescoes. And there are comparable images in Pisa's Camposanto, in the chapel of Santa Maria Novella in Florence and in the municipal and administrative buildings of a number of smaller cities. They are impressive pictorial narratives of Tuscan civic culture in the 14th century. The frescoes convey a certain social ideal and organize the experiences of the viewer into an order corresponding to the worldview of the epoch in which Lorenzetti lived. This order is a form of knowledge, of understanding.

When you have seen your fill and are back out on the Campo sipping a cup of espresso, you may suddenly feel like you have been transported back into the 14th-century city republic. And later, when you are sitting at home, in front of the evening news watching images of war, assassination and other catastrophes, you may close your eyes and think back to the images you saw in Siena. And all at once, you, too, may begin to understand.

METRIC CONVERSION

Metric Unit	US Equivalent
Meter (m)	39.37 in.
Kilometer (km)	0.6241 mi.
Square Meter (sq m)	10.76 sq. ft.
Hectare (ha)	2.471 acres
Square Kilometer (sq km)	0.386 sq. mi.
Kilogram (kg)	2.2 lbs.
Liter (l)	1.05 qt.

TRAVEL PREPARATIONS

When to Go

Tuscany is "in season" year round. More than four million foreign and Italian tourists, who have more than 120,000 beds in hotels and guesthouses at their disposal, flood into Florence and other popular tourist centers throughout the year – particularly on short guided tours on long holiday weekends. If possible, you should avoid planning your trip to Tuscany over Easter, Pentecost (Whitsuntide) and Christmas. Also the cities can be unbearable in the oppressive heat of summer, when you are better off following the lead of the Tuscans, who set aside their work in July and August and take refuge on the coast. Another alternative is to visit the cooler mountain regions where you can go on marvelous hikes, and will also find that there are, usually, plenty of diversions for art and culture lovers.

Tuscany's mild, Mediterranean climate makes it particularly pleasant during the spring and fall. Unfortunately, since most visitors know this, it can be difficult to find lodging during these months. It is also possible that visitors in April/May and October/November are surprised by sudden cloudbursts, but you will rarely experience a protracted period of bad, rainy weather, as is often the case north of the Alps.

Art lovers, more than anyone else, are well advised to travel in the winter, when the museums are likely to be empty of people. The countryside, too, has a special attraction all its own at this time of year. At higher altitudes, however, January may see temperatures around freezing, and the old stone buildings can get extremely cold. Particularly in mid- to low-priced accommodations, the heating can often be inadequate during cold winter weather.

If you want enough time to really get to know Tuscany, rather than merely dropping by for a superficial visit, you should plan to stay for at least three weeks. If you don't have much time, limit yourself to a handful of destinations. Tuscany is an area that demands time, effort and a sense of adventure if you want to really get to know it.

Clothing

Light summer clothes are always fine, but in the spring and fall you should bring along a warm pullover and some rain gear. In the winter, you will probably need warm wool clothing. And it isn't a bad idea to take along a blanket or sleeping bag, which may come in handy if you plan to stay in (cold) old country estates or hotels and pensions in the lower price category.

When setting out to visit churches and monasteries, make sure that you wear suitable clothing – no shorts or short skirts, and keep your shoulders covered. If you don't follow this code, you may not be allowed in. Most Italians feel that it is important to dress well and, above all, properly. Even in beach towns, therefore, don't run around in your swimming suit unless you don't mind being followed by disapproving glances.

Suggested Reading

The following is a selection of books that you may be interested in reading for pleasure, in preparation for your trip, or for background information about what you are likely to encounter in Tuscany:

Abrams (publisher); *Renaissance and Mannerist Art*.
Barzini, Luigi; *The Italians*.
Berenson, Bernard; *The Florentine Painters of the Renaissance* and *The Passionate Sightseer*.
Burckhardt, Jacob; *Civilization of the Renaissance in Italy*.
Fischer, Heinz-Joachim; *Tuscany* (Prestel Guide).
Forster, E.M.; *A Room with a View*.
Fruttero, Carlo and Franco Lucentini; *The Secret of the Pineta*.
James, Henry; *Italian Hours*, *Portrait of a Lady*, and short stories.
Lawrence, D.H.; *Etruscan Places*.
McCarthy, Mary; *The Stones of Florence*.
Murray, Peter; *The Architecture of the Italian Renaissance*.
Origo, Iris; *The Merchant of Prato*.
Pater, Walter; *The Renaissance*.

Facts & Figures

Tuscany is the fifth largest of Italy's twenty regions. It measures about 23,000 square kilometers and is divided into ten provinces: Arezzo, Florence, Grosseto, Livorno, Lucca, Massa-Carrara, Pisa, Pistoia, Prato (since 1993) and Siena.

The largest cities (statistics from early 1999) are Florence (population 377,180), Livorno (161,943), Prato (171,135) and Pisa (93,000).

Quite some time ago, Tuscany ceased to be a primarily agricultural region. Today, less than 10% of the population makes their living from agriculture, although the figure is as high as 20% in the provinces of Siena and Grosseto. The main agricultural products are grain and fodder, wine and olives, but there is also some cultivation of fruit and vegetables. Additional agricultural products include tobacco and the region's famous meat, and *pecorino* (cheese made with ewe's milk).

Some 60% of Tuscans are either employed in the industrial sector (engineering, shoemaking, woodworking and the textile and chemical industries) or support themselves by artisan skills, usually practiced in small or even family-owned businesses. The trade and service fields (mainly in the tourist industry) support another 25% of the population.

One-tenth of the tourists in Italy visit Tuscany. Of these, about 35% are foreigners, 40% Italians, and 25% Tuscans.

GETTING THERE

By Plane

Tuscany's most important international airport is in Pisa (Galileo Galilei). From here, the trains and buses of the Linie Lazzi run to Florence every hour. Florence has its own international airport (Peretola), which is also important for domestic connecting flights. Expansion of this airport recently began. From abroad, you can also fly into Milan and continue to Tuscany from there by train.

By Car

From central Europe, if you are coming through Germany and Austria, you can get to Tuscany by taking the expressway A 22 via Bozen, Verona and Modena. From there, the A 1 leads, via Bologna, to Florence. If you are coming from the south (Rome), the A 1 will also bring you to Florence, but from the other direction.

If you are arriving from southwest Germany or Switzerland, join the A 1 in Milan and follow it towards Modena. You can also drive from Milan to Parma, and from where you can take the A 15 over the Cisa Pass to La Spezia. From there you can catch the southbound A 12. From Viareggio, the crossland route (A 11, Firenze-Mare) runs through Lucca and on to Florence.

From France, follow the A 12 from Genoa, along the scenic Ligurian coast, through the Versilia to Pisa or Livorno.

Guidelines

You are required to pay a toll for the privilege of traveling on Italian expressways. From the Brenner Pass to Florence, the charge (1999) is about 60,000 lire. The purchase of a Viacard for 50,000 lire, available at expressway gas stations is recommended. There are special lanes for card users at the exits.

By Train

A number of Tuscany's larger cities (Massa-Carrara, Pisa, Livorno, Grosseto, Florence, Arezzo) are located on the main Italian train lines, and therefore have direct connections to a number of European cities. A number of trains end at the station of Santa Maria Novella in Florence. The trains that don't end in Florence stop at the station Campo di Marte, in the eastern part of the city.

If you want to travel to your final destination by taking a local train from one of the larger cities, you'd better bring plenty of patience, since most of these trains do stop at literally every station. On the other hand, this leisurely pace can provide you with some enchanting insights into provincial life.

By Bus

There aren't any regular international bus connections to Tuscany, but a number of private bus companies do offer organized tours to Florence and Tuscany.

GETTING AROUND

If you are planning a tour of Tuscany's cities and you already know where you want to go, it is most practical to travel by plane or train. Most of the old city centers are closed to car traffic, parking lots can be few and far between, and furthermore, most of the sights, which are generally grouped together within a city center, are easy to reach on foot. In addition, good public transportation within the cities – that is, public buses – make it quick and easy for you to get to those slightly out-of-the-way destinations.

But if want to get to know the countryside, and aren't prepared to do so on foot or bicycle, you are almost obliged to go by car. This will give you the freedom to seek out small villages and hidden corners, as well as giving you more freedom to transport wine, oil and any other local specialties you might want to collect along the way.

All of the major car rental companies have branches in Florence and the region's other large cities. It is usually quite a bit cheaper if you make a reservation in advance.

There are also three main bus networks in Tuscany that are operated by the transportation companies Lazzi Fratelli, SITA and CAP. There are also a number of smaller local buses that service individual cities and the surrounding villages. Tickets can be purchased at bus company offices or in bars and kiosks.

PRACTICAL TIPS

Accommodations

Hotels. The hotels and guesthouses in Italy are classified or categorized by stars (* to *****). This system, however, fails take into account the location, possible noise, or atmosphere. Still, you can assume that a three-star hotel will provide solid comfort at moderate prices (©©). Anything over that is considered luxury (©©©) or first-class accommodation and you can expect to pay between 150,000 (single) and 200,000 lire (double), and 350,000 (single) and 550,000 lire (double) respectively. Budget (©) accommodations range from friendly little family hotels to run-down dumps.

All in all, you can expect that in tourist centers such as Florence, Lucca and Siena you will have to pay more than you would elsewhere. Prices must be posted both in the room and at the reception desk, and breakfast is normally only served (for an extra charge) if you have asked for it.

Usually, it is better to forget about the (rather indifferent) hotel breakfast and pick up a cappuccino and a fresh *cornetto* (roll, croissant) in the nearest bar.

Reasonably priced, and often particularly nice and peaceful, accommodation is offered in a number of old monasteries, where the food is also often very good. Sometimes, however, unmarried couples will not be allowed to share a double room in these facilities. *Agritourismus* (Farm Vacations) also offers reasonably priced accommodation. Complete hotel listings are available from A.P.T. and Pro Loco, local tourist information offices.

Youth Hostels. If you hold an international youth hostel membership card, you can sleep cheaply in Italian youth hostels. It is a good idea to call ahead, and essential if you are traveling in a group of more than five people. If the hostel is full, the maximum stay is three nights. For more information, contact the Associazione Italiana Alberghi per la Gioventù, Via Cavour 44, 00184 Roma, Italy, tel: 06-487 1152, fax: 06-488 0492.

Camping. Most of Tuscany's campgrounds are only open between April and September or October. You can make reservations at, and get a campground guide from Federcampeggio, Casella Postale 23, 50041 Calenzano, Italy, tel: 055-882 391, fax: 055-882 5918. You can also get guides to the region's campgrounds at local bookstores.

Airlines

Offices in **PISA**:
ALITALIA, Galileo Galilei International Airport, tel: 050-147 865 643 (info), 050-147 865 642 (internat'l), 050-147 865 641 (domestic).
BRITSH AIRWAYS, Airport, toll-free tel: 147 812 266.
LUFTHANSA, 02 583 725 (reservations).
Offices in **FLORENCE**:
ALITALIA, Vicolo Oro 1, tel: 055-27881.
BRITISH AIRWAYS, Via Vigna Nuova 36R, tel: 055-218 655 and 055-216 769.

TWA, Via Vecchietti 4, tel: 055-284 691, 055-239 6856 and 055-238 2795.
Offices in **CAMPO NELL'ELBA**:
INTERNATIONAL FLYING SERVICES, Aeroporto La Pila, Marina di Campo, tel: 0565-977 937 / 938.

Auto Club

ACI (Automobile Club Italiano), tel: 116.

Banks

Banks are open Monday-Friday 8:30 am-1:30 pm and ca. 3:00-4:00 pm. The currency exchange counters at the Santa Maria Novella train station in Florence, and the Galileo Galilei International Airport in Pisa, are open longer, and on Saturdays. Many hotels will also change money, but the exchange rate is often less favorable than at exchange counters or in banks. For those with EC cards, it is still cheapest to get the cash you need from the automatic bank machines that are in most medium-sized and large cities.

Eurocheques can only be cashed at a bank, and they have to be filled out in lire in the presence of the teller. Many hotels and shops also take credit cards and travelers' checks.

Bus Companies

SITA, Florence, Via Santa Caterina da Siena 17R, tel: 055-294 955. **Lazzi Fratelli**, Florence, Piazza Stazione, tel: 055-351 061; Lucca, Piazza Le Verdi, tel: 0583-584 877. **CPT**, Pisa, Piazza San Antonio, tel: 050-505 511; **APL**, Livorno, Piazza Grande, tel: 0586-884 262. **RAMA**, Grosseto, Piazza Marconi, tel: 0564-25 215.

Consulates

In FLORENCE (area code 055):
Great Britain, Lungarno Corsini 2, tel: 284 133 / 212 594; **USA**, Lungarno Amerigo Vespucci 38, tel: 239 8276 / 217 605 and **U.S.I.S.** (United States Information Service) Lungarno Amerigo Vespucci 46, tel: 216 531 / 294 921. Office

hours 8:30 am-1 pm and 2:00-5:30 pm, by appointment only.

Crime

Tuscany's tourist centers are an El Dorado for pickpockets who jostle or seem to approach you with a friendly question. They can relieve you of your valuables and be gone before you know what has happened. Bands of seemingly-innocent women and children are not to be trusted either – their methods are particularly refined.

If you have a car, use attended parking lots when possible. Don't leave valuables in plain view and open the glove box so potential thieves can see that nothing is hidden inside.

Electricity

In Italy, the electrical current is 220V AC, which means North American appliances won't generally work, and UK appliances need an adaptor.

Emergencies

Carabinieri, tel: 112
Police and Emergency (automobile accidents), tel: 113

Farm Vacations

(*Agriturismo* and *Turismo Verde*)

Nowhere else do you have so many chances to spend a relaxed, back-to-nature vacation as you do in Tuscany. Countless former and still-working farmhouses offer reasonably priced accommodation, generally as self-contained apartments. This may be with or without direct contact with the host family. If you wish to, you can often pay a small fee and have meals included as part of your stay. These meals are eaten with the host family, and usually consist of good solid homemade dishes made with the farm's own products.

For addresses and additional information, contact the local tourist information offices.

Ferries

You can get the schedule for ferries between the mainland and the islands of the Tuscan Archipelago from the following agencies:

ISOLA D'ELBA:

TOREMAR, Piazza Arsenale 8, 57100 Livorno, tel: 0586-896 113; Calata Italia, 22, 57037 Portoferraio, tel: 0565-918 080; Piazzale Premuda 13-14, 57025 Piombino, tel: 0565-31 100; Banch. dei Voltoni 9, 57038 Rio Marina, tel: 0565-962 073; Banchina IV Novembre 19, 57036 Porto Azzurro, tel: 0565-95 004; Via Michelangelo 54, 57030 Cavo, tel: 0565-949 871.

NAV.AR.MA. Lines, Piazzale Premuda 13, 57025 Piombino, tel: 0565-221 212; Viale Elba 4, 57037 Portoferraio, tel: 0565-914 133 / 918 101.

Moby Lines, Via Ninci 1, 57037 Portoferraio, tel: 0565-9361 / 910 101. Florence reservation office, Lungarno Corsini 42B, tel: 055-280 959.

ISOLA DEL GÍGLIO:

Maregiglio, Loc. Porto, Via Umberto I, 58013 Isola del Gíglio, tel: 0564-809 349; Piazzale A. Candi, 58019 Porto Santo Stéfano, tel: 0564-812 920.

ISOLA DI CAPRAIA:

TOREMAR, Via Assunzione, 57032 Isola di Capraia, tel: 0586-905 069.

Sample prices for the trip to Elba:

Piombino-Portoferraio (January 1-May 30), per person: 10,000 lire; per car (depending on size): 39,000-69,000 lire. Hydrofoil, per person: 18,000 lire. During the summer months, fares are generally 2000-3000 lire (per person) and 1500 lire (per car) more expensive.

For the trip to Gíglio:

Porto San Stéfano-Gíglio (January 1-June 30), per person: 10,000 lire, per car: 40,000-60,000 lire.

Lost and Found Offices

(*Uffici oggetti smarriti*)

You can get the addresses of lost and found offices from local tourist offices, at the town hall and at police stations (*Vigili urbani*). Lost property offices are only open mornings, from 8:00 or 8:30 am to about 1:00 pm. If you leave something on a public bus or a train, go to the responsible authority, i.e., railroad, bus or ferry company.

Markets and Trade Fairs

Flower Markets: In Florence, every Thursday morning, Via Pellicceria. At the end of April/beginning of May, on the Piazza della Libertà, there is a huge sales show of spring flowers. In Pescia, the largest flower market in Tuscany is held 6:00-9:30 am, Monday to Saturday, on Via Salvo d'Aquisto). In Florence, a colorful **Flea Market** is held Monday to Saturday in the summer (Tuesday to Thursday in the winter) on the Piazza dei Ciompi. Local arts and crafts can be found every third weekend in Viareggio's Piazza d'Azeglio. On Monday afternoons and Tuesday-Saturday at the **US Market** in Livorno (Piazza XX Settembre) you can buy everything that members of the American military stationed near town want to sell, like the cheap parachutes that farmers spread under their olive trees making it easier to collect the harvest. In Florence, from the end of April to the beginning of May, the **International Artisan Congress** (*Mostra Internazionale dell' Artigianato*) is held in the Fortezza da Basso. Distributors come from throughout Italy and 30 other countries. For information, call 055-49 721.

In September on the main square in Greve, in Chianti, there is an annual **Wine Congress** for purchasers from all over Europe, at which private individuals can stock up as well. There are also permanent wine exhibitions in the Medici fortress in Siena and Montalcino's Fortezza.

Medical Assistance

If you can present form E 111 entitling you to international medical treatment,

USL (*Unità Sanitaria Locale*) centers will treat you free of charge. It is a good idea, however, to look into special travel insurance, particularly if you want to ensure a slightly better level of care.

In emergencies, call First Aid (tel: 118) or the *Pronto Soccorso* at the hospital nearest you.

Museums

Opening hours of museums are not regulated in Italy, and therefore tend to change frequently, making it difficult to state anything definite here. Most museums are closed at midday, from ca. 1:00-3:00 pm, and some are only open in the morning. In many cases are closed all day on Monday. Many museums are also closed on Christmas Day, January 1, Easter Sunday and May 1.

To ensure that you don't end up standing in front of a locked door, phone ahead for the current opening hours, or ask at the local tourist office.

Admission fees for museums are divided into three categories. The largest – including the Uffizi Gallery in Florence – now cost a uniform fee of 12,000 lire. Entrance to less spectacular establishments costs 8000 lire, while the smallest museums charge 4000 lire. Sometimes tickets that are valid for several museums are available (e.g. local museums in Florence). Local tourist information offices can provide you with more information.

Nature Parks and Mountain Huts

CARRARA (MS): **Rifugio Carrara**, Loc. Campocecina, tel: 0585-841 972.
CASTELNUOVO DI GARFAGNANA (LU): **Parco delle Alpi Apuane,** Piazza delle Erbe 1, tel: 0583-644 242.
GROSSETO: **Parco Naturale della Maremma**, Piazza Combattente Alberese 17, tel: 0564-407 098 (visitors' center) and Loc. Pianacce Alberese, tel: 0564-407 111 (administration).
MINUCCIANO (LU): **Rifugio Donegani**, Orto di Donna, tel: 0583-610 085.

MASSAROSA (LU): **L.I.P.U.**, Via del Porto 6, Massaciuccoli, tel: 0584-975 567.

PISA: **Parco Naturale Migliarino San Rossore Massaciuccoli**, Via Aurelia North 4, tel: 050-525 500.

SERAVEZZA (MS): **Rifugio Del Freo**, Mosceta, tel: 0584-778 007. **Centro Accoglienza Parco delle Alpi Apuane**, Via Corrado del Greco 11, tel: 0584-757 325.

Opening Hours

In general, stores are open Monday-Saturday, 9:00 am-1:00 pm and 4:00 or 5:00-7:00 or 8:00 pm. In the winter, most grocery stores are closed on Wednesday afternoons. In the summer, they are usually closed on Saturday afternoons. In the main tourist centers, some stores no longer close for the mid-day lunch break, and in large beach towns like Viareggio and Forte dei Marmi, you can even go shopping on Sundays.

Pharmacies

Opening hours for pharmacies are no different from those of other stores. For information about opening times on Sundays and holidays, call the toll-free number 800 420 707. In Florence there are a couple of pharmacies that offer 24-hour-service, such as **All'Insegna del Moro**, Piazza San Giovanni, 20R, tel: 055-211 343. **Comunale 5**, Piazza Isolotto 5, tel: 055- 710 293. **Comunale 13**, Stazione Santa Maria Novella, tel: 055-289 435. **Molteni**, Via Calzaiuoli 7R, tel: 055-289 490.

Post Offices

Monday to Friday, usually from 8:15 am-1:40 pm, Saturdays until 12:20 pm.

In the provincial capitals and vacation centers, some post office branches may be open throughout the day. You can also buy stamps in bars and tobacco shops. If you mail a letter or post card abroad, it should take about five days to reach its destination, but it is not unusual for it take a lot longer!

Rental Cars
(Autonoleggio)

FLORENCE (area code: 055): **Avis**, Airport, tel: 315 588; Borgo Ognissanti, 128R, tel: 213 629. **Program**, Borgo Ognissanti 135R, tel: 282 916. **Europcar**, Airport, tel: 318 609. **Hertz italiana Rent a Car,** Via Maso Finiguerra 33, tel: 282 260. **Maggiore Autoservizi,** Via Maso Finiguerra, 31R, tel: 210 238; Via Termine 1, tel: 311 256.

AREZZO: (area code: 0575): **Avis Conc. SIVOC**, Piazza della Repubblica 1A, tel: 354 232; **Hertz**, Via Calamandrei 97D, tel: 27 577. **Sixt**, Via Marco Perennio 21, tel: 353 570.

GROSSETO (area code: 0564): **Avis**, Via Telamonio 40B, tel: 451 261.

LIVORNO (area code: 0586): **Hertz**, Via Mastacchi 63, tel: 400 491. **Avis**, Via Garibaldi 109, tel: 880 090. **Maggiore Autoservizi**, Via Fiume 31/33, tel: 892 240.

LUCCA (area code: 0583): **ACI Lucca Service**, Via Catalani 59, tel: 582 626. **Gíglio**, Via Orsali 321, tel: 492 698.

MASSA (area code: 0585): **Autonoleggio**, Viale Roma 354, Loc. Marina di Massa, tel: 241 360.

PISA (area code: 050) **Program Noleggio**, airport, tel: 500 296. **Avis**, airport, tel: 42 028. **Europcar Italia**, airport, tel: 41 017. **Hertz Italiana**, airport, tel: 49 187. **Maggiore**, airport, tel: 42 574.

SIENA (area code: 0577): **Avis,** Via Martini 36, tel: 270 305. **Hertz**, Via XXIV Maggio 10, tel: 45 085.

Shopping

Tuscany is a true shoppers' paradise for anyone looking for novel souvenirs, high-quality crafts, jewelry and antiques, or culinary delicacies.

Florence is clearly the shopping center of the region. For elegant **fashion**, the best place to look is Via dei Tornabuoni,

Via degli Strozzi and Via dei Calzaiuoli. There are also countless young boutiques, **leather** and **shoe shops**, and **knitwear shops** throughout the old city, as well as on the other side of the Ponte Vecchio. Here, in the side streets around Santo Spirito, you will find most of the city's traditional artisan and restorers workshops. The Ponte Vecchio itself is a center for **gold-** and **silversmiths**. The famous *carta marmorizzata*, **marbled paper**, colored according to centuries-old techniques, is another product of a traditional Florentine craft that you can buy all over the city, including the square in front of the Duomo. The lovely old pharmacy of Santa Maria Novella, Via della Scala 16, sells creams and soaps, liqueurs and perfumes that are made according to traditional recipes handed down by Dominican monks.

Outside Florence you can also find a tempting range of unique gifts and souvenirs. In Lucca, for example, you can get marvelous **hand-woven silk**; while in Impruneta and Mercatale, south of Florence, there are hand-made **ceramic pots** for plants and flowers, as well as hand-made earthenware tiles.

Arezzo is famous for its **antique shops**. The first weekend of every month sees a huge antiques market on the Piazza Grande and in the surrounding streets of the old city, where you can buy furniture, tableware, silverware, etc. In Florence, too, a good address for antiques and odds and ends is the Piazza dei Ciompi, where you can shop on weekdays and the last Sunday of every month.

There are other interesting markets for collectors in Lucca (next to the cathedral, third weekend of the month), Viareggio (Piazza Manzoni, last weekend of the month), Pisa (Logge dei Banchi, second weekend of the month), Marina di Carrara (Piazza Gino Menconi, fourth weekend of the month, especially good for sellers), Massa (around Via Cavour, Via Dante, Piazza Mercurio, third Sunday of the month, except in June, July and August) and in Pistoia (the old factory grounds at Breda, second weekend of the month, except in July and August).

Volterra is known for its **alabaster**. Countless workshops in the town produce a variety of objects that have either been copied from old models or are wholly new forms. There is a lot of kitsch sold here, but if you seek out the smaller shops in the old city you may be able to find something pretty or original. In the city center, there is also a sales outlet for the **Union of Artisan Alabaster Workers** on the Piazza dei Priori 5, tel: 0588-87 590.

Delicious culinary delicacies can be found throughout Tuscany. Typical offerings include baked goods and spicy cakes, such as *panforte* from Siena, a dense kind of fruitcake that is prepared with honey and almonds, and the *Biscotti di Prato*, hard little cookies that are flavored with almonds and aniseed, which are a popular dessert, especially when they are dunked in Vin Santo.

In Greve, as well as in the Maremma, you can buy a number of different **sausages made from the meat of wild boars**. Typical Tuscan **cheese** is generally made from ewe's milk (*pecorino*), and can be found mainly in the Crete and the Maremma.

You can purchase olive oil directly from the producer at many regional farmhouses. If the label announces that it is *Olio extra vergine d'Oliva*, and the contents appear slightly cloudy and greenish, then you know it is of the very highest quality and will be worth the generally high price. Particularly famous is the oil from around Lucca, but fabulous olive oils can be found throughout Tuscany.

Many monasteries have pharmacies or sales outlets that sell olive oil, honey, herbal liqueurs and cosmetics products, all of which have been prepared by the monks or nuns according to traditional recipes.

Guidelines

Taxis

Florence: 055-4390. Livorno: 0586-210 000. Pisa: 050-541 600.

Telephones

You can call from public telephone booths with coins or telephone cards (scheda telefonica). Many bars have a public telephone you can use (you will know it by the yellow telephone symbol posted by the door). The Italian phone company TELECOM ITALIA (which is wholly independent of the post office) has some public rooms in larger towns that have banks of phone booths, from which you can also make international calls. Furthermore there are private telephone companies, such as Infostrada, Tiscali, that sell pre-paid telephone cards with which charges for international calls are considerably cheaper.

You can buy telephone cards at tobacconists or newspaper kiosks for 5000, 10,000 and up to 100,000 lire. Please note: even for local calls you need to dial the local area code; for calls from abroad however, you must leave out the zero of the area code.

When making calls to Italy (drop the zero in the local area code):
from USA and Canada 01139 + number,
from England 0039 + number.

When placing internat'l calls from Italy:
to the USA and Canada 001 + number,
to England 0044 + number (drop zero in local area code).

Directory assistance (domestic): 12
Directory assistance (international): 176.

Thermal Spas

Tuscany has a wealth of hot mineral springs, most of which had been discovered before the arrival of the Romans. Today, the largest spas are the Chianciano Terme and Montecatini Terme, but there are also a dozen or so smaller spas. You can get information materials from the local tourist offices. These addresses and telephone numbers may be useful:

Bagni di Lucca: Piazza San Martino, tel: 0583-87 221.

Chianciano Terme: Via delle Rose 12, tel: 0578-68 111, fax: 0578-60 622.

Monsummano Terme: Grotta Giusti, Via Grotta Giusti 171, tel: 0572-51 008; Grotta Parlanti, Via Grotta Parlanti 41B, tel: 0572-953 029.

Montecatini Terme: Viale Giuseppe Verdi 41, tel: 0572-7781.

San Giuliano Terme, Largo Shelley 18, tel: 050-818047.

Terme di Bagno Vignoni, Piazza del Moretto 35, tel: 0577-887 365.

Tipping
(*Mancia*)

Tips are included in hotel and restaurant bills, but it never hurts to round up and add an extra 5-10% to the total as a *mancia*. In bars, service is not included, so you should leave a 15% gratuity behind. Porters, too, expect you to round up; and you generally leave about 500 lire in toilets and public bathrooms. At the movies and in other theaters, it is common practice to give the usher a tip of between 500 and 1000 lire.

Tourist Information

The Italian State Tourist Office **ENIT** (www.mi.cnr.it/WOI/) has bureaus in **Canada**: 3 place Ville Marie, 56 Plaza, Montreal H3B 2E3, tel: (514) 866-7667; **USA**: 630 Fifth Avenue, New York, NY 10111, tel: (212) 245-4822; as well as in **Tuscany** (**A.P.T.** and **Pro Loco**). Local addresses and phone numbers are in the "Info" section at the end of every chapter.

GLOSSARY OF FOOD AND DRINK

Though many menus are now written in English for the benefit of tourists, you may find the following glossary helpful in deciphering a Tuscan menu.

Dishes (*cibi*)

acciughe	sardines
aceto	vinegar
acquacotta	vegetable soup from the Maremma
affettato	cold cuts
agnello	lamb
aglio	garlic
alici	sardines
anatra	duck
anguria	watermelon
arancia	oranges
aragosta	lobster
arrosto	roast
baccalà	stockfish, a specialty in Lunigiana
bistecca (ai ferri)	cutlet, sirloin
bistecca fiorentina . . .	tender sirloin from the Chiania valley
brodo	consomé
bruschetta	toasted bread with garlic and olive oil
burro	butter
cacciucco	Livornese fish soup
cantuccini	hard almond pastry, dunked in Vin Santo
caprese	tomatoes with mozzarella
carciofi	artichokes
castagnaccio	round, flat bread made with chestnut flour
cavolfiore	cauliflower
cavolo con le fette . . .	cabbage breads
cecina	chick pea flat breads
cervello al burro	brain in butter
cibreo	fricasséd chicken gizzards Florentine specialty
cinghiale	boar
coniglio	rabbit
coda alla vacinara	ox tail
contorno	side dish
costata	entrecôte
cozze	mussels
crema	creamed soup
crostata	fruit tart
crostini . . .	roasted white-bread slices with various herbs
crudo	uncooked
erbe	herbs
fagiano	pheasant
fagioli	white beans
fagioli all'uccelletto	white beans with lots of sage
fagiolini	green beans
fegato	liver
fegatelli	liver kebab
fettunta	toasted white bread with garlic and olive oil
finocchio	fennel
finocchiona	thick salami with fennel seeds
formaggio	cheese
francesina	boiled meat dish
frittata	omelette
fritto misto . .	various types of fried fish
funghi porcini	bolet mushrooms
gallina	chicken
gambero	shrimps
gnocchi	dumplings
grano turco	corn
grasso	suet
infarinata	corn chowder
involtini	little meat rolls
lampone	raspberries
lingua	tongue
lombata	tenderloin
lumache	snails
maiale	pork
mandorla	almonds
manzo	beef
mela	apples
melanzane	aubergines
menta	mint
merluzzo	cod
miele	honey
minestra	soup
noce	nuts
orata	haddock
ossobuco . veal knuckle with vegetables	
ostriche	oysters
panforte . .	very spicy cake from Siena, similar to gingerbread
panino	rolls
panna	cream
pappa al pomodoro	thick tomato soup with bread
pasta e fagioli	thick noodle soup with white beans
patate	potatoes

pecorino	ewe's cheese
pepe	pepper
peperone	peperoni
peperoncino	hot peppers
pera	pears
pesce	fish
pescespada	swordfish
pesto	basil sauce
pinoli	pine nuts
piselli	peas
pizzaiola	spicy tomato sauce
pollo arrosto	roast chicken
pollo alla diavola	hot and spicy roasted chicken
polpetta	meat balls
pomodoro	tomatoes
porchetta	suckling pig
prosciutto	ham
ragù	meat sauce
riso	rice
rognoni	kidneys
rognoncino	calf's kidneys
rostinciana	spareribs
sale	salt
salmone	salmon
salsa (verde)	(green) sauce
salsiccia	pork links
saltimbocca	calf medaillon with sage
scaloppine	loin of veal
scottiglia	pot roast including various meats
seppia	octopus
sogliola	sole
spezzatino	goulash
allo spiedo, spiedino	kebab
spigola	perch
succo	juice
sugo	sauce
tacchino	turkey
tartufo	truffels (also ice cream)
tonno	tuna
torta d'erbi	herb tart
tramezzino	sandwich
triglia	sea barbel
triglie alla livornese	sea barbel, Livornese style
trippa alla fiorentina	tripe in Florentine style
trota	trout
in umido	steamed
uovo	egg
uva	grapes
verdura	vegetables
vitello	veal
vitello tonnato	veal with tuna sauce
vongole	scallops
zucchero	sugar
zuppa di farro	wheat soup

Drinks (*bevande*)

acqua fresca	tap water
acqua gasata	bubbly water
amaretto	bitter-almond liqueur
amaro	bitter
aranciata	orangeade
bicchiere	glass
birra (alla spina)	beer (on tap)
caffè (espresso)	espresso
caffèlatte	café au lait
cappuccino	espresso with foamed milk
ghiaccio	ice cubes
grappa	lees schnaps
latte	milk
latte macchiato	milk with a shot of coffee
mezzo litro, quarto di litro	half, quarter liter
sambuca	aniseed liqueur
spremuta d`arancia, di limone, di pompelmo	freshly-pressed orange, lemon, grapefruit juice
spumante	bubbly wine
tè (al limone, con latte)	tea (with lemon, with milk)
vino abboccato, amabile	sweet wine
vin santo	sweet dessert wine
vino secco	dry wine

AUTHORS

Ulrike Bossert was project editor and co-author of this book. She studied both German literature and Romance languages and literature in Heidelberg, with a special focus on Italian literature. She has also studied in Italy, and now works as a freelance television journalist and author in Munich. She also edits the Italian editions of Nelles Guides. She was also project editor for *Nelles Guide to Rome*. For *Nelles Guide Tuscany* she wrote the chapters on history, Florence, Chianti, Siena and Arezzo, cuisine and hiking.

Christiane Büld-Campetti has studied German and Dutch in Münster and Amsterdam, and has worked for ten years as an editor for the Bavarian Radio. She lives with her Florentine husband in an old farmhouse near Florence. She provides German radio stations with reports about Italy and its people, as well as Tuscan cultural events. For this book she wrote the chapters on the Maremma, the Tuscan Archipelago, the coast, Versilia and Lunigiana, the Garfangnana, and the features on Tuscany's arts and crafts, festivals, feasts and foreigners.

Dr. Stephan Bleek studied history, political science and sociology in Munich. For many years he has worked as a TV journalist and film author for Bavarian Television. Because one of his focuses is cultural history, he frequently travels to Italy, particularly Tuscany. He wrote the chapters on frescoes and wine.

Caterina Mesina studied history, Italian and German literature in Freiburg. For many years she has led study groups to Italy. She writes travel books about Italy and recently published a book of photographs of Tuscany. She revised and updated this *Nelles Guide Tuscany*.

PHOTOGRAPHERS